01303 237618

THE
HYTHE & SANDGATE
RAILWAY

Sandgate branch trains cross at Sandling Junction, both waiting for the 'clear road' from their respective starting signals. Notice the huge twin-posted down main line starting signal. Up until now this rare negative had never been printed. *Imperial War Museum*

THE HYTHE & SANDGATE RAILWAY

Brian Hart

WILD SWAN PUBLICATIONS LTD.

© Wild Swan Publications Ltd. and Brian Hart 1987
ISBN 0 906867 53 3

Respectfully and fondly
dedicated to
PETER DAVIES
to whom all
Folkestone owes so much

Title page: The once labour-intensive railway industry is well illustrated here in this view of the station staff at Sandgate, taken on the spot where the former 'gents' stood. The station master, seated in the middle, is understood to be Frederick Porter (here 1904-12). Behind him, third from left, stands Robert Force, whilst on the far right, back row also, is T. Faircloth. In the front row, extreme right, is Tom Owen and next to him is driver Sid King. Sitting cross-legged is the newspaper lad with 'W. H. Smith & Sons' on his cap, but the identity of the dog remains a mystery; perhaps he is Hythe station's 'Rufus'!
Lens of Sutton

Designed by Paul Karau
Printed and bound by Butler & Tanner, Frome

Published by
WILD SWAN PUBLICATIONS LTD.
1-3 Hagbourne Road, Didcot, Oxon OX11 8DP

Contents

THE HYTHE & SANDGATE RAILWAY

INTRODUCTION	vii
A NEW ROUTE TO THE CONTINENT	1
A ROYAL INAUGURATION	7
OH! WHAT A DAY HYTHE IS HAVING	11
ONWARD!	17
THE DREAM FADES	39
A TRIP TO THE SEASIDE	63
THE PRIDE OF KENT	77
GATHERING CLOUDS	85
THE END OF A DREAM	99

APPENDICES

Track Plans and Elevations	110
Signalling Plans	118

THE HYTHE & SANDGATE TRAMWAY

INTRODUCTION	123
A BRIGHT AUGURY	125
DAYS OF ADVERSITY	129
THE GREAT CRISIS	143
A FATEFUL SEQUEL	151
ACKNOWLEDGEMENTS	168

Preface

When asked to seriously consider compiling a history of the Sandgate Branch I must admit I viewed the prospect with more than a hint of trepidation. It was, after all, rather an unknown subject and one barely touched upon by transport historians. At first I thought I would be fortunate to find sufficient information to fill a small booklet. How wrong I was.

Perhaps because I was born less than a couple of miles from Sandgate station, and the overgrown remains of the line featured in my childhood wanderings, I have always nurtured a fondness for this particular lost railway. Indeed, even though my first passionate interest was, and always will be, the Elham Valley Line, the Sandgate branch never trailed very far behind and so I was able to look forward to this challenge with growing enthusiasm.

The bedrock for any historical book invariably consists of written facts and figures. These are often readily available to the determined researcher who has plenty of time and patience to spare. Such information can extend to great depths and intricacy and inevitably a discriminating frame of mind is necessary. I have therefore recorded as much technical information as I feel the book will allow without it becoming drearily dull and dusty. In my opinion, the more serious student can easily gain access to, for example, locomotive and stock workings, signalling rules and regulations, etc., from numerous sources. Accordingly, I have simply summarised how the branch was operated. In regard to the tramway, I have stripped away much of the jargon that accompanies the substantial amount of legal and parliamentary documentation available. My prime intent has been to try and relate why railway and tramway were built, why they went where they did and why they eventually closed.

Paramount above all else has been my desire to attempt to recapture the spirit of that age and here I must beg forgiveness if I have over-indulged at times! Hopefully though the same images will flash into the reader's mind as appeared in mine when setting down the words within these pages. I hope, too, that all will agree that in spite of the remarkably short length and unfulfilled dreams of both railway and tramway, their stories are worth recording and that each deserves a place in the transport and sociological annals of Kent.

A beautifully clean 'O1' class No. 385 approaches Rectory crossing, Saltwood, with a train from Sandgate on 17th June 1924.

F. J. Agar/R.C. Riley Collection

Introduction

On a rather damp and chilly autumnal day I stepped from an East Kent double-decker bus onto the Esplanade at Sandgate. The sea was calm, but grey and unfriendly, whilst a stiff breeze blew in across the bay from Dungeness. Turning, I prepared to cross the road, pausing briefly to reflect that I was about to step across the route of the former Hythe and Sandgate tramway which, for thirty years, gave such pleasure to holidaymakers of all ages and classes. Leaving behind as quickly as possible the more loathsome reminders of the present day, I reached the mossy, overgrown approach road leading up to where Sandgate station once stood.

It had been in my mind to visit the site now that the bus garage had been demolished to make way for a housing development. All remains of the station would soon disappear beneath wall to wall carpets, patio gardens and rotary clothes driers. A swathe of elder, bramble and buddleia enveloped the old 'up' platform making it a difficult task of exploration. Determination, however, soon had me standing relatively scratch-free upon the remnants of the 'up' platform. Its remains comprised obscure lumps of iron, rail-posts, rotting wood and the like, scattered around the concrete base of the old gents' lavatory and lamp room. A few fragments of buff and green timbers remarkably survived, as did an ancient wooden lavatory seat – delightfully covered in a most brilliant shade of viridescent moss! I picked up a few pieces of coal and ballast, holding them in my palm and wondered what this scene had looked like when they'd first fallen there. Where the engine shed once stood a group of sloe and elder bushes had taken root, whilst blackberries abounded in this quiet little haven where only rabbits played. I decided to sit down to eat my sandwiches, amidst the cheery scarlet pimpernel, yellow vetch and ubiquitous daisy which carpeted the ground where once the 'up' line stretched. I reckoned I was sitting on the spot where locomotives once stopped to have their tenders or tanks filled from the water tower. It was difficult not to drift back...

On a glorious spring day in almost any year during the 1890s the Sandgate signalman would rise from his bed, wash and shave himself at the scullery sink while glancing out of the window at the clear blue sky which heralded yet another beautiful day. Dressed in an old shirt with fraying cuffs, he quietly breakfasted before winding his watch and popping it into his stained waistcoat pocket. Kissing his wife goodbye, he stepped out into the first warming rays of the early morning sunshine. His scuffed but polished boots crunched unhurriedly upon the patches of gravel as he made his way up the path to the station. With each step the foreground fell away, allowing his gaze to reach out to the sharp horizon where the glinting English Channel meets the sky. He paused for a moment just to watch the sea gently rising on a swell, its glassy form sparkling in the sunlight, yet with hardly a wave breaking upon the shoreline. The air was crisp and fresh, tinged with a salty tang that was every bit as invigorating as any mountain breeze. He resumed his climb when his momentary day-dream was interrupted by an engine whistle which announced that the crew were finished with coaling and watering and were ready to begin the day's business. The fireman's day had begun earlier when he'd stepped into the dim cold gloom of the shed to light and prepare the engine in readiness for the first goods train of the morning. Unlocking his box, the signalman would first check his watch against the clock whose regular beat was somehow comforting in the lonely hours. His hand reached out for the instrument to tap out the bell-code, 5–5–5, to his counterpart at Sandling Junction Cabin No. 2, informing him his box was now open. Having raked out his stove, he lit a fire while the dust from the ash still lingered in the sunlit interior, and placed the heavy black kettle on top for his first railway brew. Wiping his hands on the chequered duster, he strolled along the 'down' platform and across the rails where a Cudworth '118' simmered away, glinting in the early light as the fireman proudly polished its brasswork. There was often plenty of time for a chat at this time of the morning, even idle gossip, but at length, a glance at the clock beneath the awning showed the hands approaching 6.45 a.m. so, leaving his colleagues, the signalman made his way back to the box to set the road. Obediently the horizontal arm of the 'up' home starting signal dropped into the lower quadrant and the engine and brake vans set off. The signalman stood gazing from his steps as it passed by, waving to the crew, before watching it disappear round the curve, its wisps of white steam brilliant against the blue sky. He then turned towards his kettle which was by now also merrily steaming away.

The drone of an aeroplane brought me back through ninety years and, gathering my few belongings, I said goodbye forever to the last vestiges of Sandgate station. Finding my way back onto Seabrook Road, I glanced between the gaps in the houses to see the railway embankment running parallel. How many landladies had paused when pulling back the heavy curtains to watch the early morning train pass by? Making my way up Cliff Road I gazed out across to the seafront where stands the Hotel Imperial, but my attention was soon drawn back to the railway on finding the overbridge intact. A new house now straddles the trackbed on the Hythe side, its garden across the filled-in cutting blocking the opening of the bridge. These select surroundings were, when the railway arrived, little more than pastures where 'Daisy' or 'Gertrude' interrupted their monotonous cudding to peer through the fence as the first train of the day passed beneath the overbridge, blowing a sudden cloud of steam as it emerged on the other side. At this point the beat of the engine was strong and hard as it pounded away up the 1 in 59 bank. On the footplate, the fireman kept a look out along the short distance between the two stations while the driver gave a long blast on the whistle as Hythe was approached.

I could not help but momentarily pause to admire the bridge which sadly now lies hidden and dejected. It deserves to be looked at and appreciated and not used as a convenient dumping ground for rubbish by residents who ought to know better. Pleasant grey ragstone blocks, interspersed with layers of brick, present a most attractive prospect, underlying the care and dedication to perfection and beauty in all things which accompanied our forebears' achievements.

Resuming my walk, I found myself soon approaching the site of Hythe station which has now been completely obliterated. Thankfully, the former station master's house survives as a reminder but elsewhere rows of bungalows border new roads and sterile cul-de-sacs. Pausing for a moment, I imagined that first train dashing through the station, all signals 'off' as Hythe signalbox would not be opened until the first 'down' goods. On this spot so many faces had eagerly peered in wonderment at the royal personages who had stepped out of the trains in those far off days.

The eastern abutment of the old bridge across Blackhouse Hill survives, as does the breathtaking scale of the stone wall which rises up towards the old 'up' side approach road. A tiny footpath beckoned me onward where, once over a wooden stile, the lush green meadows of Saltwood valley stretched ahead, bordered on my right by the huge railway embankment. Bridge 2128, carrying the line across a farmtrack, remains but its brickwork stands decaying, and its span looks noticeably warped. At this point I rested for a while to enjoy the warm sunshine that had scattered the earlier grey gloom. A breeze rustled through the nearby cornfields and grasslands; was it really only the wind, or might it be the lost echo of a train hurrying up from Hythe? A skylark incessantly twittering high up in the bright blue yonder caught my attention, leaving my eyes to fall upon the soft outline of the North Downs, with their wooded slopes at Etchinghill. Southwards, Saltwood Castle dreamed away in the fresh autumn air, peeping at me through the trees as I made my way over the former occupation crossing. Leaving the railway, I ventured into the village to find a local shop where I might find some sort of refreshment. Ah, the English village stores, it's unique smell of soap, fresh bread and earthy vegetables, replete with its statutory refrigerator lurking in a corner, merrily humming and buzzing away to itself. How carelessly we under-value the comforting sense of security and routine offered by these precious social centres. Having made my purchase, I spent ten minutes or so resting on one of those wooden benches, donated by some kind soul. The store's young cat decided I was obviously the sort of person who couldn't possibly resist feline charms and came bounding across the grass to greet me. 'Kitty' enjoyed all the fussing, tickling and scratching, not to mention the odd crumb of biscuit and I in return enjoyed her friendly rubbing and nudging. Bidding farewell to my new friend, I followed the dry, dusty track that led past the old church and on to the railway.

I soon reached Rectory Crossing but sadly, of course, there were no trains for me to sit and wait for. The childhood pleasures of sitting amongst ox-eye daises on sunny summer days, waiting for the signal wires to rustle, initiating that pounding of the heart, are now just memories. The ordinary, everyday train with its dirty old engine is something we shall never set eyes upon again.

At the start of Saltwood cutting one of the two three-arch bridges still spans the overgrown trackbed, but further on the second bridge has disappeared amongst the infill which seems likely to engulf both. Standing upon its broken parapets I looked towards the hillside, hoping to see the portals of Hayne tunnel, but it was impossible. I therefore skirted round to venture into the chestnut woods, climbing uphill amongst rhododendrons which had escaped from the confines of the adjacent ornamental gardens. Glancing all around, I was still unable to find any trace of the old railway or the tunnel mouth. Then, peering down into the very depths of the valley, my eyes fell upon some brickwork which could mean only one thing. Yet what a depth it was and only then was I struck by the sheer effort put in by those workmen who had excavated this portion of the line. The descent towards the tunnel mouth was risky and, upon reflection, quite foolhardy, but my curiosity had the better of me. Eventually I reached the brick portal where I scrambled round to gain a better view. Even though it is possible to look through the tunnel it is quite impassable since a blocked culvert has flooded the trackbed in places to a depth of four or five feet. Ninety or so years ago it all looked so different....

The look-out glanced at his watch, its shiny silver case glinting in the few rays of sunshine that penetrated into the deep cutting. His men were busy raking out the ballast with their forks. Some had already removed their thick, coarse jackets as they toiled and sweated even though a cooling breeze wafted out of the tunnel. Raising the warning trumpet to his lips, the look-out blew a warning, telling the men to pause from their work and step aside for safety. Already the sounds of the approaching train were apparent as the locomotive worked hard on the 1 in 54 stretch past Saltwood Castle. Looking through the two tall three-arch bridges, they watched it appear round the bend before clouds of white steam billowed up through Saltwood overbridge. Within a few moments the train pounded past, hot and oily, with that distinctive smell, and a wave and a grin were exchanged with the crew. While his men resumed their task, the look-out watched the train disappear into the blackness of the tunnel which continued to breathe smoke long after the train had gone.

This time, a startled cry from a pheasant in the woods broke my daydream, whereupon glancing at my watch I decided it was time to press on. With no chance of walking through the tunnel, I had little choice but to retrace my steps and scramble precariously up the crumbling hillside, to wander over the hill and down the other side. The pathway through the trees was littered with fallen chestnuts, but of course there were no railwaymen gathering them as they once did. The opposite portal was easily found and what a grand prospect it is to behold. Surely, this was never intended to remain a mere branch line, for the brickwork is highly decorative and unusually so, especially for the impoverished South Eastern Railway. How different it all might have been had Sir Edward Watkin finally achieved his ambition. Instead, his dreams now lie as dead as the leaves carpeting the empty route where once shiny rails carried princes, generals and artisans.

A mossy trackbed led me past a broken 'whistle' sign and into the reality of the 1980s where modern electric trains now dash through Sandling station. Only the 'down' platform survives on the branch, and the only remaining building left standing at this once imposing station is on the 'up' main platform. There is little else left to remind us of this short but colourful branch. Those who do spare it a cursory glance from the air-conditioned comfort of a modern compartment might wonder where it once led, perhaps thinking it just an unremarkable little branch to somewhere or other. How wrong they are.

Rather than dwell upon its sorry state today, or its unfulfilled dreams, I prefer with the aid of photographs to peep behind the curtain of time and gaze upon the Hythe and Sandgate Railway – a new route to the continent!

CHAPTER ONE

A New Route to the Continent

ONCE described by the Southern Railway posters of the 1920s as 'The Pride of Kent', Hythe evolved into a highly respectable, if somewhat demure, seaside resort. Yet its reputation up until the arrival of the railway is somewhat dubious if we are to believe what was once written about it. 'Years ago it was described as the filthiest and most immoral town in Kent. Today, it is an example of cleanliness and spruceness, whilst its morals are, let us suppose, about the same as those of other places.'

The name derives from the early Saxon language, meaning a harbour or haven, for in its day Hythe ranked far higher than neighbouring places. Folkestone, for example, was nothing more than a ramshackle fishing hamlet. As one of the original Cinque Ports, Hythe's status gradually dwindled with the receding sea. Leland penned: 'Hythe hath bene a very greate towne yn length ande conteyned IIII paroches, that now be cleyn destroied.' Shortly after the reign of Elizabeth I, the diminishing channel to the sea was entirely silted up and blocked with the shingle beaches that had accumulated. Its sole claim to any marine activity from thence forward lay in the local fishing smacks perched high upon the stony banks. However, Hythe may boast at being the home of Francis Pettit-Smith, the inventor of the screw propeller who, oddly enough, began his life as a humble cattle farmer on nearby Romney Marsh. Lionel Lukin, the inventor of the first insubmersible lifeboat, also lived here and lies buried in the churchyard. There is even a railway connection too, for General C. S. Hutchinson, who later became an Inspector of Railways for the Board of Trade, spent his boyhood in Hythe where his father was a local medical practitioner.

Probably its most famous connections rest with its military history, begun in earnest when the panic of invasion by the ambitious Napoleon Bonaparte gripped the nation. Being just an uncomfortable twenty-six miles away from his ever-expanding empire, a line of seventy-four defensive 'Martello' towers were erected in 1804, stretching from Wear Bay in Folkestone to Seaford in Sussex. Simultaneously a canal was excavated from Seabrook, east of Hythe, as far as Rye for the conveyance of troops and stores to supply the forts, but it was never thoroughly completed. The School of Musketry, established in 1854, incorporated a rifle range set up on the lonely wasteland of shingle and scrub at Palmarsh, home of the windswept thrift and ubiquitous yellow-horned poppy, almost the only tolerant residents of such a salty, barren landscape.

Whereas Hythe evolved into a military base, neighbouring Sandgate, on the road to Folkestone, remained very much a small independent town until it was amalgamated into the Borough of Folkestone in 1934. Its origin stems from the first settlers who chose to live at this sheltered spot beneath the hills, whilst its name is understood to imply an opening in the hills near the coast. For many years the road leading down the hill from Folkestone comprised but a rough track over deep and loose sand which made the going particularly unpleasant in the winter months. Near the bottom was situated one of the unpopular toll gates and, not surprisingly, some contentment was felt locally with its abolition in 1877. About 1770–90 some dozen or so war vessels are believed to have been built on its beaches, but nowadays only small fishing boats or pleasure craft grace the waterline. The castle, built about 1539 by Henry VIII in order that he might 'Stand upon his own gardes and defence agaynste the intolerable yoke of Popish tyranie', remained relatively intact for almost three centuries. Then, in 1805, its outer walls were demolished in an attempt to more or less make it conform with the general design of the Martello towers. For many years Sandgate was the favourite retreat of H. G. Wells, John Ruskin, and William Wilberforce. Wells so loved the place that he lived here for a number of years in the splendid 'Spade House' which he had built half-way up Sandgate Hill.

The arrival of the railway into the fair land of Kent understandably caused much excitement, be it favourable or otherwise. As the county nearest the continent, it was only a matter of time before the iron road would make for the coast. By the time the navvies were laying down the 'straight, true road' between Redhill and Ashford, the South Eastern Railway, as it was now titled, prepared itself for the final few miles to its seaport goal. Anyone maintaining a watchful eye on the progress of this new line as it darted like an arrow across the Kentish heartland could well have been forgiven for supposing that the line of stumps east of Ashford would continue in a like manner, straight into Hythe. It may have come as a bitter blow to the township as the railway swerved to by-pass them, continue to Folkestone and eventually Dover where deep water offered suitable sites for harbours. Even Folkestone, still a huddle of rude dwellings centred upon a tiny silted-up and derelict harbour, offered more potential than Hythe which, solely through geological misfortune, could not tempt the railway entrepreneurs.

A temporary station was opened at Folkestone on the western side of the Foord valley on 28th June 1843 with a promise that a station would soon be established between there and Ashford for the benefit of Hythe. Seven months later, on 7th February 1844, 'Westenhanger & Hythe' station opened but this can only have rubbed salt into the wound. Not only was it a simple wooden station in the fashion of the South Eastern Railway at its meanest, but it was sited over $3\frac{1}{2}$ miles from Hythe, and most of that up hill. The initial complaints to the railway were characteristically brushed aside by a company which, perhaps understandably, had more than enough on its plate at the time. The drainage and construction works at Folkestone harbour, recently purchased for £18,000, demanded much attention, investment and engineering skill if a continental railway route was to be established. However, with the opening to passengers, on New Year's Day 1849, of the branch line from Folkestone (Junction) station down to the harbour, the SER became, it appears, more approachable and were willing to lend an ear to new ideas, although not without conditions. On 25th November 1851 a newspaper reported:

'Great efforts are being made to procure a branch railway to the town. At present Hythe is distant three miles and a quarter from the station, whereas it is only about a mile in a direct line from the main line. It is therefore proposed to have a line to Hythe, to commence at the eastern end of the Saltwood tunnel, and thence to the town by the beautiful and picturesque valley, leaving the

The town of Hythe from the hillside. On the seafront can be seen villas and, on the left, the Seabrook Hotel, opened in 1880.
Eamonn Rooney Collection

castle on the right. It is expected that a public meeting of the inhabitants will shortly take place, to consider the best mode of effecting the object desired, as the South-Eastern Company have offered to make the line, if the land be presented to them free of cost.'

Perhaps the SER were playing it hard, knowing full well that an outright refusal to build a branch to Hythe would create such ill-feeling whereas such a preposterous notion that the land be handed over free of charge created a *fait accompli*.

Not content to let the matter rest there, on 1st April 1852 a Hythe resident, Colonel Sandilands, reached for his pen and wrote a personal and influential letter to the SER Board asking them to seriously consider a branch to Hythe and Sandgate. The South Eastern's secretary encouragingly replied that the directors would be only too pleased to view whatever plans and sections might be drawn up and they'd welcome any information the colonel himself might care to contribute. In carrying out their promise the SER instructed Mr. Drane, their chief engineer, to survey this proposed new line. The route chosen in this instance began at the western side of Saltwood tunnel, incidentally the precise spot where the junction was to be formed in later years. On leaving the main line the branch swung very sharply southwards, through the Slaybrook and Brockhill estates, then gently curved south-eastwards to pass conveniently behind the site of the School of Musketry, recently established, before terminating close to the centre of Hythe in the vicinity of Hillside Street. The availability of land apart, the line would have presented numerous difficulties to engineer, as pointed out by Mr. Drane. It is therefore not surprising that when another request for a branch arrived at the SER headquarters, this time from a Mr. Watts, that he received the same reply: 'A carriage road is the best facility for the Hythe district and we are not disposed under the advice we have received from our engineer to assist in construction of a branch railway.' To this end a plan was drawn up which showed a new road coloured-in from Hythe, through Slaybrook, to Sandling Park bridge where a 'new station' was marked.

Having met with no success whatsoever, the locals had little option but to contend with their reliance on road transport which was both slow and expensive. It seems the railway company were equally at the mercy of domineering landowners too, for in the spring of 1853 the Goods Clerk at Folkestone wrote to the Board complaining of the high charge of tolls levied by Lord Radnor along the Sandgate Road.

A few months later Mr. W. Deedes, the owner of Sandling Park Estate, tried another tactic with the SER by proposing that the small station at Westenhanger be moved to a more convenient site, suggesting Bargrove bridge, immediately north of Hythe and east of Saltwood tunnel. Backed by Colonel Sandilands, this idea received as much response as the branch line for, after viewing the report by Mr. Drane, the SER replied: 'No steps can be taken until a new road from Hythe shall have been completed.' This referred to the road, or rather muddy lane, which climbed steeply out of Hythe and twisted and turned over the hills, across the railway to Beachborough Park before continuing through the Elham Valley.

Three more summers came and went without any progress towards a new station, let alone a branch line. In an effort to get things rolling once again, the Mayor of Hythe, Thomas Denne, called a public meeting at the Town Hall to ascertain the support for better railway communication. Raikes Currie, the Borough's Member of Parliament, rose to propose that nothing less than the construction of a branch railway line would be adequate. This met with spontaneous loud applause and was carried unanimously. Mr. Henry Mackeson, of the local brewery family, then rose and proposed a second resolution suggesting that success might be achieved were they to press for an extension to Hythe, not from Sandling Park, but from Folkestone. With Shorncliffe military camp having just been established, the government were bound to insist upon a line into the camp and this could be extended to Hythe. At this point Mr. James Watts rose and explained he'd already led a deputation to the SER Company, whereupon a desultory discussion of a somewhat personal nature broke out which necessitated an intervention by the chairman to call several red-faced gentlemen to order. All did manage to agree, however, that it was a railway they wanted and nothing else would suffice. The resolution to that effect duly arrived at the Tooley Street headquarters of the SER on the 30th October where it was likely dumped inside a cabinet along with its counterparts.

In spite of these efforts nothing happened, simply because the SER were busy elsewhere in far more profitable ventures, and plainly an inducement comprising more than petty local business traffic would have to be found. Just such a carrot was about to be dangled when on 28th October 1858 the General Manager submitted a report to the board which he'd received from a Mr. Knight. Was this the spark that would ignite the flame of ambition in the SER and cause it to burn, albeit irregularly, for close on half a century? Its aim was to bring to their attention 'the advantages of constructing a branch from Westenhanger to Folkestone with a view to the improvement of the tidal service'. The appeal of this new coastal route is apparent and understandable, for the SER were only too mindful of the awkward nature of working the present steeply-graded harbour branch. The exchange of engines, the reversals, not to mention the lost time and inconvenience to passengers – all would become a thing of the past if this new line could be built. It would indeed be, as claimed, 'A new, and first class route to the Continent'.

The idea spawned similar plans for alternative routes. One suggestion involved a junction at Cheriton Street, running parallel to the main line before dropping down into the Foord valley to pass beneath the lofty arches of Cubitt's viaduct and into the harbour by means of Tontine Street. Due to the enormous cost, approximately £55,000, this route fell out of favour, whereas a direct coastal route costing about £12,000 had its obvious appeal. Still keen on a junction at Cheriton, the SER went so far as to introduce a bill into parliament for the 1861 session which, as described by their counsel Mr. Littler, 'was for a more easy and expeditious communication with the continent'. The proposed line began just east of Cheriton, followed the path of Coolinge Lane until it reached the eastern extremity of Sandgate, about halfway up Sandgate Hill, whereupon it curved eastwards to run along the Leas undercliff as far as the harbour. The Bill merrily set off on its way, unhindered in the House of Commons, but came to a grinding halt in the House of Lords, who threw it out on the opposition of their colleagues who had vested interests in Folkestone. While support for the line came from such humble bodies as the Sandgate Local Board of Health, keen to have a station where the railway would cross Sandgate Hill, it was the rich and powerful who held sway. Notable characters against the railway were Sir John Bligh and General Hankey. The General expressed a hearty distaste at seeing trains pass by his kitchen window! In an effort to appease him, and others, the SER offered to landscape the slopes and banks, screen the railway where possible as well as suitably embellishing all the civil engineering structures. Unquestionably though, the main opponent was Lord Radnor who owned a sizeable proportion of Folkestone. At that time the town was rapidly expanding and growing into a watering place for the upper classes which brought about a sharp increase in land values. Although probably more worried about depreciation of his assets than discomfort to his patrons, he claimed: 'Such an intolerable nuisance would be too high a price for Folkestone to pay for improved communications with Paris.' He went on, adding, 'a volume of dense smoke constantly pressing into their nostrils and clouding their view along the cliff as they walk along the Leas.'

A local solicitor, Richard Hart, then suggested that the line be built for the most part in tunnels which would solve the problem of interference with Radnor's land whilst protecting access to the seashore which many people feared they'd lose as the railway would sever the beach from the town. Alarmed by the enormous cost of building such a line in tunnels, the SER lost their impetus and allowed the scheme to be shelved; besides, it had many other problems on its hands.

One such predicament, although small at this time, is worthy of mention since it involved a group of local landowners in the Elham Valley who held a meeting at Elham in August 1862 to 'take into consideration the expediency of forming a line of railway from Hythe to the London, Chatham & Dover Railway'. Quite likely they were prompted to contemplate this scheme by the opening two years previously of Canterbury station on the LC & DR's new railway between London and Dover. The SER remained unruffled at this threat into their territory but kept a watchful eye on matters all the same.

Seemingly as a desire to give something to the Sandgate locality, the SER opened a new station in the western end of Folkestone on 1st November 1863 and called it 'Shorncliffe & Sandgate'. That it was a mile or so from both places didn't really seem to matter. Alone amongst the fields and meadows it comprised little more than a small wooden building on the 'up' side with a waiting canopy on the 'down' side. Improvements of a sounder nature were made at Westenhanger where two years earlier the original station, very dilapidated and nearly falling down, was demolished to make way for a fine and imposing brick structure built on the same spot.

It is evident that the SER was still keen to pursue the construction of the Sandgate branch for in February 1864, Francis Brady, their newly-appointed chief engineer, visited Sandgate where he outlined the railway's latest scheme. It was proposed to commence the line east of Saltwood tunnel, near the Honeywood bridge, running past Saltwood castle thence along the back of Hythe to finish beneath Shorncliffe camp where the station for Sandgate would be provided. By the autumn the plan was slightly altered with the junction transferred to the other side of the tunnel at Sandling Park. Brady submitted an estimate for £25,000 for the line which included building both Hythe and Sandgate stations as well as providing a goods warehouse at Hythe. Serious consideration was, however, postponed until the Board had scrutinised the receipts from Westenhanger and Shorncliffe stations.

In 1865 the 'Elham Valley Light Railway Company Limited' issued its prospectus which entailed 'affording a direct railway communication between the city of Canterbury and

THE HYTHE & SANDGATE RAILWAY

'Shorncliffe & Sandgate' station photographed in 1871, looking east towards Folkestone. Station master James Keefe stands with his dog on the up platform.
Tonbridge Historical Society

the cinque port of Hythe, together with the adjacent watering place of Sandgate'. Fearing an eventual invasion by the hated LC & DR who might buy out the EVLR, the SER galvanised itself into action by ordering its surveyors and engineers to prepare the Sandgate branch surveys and drawings 'without delay'. At last it seemed as though the residents of the two towns would achieve their railway, yet fate played one more trick when the EVLR stumbled into numerous financial difficulties. In October 1866 the EVLR Company's secretary wrote to the SER informing them that they were obliged to abandon the Hythe section of their railway to Canterbury. Within a few months the EVLR Co. collapsed altogether which allowed the SER to lapse into its lax attitude over Hythe and Sandgate. Quite possibly the SER imagined that was the end of this independent upstart, but how wrong they were and little did they realise then what an embroilment they'd be forced into in the 1880s. In fact all that happened was that the Elham Valley scheme lay moribund for nearly twenty years.

Two more years elapsed in which feelings of indignation and impatience were mixed with a sense of resignation at ever achieving the ultimate goal of a railway line. In the spring of 1868 the Sandgate Local Board of Health wrote to the SER pointing out that whilst they held no high hopes for seeing the railway built, might the SER at least provide an omnibus connection between the town and Shorncliffe station with which they shared the nameboard?

Although the powers granted to the SER in 1864 to allow the construction of the Sandgate branch were extended in 1867, nothing of substance took place and indeed the capital account of the company scheme was closed. But the idea still burned on and was far from dead.

In 1866 Watkin had succeeded the Hon. James Byng as chairman of the South Eastern Railway and from then onwards the affairs of the company were, to a large extent, carried out in a manner that reflected Watkin's own fiery nature.

Two years later, in May 1868, there appeared in the Minute Book 'Saltwood Valley & Hythe Line' which headed a brief report revealing that the recently-knighted Watkin had accompanied James Byng to Hythe where they had met Mr. Wilks, the Clerk to the Justices, to view the plans put forward by local landowners and others interested in the scheme. These plans were requested to be brought before the SER Board once they had been finalised. A fortnight later, however, a rival scheme was delivered to the Board with an accompanying letter from a Mr. Joseph Yeoman who intimated that the line through the Saltwood Valley to Hythe as proposed by Mr. Wilks could not be carried out as he had already made arrangements for taking a considerable portion of the land for building purposes. Yeoman then promptly laid his cards on the table when submitting his own plan for a railway to Hythe and Sandgate including a rather naive proviso that the landowners should provide all the means for its construction.

The SER decided that it would be wise and prudent to interview both Wilks and Yeoman and accordingly separate meetings were arranged for the 6th August. No intimation of any decision which they may have reached at that point was given to either gentleman, but it appears the SER had already made up their mind. Probably envisaging an unfavourable reply, Yeoman sought to press his case a fortnight later with the following letter:

> 'I will undertake to provide the land for the line, station and road approaches, construct the line from a point near Saltwood tunnel (on the main South-Eastern line) to Hythe and Sandgate as shewn on plan furnished to you. The Co. to guarantee a perpetual dividend of $3\frac{1}{2}\%$ on £70,000.
> The execution of the work to meet the satisfaction of the Govern-

ment Inspector. A provision of £3,000 for stations and roads is included in the £70,000.'

A further letter, dated 29th October, informed the Board that he was 'now in possession of the land' and requested that they formally, and immediately, adopt his scheme. Yeoman was cold-shouldered but this didn't dampen his enthusiasm for in the following February he wrote again stating that the land arrangements had now been settled and would the SER be interested in working the branch once it was completed? Despite Yeoman's persistence, the Board had no intention of being rail-roaded into an early decision, and a couple of weeks later it was revealed that Watkin had been to see Wilks to propose that the SER be relieved from any obligation to build the branch. Wilks, undaunted, then announced his intention to join another company for the construction of the line whereupon it was explained that it might be necessary for this new company to arrange with the SER over powers to obtain land, as well as the sanction of the Board of Trade.

As the spring of 1869 blossomed it became clear that the two townships were not going to relinquish their desire for a railway and, in April, Watkin met a Mr. George Smith who informed him that local parties were keen to form a company under the Railway Facilities Act 27 & 28 and to take up the SER powers obtained in 1864. Agreeing that the South Eastern Railway should work the line once complete, the Board gave the project their blessing. So many years of fruitless effort, hard work and dashed hopes had gone by since the idea was first mooted that any sceptics could have easily been forgiven, but this time it really seemed as though something might be forthcoming.

An arrangement between the two parties was entered into in which the SER would lease and work the branch in perpetuity, paying for the Hythe & Sandgate Company out of the gross traffic receipts arising from the line, a sum equal to $4\frac{1}{2}\%$ on the cost of the line and not exceeding £65,000. All went smoothly until Watkin predictably blew his top at the price being asked for the land which was, in his opinion, far more than its intrinsic value.

The dawn of a new decade was a turning point in the stuggle for on 25th January 1870 the 'Hythe and Sandgate Railway Company Limited' was registered and comprised seven directors: The Hon. James Byng, James Whatman MP, Alexander Beattie, Henry Bean Mackeson, Gilson Hornan, Edward Leigh-Pemberton MP, and George Smith. The first meeting was held at Tooley Street on 3rd March at which it was agreed that although the Hythe & Sandgate Rly Company would be the owners of the land, the SER would provide the finance for this purpose.

The route of the new railway took it through the land of several large estates belonging to: Col. William Deedes, William Tournay Tournay, Rev. Tatton Brockman, Henry Rigden, Sir Courtenay Honeywood, Sir Edward Dering, Edward Hugessen and Her Majesty's Secretary of State for War. The Scene Estate, bordering the railway, was offered to the SER for approximately £100 per acre, of which 500 acres were bought. This large acreage was a bargain, for not only would its value increase with the building of the railway, but it contained a frontage to the English Channel of almost a mile – perfect for attracting seaside development. To this end the Seabrook Estate Company was formed, the directors of which were almost all involved with the railway. Having now secured this land, the SER were ebulliently confident that once the rails had reached Sandgate 'there would be no difficulty in getting an extension to the harbour'. Indeed, it appears that the very existence of the branch was pinned entirely upon this one hope.

In the meantime the shareholders of the Seabrook Estate Company were likely rubbing their hands in glee at the fortuitous prospects before them. Not only had work already begun on keeping the sea at bay with a new sea wall, but new roads were being drawn up, along with residential development and a large hotel on the seafront. The jewel in the crown however was the firmly held belief that it was only a matter of time before the new line became the main route to the continent, leaving the present line to Folkestone for just local traffic.

The seal of the company was instructed to be obtained by Mr. Shaw the SER's secretary. Costing £12 it featured the arms of the South Eastern Railway and the town of Hythe.

The sanctioning of the railway was not without its difficulties. Primarily these were objections from Lord Redesdale to certain sections of the Bill, but eventually all opposition was withdrawn, the dust settled and by the summer an air of excitement was felt in the district with locals expecting the arrival of the railway navvies at any time. However, further troubles persisted, caused mainly by negotiations with the War Office for land at Seabrook for which they were asking £350 per acre or that the SER should lease the land. The SER retorted by refusing to instruct their proprietors to build the line unless the land was made available at a moderate price.

In July 1871 Watkin told the Board he'd hoped to report on the progress of the branch but matters were still unsettled in negotiations with the War Office. He then went on to outline an interesting scheme put forward by Colonel Jervois for a railway between Hythe and Ham Street. Subsequently the SER offered £40 per acre for the land running adjacent to the Royal Military Canal but the War Office refused, claiming it was worth at least four times that price. Watkin, never noted for his tensile temper, raged that the line would never pay, would cost at least £100,000 for a single line railway and added that his negotiations with the War Office were 'tedious, troublesome and useless!'

Another six months of exchanging letters then followed in which the SER made the suggestion that:

'Her Majesty's Secretary of State for War and the South Eastern Railway should agree upon the acquisition of the northern side of the military canal from a point near the intended 'Shorncliffe Camp Station' on the proposed Hythe & Sandgate Line to Ham Street where the canal crosses under the Ashford & Hastings Branch.'

They went on to add:

'The use of the canal bank and contiguous property would enable troops and stores from Shorncliffe and Hythe to be conveyed continuously to all parts of England, Wales and Scotland without marching and should the War Office and the South Eastern Railway co-operate, a short piece of line three miles from the end of the Hythe & Sandgate Line to Folkestone – and another piece of line from Dover to Deal, would complete a direct coastal line available for operations of defence all the way from London to Portsmouth and, with a detour here and there, all the way to Penzance.'

The directors stressed that they considered these facts pointed 'to a matter of great national interest' but a cynic might well be forgiven for suggesting that all they really intended was to procure the support of H.M.'s Secretary of State for War in order to back their line to Folkestone Harbour! The seeds of the scheme fell on stony ground and, apart from making the august columns of the *Illustrated London News*, little else was ever heard of the 'Hythe & Ham Street Railway'.

Spurred on by the prevailing optimism pervading their London Bridge headquarters at that time, the Board summoned Francis Brady on Leap Year's Day 1872 requesting that he prepare the working plans as soon as possible in order that tenders for the line's construction might be invited. Watkin then embarked upon a crafty ploy of true Watkinsian nature. He wrote to Edward Cardwell, the Secretary of State for War, requesting that as there were likely many soldiers stationed at the camp at Shorncliffe, they might be usefully employed upon constructing the new branch line to Sandgate which was to serve their camp. The request was duly passed to Major D'Aunt, who was no fool and saw through this thinly disguised attempt at enlisting cheap labour, so he politely declined Watkin's offer saying:

'In consequence of the musketry instruction which is at present being carried on, considerably reducing the number of men for parades etc, and that as this is the "dull" season and the regiments in garrison being composed principally of young soldiers, Colonel Parke commanding the troops is unable to make any arrangement at the present time with regard to soldier labour on the Hythe and Sandgate Line.'

Alas, poor Watkin, every shovelful to the Pride of Kent and beyond would have to be paid for, but at least the first would be dug free of charge, and that would be hewn by nothing less than a royal hand.

Shorncliffe station master James Keefe standing with his dog outside his railway-built home 'Rose Villa' in 1871. The house, now named 'Wilderness', still stands to this day virtually unaltered. *Tonbridge Historical Society*

CHAPTER TWO

A Royal Inauguration

NAMING Prince Arthur of Connaught, a grandson of Queen Victoria, as the royal personage chosen to perform the ceremony of the cutting of the first sod of the Hythe and Sandgate Railway, caused considerable excitement in the borough. A local newspaper commented that this was indeed an honour for Hythe since the railway would be the first in the land to have been begun by a royal hand. Much confidence and optimism accompanied the undertaking which it was felt would transform Hythe, causing it to out-rival nearby Folkestone and 'put neighbouring Dover completely in the shade'. Envisaging such development it was perfectly plausible that with the transformation of Seabrook the townships of Hythe and Sandgate would be almost as one, giving Kent its 'Brighton' or its 'London-super-Mare'.

The date for the ceremony was set for Thursday, 11th April 1872, and it must have seemed that the gods themselves were favourable to the venture for the preceding two days were untypically English, being gloriously sunny and dry, thereby allowing all the decorations and preparations to go ahead unhindered. As Thursday dawned, yet another warm, cloudless day tinged with the fresh sparkle of spring, the station master at Shorncliffe was busily engaged with final preparations, while 72 miles along the line at Charing Cross the special train was assembled and cordoned off from the other platforms. Shortly before departure, the dignitaries gathered on the platform and shook hands before sinking into the cushioned comfort of the first class compartments. Here, among the many invited guests, were Sir Edward and Lady Watkin, the Lord Mayor of London, the Sheriff of London, as well as the directors and officials of the Hythe & Sandgate and South Eastern Railway Companies. At precisely 11.00 a.m. a shrill whistle announced the departure of the train which rumbled over Hungerford bridge, leaving behind the hustle and bustle of the capital to cross the green hills and vales of Kent where a smart non-stop run to Shorncliffe was achieved in ninety minutes. Soon after the passengers had discharged, the royal train from Dover was seen approaching from the east, bearing His Royal Highness Prince Arthur, Mr. C. W. Eborall, the general manager of the SER, and numerous military officials. Gracefully pulling in at 12.35 to the pre-determined spot, Prince Arthur was warmly received by Sir Edward Watkin and the Hon. James Byng who introduced the Prince to Baron Meyer de Rothschild, the MP for Hythe, as well as a multitude of military 'top brass'.

The station looked most attractive and the newspaper reporter commended Station Master James Keefe for his splendid efforts in transforming a normally unattractive edifice into its present glory with evergreens, flowers and flags adorning the walls and fixtures. In the waiting room, which resounded to the assembly's footsteps, there hung a banner proclaiming 'God bless the Union' which was intended to refer to that between the SER and the H & SR companies, even so the newspaper couldn't resist the uncharitable gibe that it was a remnant from the 1863 celebrations when England and Denmark were united.

Entering the waiting carriages, the Prince in an open landau pulled by four handsome greys, the procession set off southwards, cheered on by a rapturous crowd of 500 lining the station approach. Led by a brass band and a guard of honour comprising the 3rd Platoon Prince of Wales' Dragoon Guards, they rode along the lane, whilst in the distance a boom of guns from the adjacent hillside sounded a royal salute. Dropping down into Sandgate the cavalcade was greeted by cheers, waving handkerchiefs and hats as they drove under the first triumphal arch which bore the inscription 'Welcome to Sandgate'. A plethora of bunting, flags and flora was to be seen everywhere, adorning every house and shop, whilst a large banner was stretched across the High Street reading 'Success to the Hythe & Sandgate Railway'. Further arches had been erected in front of the Duke of York and Royal Kent hotels whilst, commencing at the Esplanade and lining the entire route, were no less than 110 flagstaffs, 40 feet in height, painted royal blue and capped in gilt. These had been erected by a gang of SER labourers under the charge of the Permanent Way Inspector, Mr. Latham. At the foot of the Military Road in Seabrook stood a lofty arch cleverly bedecked and interlaced with bright yellow furze and evergreens from the surrounding hillsides. Upon its apex was fitted a shield bearing the royal coat of arms. At the eastern approach to Hythe another triumphal archway had been erected bearing 'Welcome to Hythe' whilst dwellings similarly decorated, proclaimed messages of patriotism and success. One such was Mr. Worthington's premises with 'Welcome Prince Arthur' emblazoned across the entrance of his coachworks.

The bells of the parish church had been rung at 10 o'clock, their merry peal beckoning thousands of people throughout the morning until it was reckoned that over 10,000 people were now gathered in the town on this auspicious day. At Cannon Gate the cheering reached a tumultuous crescendo as the Prince's carriage drew up to the appointed place for the ceremony. Not one cloud had threatened the day, while a gentle breeze kept the temperature comfortable. However, an overnight shower would have been welcomed for it was noticed that the chalky white dust of the road had 'made the guests appear as though they'd spent an hour or two in a flour mill'!

A reception marquee stood by the entrance to the site which was reached by a path lined with little flagstaffs 'ornamented with baronettes of every hue and clothed in evergreen' behind which excited crowds, all anxious for a close glimpse of the royal personage, jostled for a spot. It was seen that the Prince was most touched by the warm reception he'd received for which he bowed and raised his hat in gratitude. At this moment the band struck up the National Anthem, after which the Rector of Saltwood – the Reverend W. F. Erskine-Knollys then asked for a blessing on the undertaking followed by the Lord's Prayer. A cluster of schoolchildren then gave a hearty rendition of the National Anthem, accompanied with gusto by some members of the crowd, before the propitious moment arrived. Francis Brady then had the honour to step forward to present the ceremonial spade to the Prince before leading him to the barrow. The implements, furnished by Elkington & Co. of 22 Regent Street, London, were both of oak, ornately carved and polished and embellished with silver plaques each stating they were used by HRH Prince Arthur 'on the occasion of cutting

SOUTH EASTERN RAILWAY.

H.R.H. PRINCE ARTHUR

WILL CUT THE FIRST SOD

OF THE

Hythe and Sandgate Railway

On Thursday, 11th April, 1872.

Return Tickets

(1, 2 & 3 Class)

AT SINGLE FARES,

WILL BE ISSUED

To SHORNCLIFFE

BY TRAINS

Leaving DOVER at 9.0 a.m. & 12.0 noon,

AND

Leaving ASHFORD at 11.15 a.m.

RETURNING from SHORNCLIFFE by any Train of the same description and Class on the same day.

CHILDREN UNDER TWELVE, HALF-PRICE.

NO LUGGAGE ALLOWED.

London Bridge Station, April, 1872.

(By Order),

C. W. EBORALL, General Manager.

(20)

McCorquodale & Co., Printers, "The Armoury," Southwark.

Courtesy David Banks

A ROYAL INAUGURATION

Prince Arthur cutting the first sod.

the first sod of the Hythe & Sandgate portion of the South Eastern Railway, April 11th 1872'.

Sir Edward Watkin then addressed the crowd, recalling the great start of the railway age and the day he'd witnessed the opening of the Liverpool and Manchester Railway – a day tragically marred by the dreadful accident which killed Mr. Huskisson. Pointing to the long stretch of beautiful beach, he prophesied that the day was not far distant when houses would extend as far as the eye could see and up to the hills behind them. With the population of London increasing by 200,000 every year, he predicted thousands would flock to this haven for recuperation where many would be tempted to permanently reside in the salubrious air and lush surroundings of this patch of Kent. Whether any of the assembly shared his enthusiasm at this prospect is highly debatable but he received a warm response nonetheless, although nothing compared to the rapturous cheering as the Prince stepped forward, took the spade in his gloved hands and thrust it deep into the ground. There followed a moment of silence, broken only by a sharp crack as the spade's handle embarrassingly snapped in two. For an instant the Prince hesitated, some children sniggered, whilst older folk shook their heads but, undaunted, the Prince seized the lower half and turned the first turf of the Hythe and Sandgate Railway into the barrow before wheeling it a few yards along a plank and tipping it to one side whereupon tremendous cheering broke out. As the crowd disbanded, the guests making their way to the Town Hall, much comment was exchanged upon this unfortunate incident. One old gentleman warned 'It's a bad omen, depend upon it, what I say is: It means no good.' and one old lady sighed 'I would rather have given ten pounds than it should have happened.'

The exterior of the Town Hall boasted a gigantic representation of the Prince of Wales' feathers, lit by gas which, as was stated, would consume 1,200 cubic feet an hour. Inside, decorations of shields, trophies and arms adorned the walls, interspersed with white and crimson drapery. The Mayor of Hythe received the Prince and read the address, after which the assembly partook of a sumptuous *dejeuner* 'served in the best style' by Mr. Sydney Benser, the proprietor of the Charing Cross Hotel.

After they had eaten, Sir Edward Watkin rose and proposed a toast to the health of Her Majesty, saying it was a toast which 'found an echo in the hearts of every Englishman' and that 'no sane man wanted to alter the form of Government in this country'. He added: 'Her Majesty is a woman distinguished amongst women; one who sets an example which every mother in the country must wish to emulate. Therefore I give "The Queen" – and God bless her!' The toast was drunk upstanding and with much enthusiasm. The health of Mr. Eborall, the general manager of the SER, and Mr. Francis Brady, was then proposed by Sir Edward, who spoke of the two gentlemen being at the head of their profession, observing that the managers of the SER would never be satisfied in carrying on the work of continental communication until passengers could cross the Channel without suffering from sea-sickness and other inconvenience. He intimated that the coming of the Sandgate railway would pave the way for 'the eradication of sea-sickness' (cheers and applause) and finished by saying: 'If the people of England and France will only look upon the question as Count Cavour looked upon that glorious Mont Cenis tunnel, England would not long be separated by sea from the Continent.' The wily Watkin was not the first, nor would he be the last, to realise the huge political status this project would endow.

Mr. Eborall then spoke of his time connected with railways, which amounted to more than three decades. He told the assembly he believed that within a few years beautiful marine villas would spring up on the land in the vicinity where the ceremony had taken place and that it would become one of the finest watering places on the southern coast, vying with Eastbourne, Hastings or Folkestone (applause). Hythe had been languishing for years for want of a railway, he said, and he was the first to suggest that one be made there. He added that he believed it would be of great advantage to the place as well as adding considerably to the revenues of the company.

Prince Arthur then rose and said: 'I am sure we could not leave this room without drinking one health. It is that of Sir Edward Watkin (cheers). I am sure from what we have seen today, we shall be only too glad to drink the health of a gentleman who has done so much for the railways in Kent especially, as well as for railways in general. We will not only drink his health as a gentleman, as a friend, and as chairman of this company, but as one of the great engineers of this Company!' (loud cheers).

While the guests were enjoying their afternoon, the local children from the parishes of Hythe, Cheriton and Newington were, 'without distinction of creed or condition', treated to a grand tea where they could feast themselves to their heart's content. Charity was evidently the order of the day for Baron Rothschild presented a gift to the poor consisting of a $\frac{1}{4}$lb of tea for the women, whilst the men were each allowed 3 pints of beer.

Bidding farewell to their hosts, the royal cortège set off once again amidst renewed cheering, arriving at Shorncliffe station at 4 o'clock where a simmering engine waited with the London train. The Prince continued in his carriage through Folkestone and on to Dover, where he was stationed in barracks.

As dusk fell, the numerous devices were illuminated by gas jets, which astonished the crowds with their brilliant displays, as did the colourful array of Chinese lanterns. A sumptuous banquet, provided by the Seabrook Estate Company, delighted the guests, as did a selection of vocal music of popular songs and airs of the day. There was even a rendition of the song especially composed for the occasion, entitled 'Hythe and its beautiful sea'. After the dinner there followed further toasts and speeches. The Reverend P. Ward remarked that the people of Hythe had waited very patiently for this railway – 'almost as long as Jacob waited for the fulfilment of his desires from Laban' and he hoped that all their expectations would now be gratified. He went on to express a hope that 'on this railway, God's day would not be desecrated, but that special trains would run on weekdays'. Watkin replied that it was their policy to reduce Sunday travelling to a minimum but the reverend gentleman should bear in mind that on Sundays, as on other days, some communication must be kept up (hear, hear).

Alderman Mackeson then thanked the SER for consenting to make the Hythe railway and compared the speedy journey from Charing Cross that morning to the hitherto modes of transport. He went on to praise them further: 'Why, the South Eastern Railway had been called the "railway race-course of England" and I am quite sure that so long as it retains Sir Edward Watkin at its head it would be one of the first and best managed railways in the kingdom' (applause). Alderman Mackeson concluded by proposing 'The health of Sir Edward Watkin' and 'Prosperity to the Hythe and Sandgate Railway' whereby the toast was drunk with *Kentish Fire*.

Throughout the evening, and late into the night, the roads in Hythe were thronged with pedestrians and vehicles, making it a day to remember. For the old it was a sight, the like of which, their now-dimming eyes had probably never witnessed, whilst for the children, their bright eyes must never have been so alert, filled with the wondrous shows of the day as they laid their tiny heads on the pillow that night, desperately searching for sleep.

Summing up, the newspaper report stated:

> 'The work of the line will be pushed forward with all possible despatch. There will be no tunnelling but some rather deep cuttings. It is expected that the branch will be opened for traffic by May 1873.'

Here was optimisim indeed.

A group of SER employees, probably foremen, at Westenhanger in 1873 during the time when the Sandgate branch was under construction. Of note is the remarkable man-powered trolley. Left to right: Messrs. Frost, Neave, Hook, Bellingham (fifth unknown).
Tonbridge Historical Society

CHAPTER THREE

Oh! What a day Hythe is having

WITH tenders for the construction of the railway having been invited in the weeks preceding the royal visit, the SER sifted through the eleven offers received, ranging from the lowest, £43,769 0s 0d from Philip Stiff of Dover, up to £84,406 17s 9d from Messrs Aird & Co. After apparently little deliberation the contract was awarded to Philip Stiff, as late as the day before Prince Arthur's visit but, as the SER would ruefully learn, the cheapest was not always the best.

Work began in earnest at Saltwood and by the 15th June 1872 the *Folkestone Chronicle* reported: 'In order to expediate the construction of this line, workmen are now engaged night and day.' Curiously enough the contract between Stiff and the SER was not executed until 31st July and even by then much of the required land had yet to be purchased. The War Office were asking £350 per acre for land at Seabrook where it was planned to build Sandgate station. Watkin had no option other than to agree to this 'exorbitant price', whereby a cheque for £1,981 17s 6d was grudgingly handed over.

The construction of the line presented no great problem and the gang of men employed by Stiff soon had a temporary line of rails at Sandling Park where they were busily excavating the tunnel beneath Hayne Wood as well as the cutting beyond. Little is known of the two engines used in the line's construction, except that one was a six-coupled locomotive with 11″ cylinders, built by Manning-Wardle, whilst the other was a four-coupled locomotive with 9″ cylinders, built by Brotherhood & Co. of Chippenham. As with most railways through undulating countryside, the spoil from the cuttings was conveniently transported along the formation to build the embankments. This was done at Saltwood where a high embankment had to be created to reach the opposite hillside where the foundations for Hythe stations were being stumped out.

The onset of winter naturally slowed the progress of the works, even so any hope of having the line completed by May was clearly pie in the sky. Despite the usual spate of storms, which were notoriously violent in the last century, no significant damage occurred at the workings, but a serious landslide a stone's throw away on the main line near Saltwood tunnel caused disruption to trains. Following some atrociously wet and stormy weather which, as usual, brought about a few slips on the SERs main line through the Warren, the Honeywood stream became very swollen with the rain percolating down through the Etchinghill escarpment. The force of the water seeking its path to the sea caused a culvert to collapse, removing with it a large portion of embankment. The 'up' main line sank some three feet whereupon Francis Brady was hurriedly summoned to oversee the reinstatement of the railway. All traffic had to be run at a walking pace along the 'down' line with a pilot engine in assistance. This engine was stationed between Shorncliffe and Westenhanger. Lights were kept burning near the scene throughout the hours of darkness, whilst a large bonfire blazed at the exact point. The brook, within a matter of hours, had turned from its traditional babblings into a raging torrent. The SER did their best to ensure that the culvert taking the Honeywood stream under the Sandgate branch was of sufficient width to accommodate a recurrence of that stormy week. However, problems of a different nature cropped up many years later on another culvert when the entire length of brickwork cracked and only immediate action prevented a total collapse.

On the 1st April 1873 there occurred the only fatal accident which claimed the life of one of the workmen. William Griffey was severely hurt in the Saltwood cutting and, even though no details were given, his injuries imply an incident with the wagons or other mechanical means. He was carried to the infirmary where he remained for a number of days before finally succumbing to his wounds. At the inquest held at the Town Hall the Coroner, Mr. W. S. Smith, recorded a verdict of accidental death, where it was revealed that the poor man had left a wife and six children. It would have doubtless been difficult for a man in his position with eight mouths to feed to have provided for them in case of his death. His wife, who had only just given birth two days before the accident, was left quite destitute and the poor wretch must have been beside herself with fear for the future. A fund was organised for the family 'in the hope that she might find employment' and to this the SER donated £10, but it was a harsh and cruel age in spite of its splendour and pomp and I often wonder what happened to them.

During the construction it was reported that the Rev. Erskine-Knollys, the Rector of Saltwood, visited each navvy once a month and gave him $\frac{1}{2}$oz tobacco. At such times never a swear word was heard in his presence!

With the earthworks nearing completion, the station layouts at Hythe and Seabrook were mapped out by Brady for approval by the Board. The station at Hythe was at a convenient point between railway and road, situated just east of the bridge, currently being built, which spanned the road leading up from the town and over the hills to Beachborough. It meant, however, a long walk uphill for the townsfolk who must have wished the line could have described a wider arc by sweeping in nearer the town centre and its remoteness was undoubtedly a contributory factor to the line's future misfortune. If Hythe was poorly sited then Sandgate residents had even more cause for complaint, for their station was almost a mile away to the west in neighbouring Seabrook. Nevertheless, it should be borne in mind that the railway was not built to specifically serve the two towns, as pointed out in the *Folkestone Express*:

> 'Although the station will be further from the centre of the town than is desirable, that inconvenience may find a remedy by and by; indeed, such may be the impetus given to commercial speculation, that before long the multiplied buildings may so surround the station at Seabrooke that it will not be far from central. And then we cannot suppose for a moment that Seabrooke will be a terminus for ever. We can almost imagine we see the continuation of the branch to the Folkestone harbour, a thing which only wants time to accomplish.'

As Brady's plans didn't include station masters' houses, he was instructed to amend them and supply estimates for construction. For Hythe he estimated £2,100 whilst at Sandgate he reckoned on £2,900. These were approved, at which he was instructed to carry out the work forthwith. In the meantime the SER agents were buying up land wherever it became available, including plots east of Sandgate station and in the town itself where the route would run.

The green leaves of the trees in this beautiful landscape turned to their customary blaze of red and gold before falling to the ground as yet another winter approached. On the 1st January 1874 the Board wrote to Brady at his lodgings in Hythe, enquiring when he expected the line to be completed. Brady replied that the contractor was pushing the work as much he could and that it was confidently expected the line would be finished for opening on May Day. As to his own efforts he replied:

> 'With reference to your letter of the 1st instant I beg to say that the framing for the stations on the Hythe and Sandgate branch is being prepared by our workshops and is now in a forward state so that we should be in readiness for the opening of the line when the contractor's works are completed.
>
> I am, dear Sir Edward, yours truly, Francis Brady.'

At the end of the month, the secretary told a meeting of the directors that the new line was progressing well and would be opened in the course of the summer. This pleased Watkin as it meant maximum publicity would be achieved with the high season of visitors to the south coast as well as a chance to earn some revenue before the slacking of traffic caused by the winter. Perhaps the most surprising item which appeared in the minute book at this time, caused either through difficulties in purchasing land or a sense of the fight ahead, was the following sentence: 'The question of its extension is a matter for grave deliberation.'

In March, John Shaw, the secretary and manager of the SER, wrote to Brady seeking further news of progress, to which Brady replied that it would take a further three months to complete the works but he expected all would be ready for an opening late in June. The cause of the delay was a slip in the cutting near Hayne tunnel but this had since been remedied with work progressing satisfactorily. Adding that the station buildings were in course of erection and would be roofed in shortly, he went on to mention that the permanent way had been commenced at Sandling Park junction, with the points, crossings, signals, locking apparatus and signal cabin 'all in a forward state'. Also completed at that time were the two three-arch bridges spanning Saltwood cutting as well as the tunnel lining, while the bricklayers were putting the finishing touches to the embellished portals.

June came and went with still no sign of completion which prompted an impatient Watkin to consult with some of the directors of the Hythe and Sandgate Company concerning the position of Philip Stiff, the contractor, and stressed that it was most desirable that work be hurried along. In the end an agreement, dated 29th June, was entered into whereby a mutual release from the original conditions of the contract was adopted, with Stiff accepting £6,500 as well as agreeing to hand over all tools, machinery, sheds, materials etc, to allow the SER to finish the job. Once complete, the SER would 'return all engines, waggons, rails, barrows, and other plant without liability for wear and tear'. Stiff was paid £5,000 on the third day after possession, whilst the balance would follow on the day of opening.

Having engaged the SER labourers, the construction of the line rapidly progressed with all due speed as the running rails were laid down along the entire branch. On the evening of 4th August a minor collision occurred between some ballasting trucks and timber wagons but there were no casualties and the damage was soon rectified. A few weeks later a request was sent to the Board of Trade, seeking an inspection of the new line. On 29th August John Shaw told the Board that he'd accompanied Colonel C. S. Hutchinson, the Board of Trade's Inspector of Railways, where the colonel had refused to sanction public opening until certain details had been rectified. These, said Shaw, were now being done.

> Sir,
> I have the honour to report for the information of the Board of Trade that in compliance with the instructions contained in your minute of the 21st, I have inspected the Hythe & Sandgate Branch of the South Eastern Railway.
>
> This branch line which is 3 miles 5 chains in length and is double throughout leaves the main line at a point about a mile on the Dover side of Westenhanger station and terminates near Sandgate. The new stations are Hythe and Sandgate and the traffic is intended to be worked between Westenhanger and Sandgate.
>
> The steepest gradient on the line has an inclination of 1 in $54\frac{1}{2}$ and the sharpest curve a radius of 13 chains.
>
> There are some heavy cuttings and embankments. The permanent way consists of double-headed wrought iron rails in 24 ft. lengths weighing 81 lbs to the yard, fished at the joints, the chairs are of cast iron weighing 32 lbs, each fixed to its sleeper by two wrought iron spikes: the sleepers are rectangular in section and measure 9 ft × 10 ins × 5 ins; they are laid at an average central interval of 2 ft 8 ins; the ballast is composed of shingle and is slated to a depth of 18 ins below the under surface of the sleepers.
>
> The fencing is of post and rail.
>
> There are 5 bridges over the line, 5 under it, a tunnel of 94 yards long and 3 large culverts. The overbridges are constructed in 3 cases entirely of brickwork, and in the other two with brick abutments carrying cast iron girders, the largest span being 28 ft. One of the under bridges is constructed entirely of brickwork (span $26\frac{3}{4}$ ft); the other 4 are brick abutments carrying in 3 cases cast iron girders, largest span $28\frac{1}{2}$ ft, and in the 4th wrought iron girders, span 40 ft. The tunnel is egg-shaped in section and is constructed entirely of brickwork. These bridges &c appear all to be substantially constructed and to be standing well except in the case of the culvert at 1 mile 23 chains where a slip in the bank carried away a portion of the original culvert and for which at present a heading supported by timber has been substituted. The dislodged portion of the culvert is in course of reconstruction. The girder bridges gave moderate deflections under a rolling load of Engines and the girders possess sufficient theoretical strength.
>
> The following requirements came under my notice:
>
> 1. **At Sandling Junction**. The distant signals require repeating so that the repeaters may be seen in the cabin. The lamp of the Up Main Distant should be lowered so as to be better seen from the tunnel.
> 2. The lowest row of telegraph caps in the tunnel should be raised above the level of the tops of the carriage doors.
> 3. A railing should be placed on top of both parapets of the bridge at 1 mile 54 chains, close to Hythe station.
> 4. **At Hythe Station**. The Up Home signal should be moved back to clear the fouling point of a siding; No.1 siding points should be unlocked with the Up Starting signal and both Up and Down sidings provided with catch points.
> 5. **At Sandgate Station**. A chock block worked from the signal cabin should be provided in the centre line. There is still a great deal of ballasting, fencing and other substantial work to be done before the line can be opened and I must report that by reason of the incompleteness of the works, the Hythe & Sandgate Branch of the South Eastern Rly cannot be opened for passenger traffic without danger to the public using the same.
>
> C. S. Hutchinson, Lieut. Colonel, R. E.
> 29th August 1874

The London train steaming into Hythe on the opening day – 9th October 1874. *Illustrated London News*

On Tuesday, 8th September, Watkin went down to see the new branch. Accompanied by Shaw and Brady, Watkin found the works sufficiently complete as to urge that October 1st should be the date of public opening. It was also noted that the present road to Hythe station was in a lamentably poor state, practically useless for vehicles, so a new road was authorised on land belonging to the Seabrook Estate Co. At a further meeting, on 24th September, Shaw proposed to have the formal opening on Friday, 9th October, saying he'd informed the Mayor of Hythe that His Royal Highness the Duke of Teck would officiate at the ceremony. Two days later, Colonel Hutchinson again visited the line, to which he gave his approval for opening.

Sir,
I have the honour to report for the information of the Board of Trade that in compliance with your reference of the 12th inst. I have reinspected the Hythe & Sandgate Branch of the South Eastern Railway.

Since my inspection on the 29th inst. the deficiencies then alluded to have been for the most part made good. The repeater of the Down Distant signal at Sandling Junction has not yet been fixed and a locking bar is required at the facing points. The rails of the parapets of the bridge at Hythe station require lengthening at each end.

At Sandgate Station the short siding joining the Up line requires an interlocked chock block or catch siding. The trailing points with which this siding joins the Up line should in their normal position be open for the siding so that they might catch any runaway vehicle breaking loose on the incline.

Until the bank near Saltwood Castle has become thoroughly consolidated and the culvert through it is finished, a very cautious speed should be observed in running over the bank. In consequence of the steep gradients with which the branch has been constructed, great attention should be paid to providing trains of all descriptions running on it with ample brake power.

Subject to the completion of the matters alluded to (which there will be ample time for before the 9th approx, the day proposed for the opening) and to the above remarks, the opening of the Hythe & Sandgate may, I submit, be sanctioned.

C. S. Hutchinson, Lieut. Colonel, R. E.
26th September 1874

Whilst all this was going on, the SER had another go at cracking the nut that would get them into Folkestone via the Leas. A deputation visited Folkestone where they met members

'Reading the address at the opening of the Hythe & Sandgate Railway'.

of Folkestone Corporation, inviting them to contribute towards the cost of building the line, but this met with no success. They followed this by approaching Radnor, asking that his lordship might present the land free of charge (!). Radnor implied that while he was not opposed in principle to the railway, he did expect the full value of the land to be paid. On hearing this, Watkin advised that the outlay could not be recommended at present. With the benefit of hindsight, perhaps this was the ultimate mistake, for at that time Radnor appeared to be reasonably favourable to the SER. An opportunity like this was never to come the way of the SER again despite their persistence and acts of persuasion.

The morning of the great day began with dark clouds ominously threatening to ruin the day's events but it seemed as though the ringing of the church bells early in the morning frightened them all away for the skies cleared, allowing the sun to beam and warm the chilly autumnal air. In Hythe, many people were busy putting the finishing touches to their decorations, whilst a myriad of banners had been strung up across houses and shopfronts, proclaiming such joyous messages as: 'Long-looked for – come at last', 'Success and prosperity to Hythe', 'Never to be forgotten', 'Welcome Sir Edward Watkin', 'Welcome Prince Teck', 'God Save the Queen', 'S.E.R.', 'Oh! What a day Hythe is having' and many more, including 'Onward' – the motto of the South Eastern Railway Company. It was stated that over 3,600 yards of evergreen had been used in the decorations which also ran to a line of Venetian masts, 'the like of which Hythe has never before seen'. In fact it was reckoned that the quality and quantity of decorations even exceeded those of two years ago when Prince Arthur had visited Hythe. It is worth mentioning that originally Prince Arthur had been approached with a view to opening the line but as he was unavailable the Duke of Teck graciously offered to step in his place.

The first item of excitement on the day was the departure at 10 o'clock from the new Sandgate station of the very first public train for those desirous of making the inaugural trip. It was noticeable, however, that very few Sandgate residents boarded the train, not even the chairman or members of the local board had bothered to put in an appearance. At Hythe, however, it was a far different picture with a goodly number eagerly waiting on the 'up' platform as the sound of the engine pulling up the 1 in 59 gradient reached their ears before it appeared in the cutting to steam into the station amidst much cheering and clapping. Considerable excitement must have been felt by the townsfolk as they boarded the train for a non-stop run to Ashford. Leaving Hythe they had their first glimpse of the new panoramic view of the town, whilst presumably embankments, cuttings, bridges and a tunnel provided all the items that any self-respecting railway should possess!

On arrival at Ashford more passengers joined the train until every available seat had been filled. On the return trip the train ignored Smeeth but stopped at Westenhanger before setting off again, over the new junction at Sandling Park, to pull into Hythe at exactly 11.40 a.m. Alighting from the train, the lucky travellers were greeted by a commotion of over 1,000 children from the schools at Hythe, Saltwood, Sandgate, Cheriton, Lympne and Newington, marching past with banners and flags flying to the accompaniment of the Ashford Rifle Band, on their way to take up their positions in readiness to cheer the arrival of the royal train. The faces of the little ones were radiant with joy, for it was a holiday from school which would later include games on the green, followed by a grand feast at the National Schools paid for personally by Sir Edward Watkin. By now close on fifty carriages had lined up along the roads close to the station where all the footpaths and available spaces were swarming with hundreds of people. The 'down' platform at the station was buzzing with the excited chatter of children whereas on the opposite platform the dignitaries assembled in all their fine clothes of office. The sound of rustling wires, as the signal arms were lowered to 'road clear', only increased the tension and excitement which was fit to burst with the imminent arrival of the train from London. All of a sudden a piercing whistle from the west announced the approaching train which majestically drew into the 'down' platform under the careful guidance of SER engine driver W. Watkin. The engine was festooned with laurels and flags, whilst its carriages gleamed and shone for they contained His Royal Highness the Duke of Teck, and suite, as well as Sir Edward Watkin, the Hon. James Byng, John Shaw and others associated with the railway. The hiss from the engine was momentarily drowned out by the spontaneous cheering and clapping, then, with a whistle that probably made everyone jump, the train set off for Sandgate.

Only a few people had gathered at the terminus station, indeed the town had made no preparations for celebrating the day and it was reported that only one flag was to be seen fluttering in the vicinity, at the home of Mr. Pledge, the chairman of the Sandgate Local Board of Health. The whole party alighted on arrival at Sandgate while the train was made ready for the return trip to Hythe. In the meantime a conducted tour of the station was held with the Duke being escorted into the waiting room to be shown the booking office by Watkin who, in all probability, was likely stressing the temporary nature of things, adding that before long the trains would be running through to Folkestone harbour. Re-entering the train, a start was made back to Hythe where the crimson carpet had been rolled out across the platform while the dignitaries nervously cleared their throats and checked their adornments. As the train eased to a halt the cheers from the crowd rose to a tremendous climax as the compartment door was opened for His Royal Highness to step out onto the platform while necks strained in the crowd to catch a glimpse.

After the preliminary salutations had been exchanged the party stood beneath the 'up' platform canopy where the Recorder stepped forward to read the address:

> 'May it please your Serene Highness, We, the Mayor, Aldermen and Burgesses of the Borough of Hythe, beg to offer to your Serene Highness a most cordial welcome on the occasion of your visit to our ancient town.
>
> We beg to express our grateful acknowledgements to your Serene Highness for consenting to open the Hythe and Sandgate Branch of the South Eastern Railway, which we trust will materially promote the prosperity of our town and neighbourhood.
>
> We regret that Her Royal Highness, Princess Mary Adelaide, is

Front cover of invitation to opening of the railway

OH! WHAT A DAY HYTHE IS HAVING

HYTHE & SANDGATE BRANCH TIMETABLE ON OPENING OF LINE 1874												
WEEKDAYS: UP												**SUNDAYS**
Dep. Sandgate	6.15	8.00	8.55	10.30	12.05	1.10	4.30	5.50	6.25	7.15	9.00	7.45 6.40
Arr. Hythe	6.19	8.04	8.59	10.34	12.09	1.14	4.34	5.54	6.29	7.19	9.04	7.49 6.44
Arr. W'Hanger	6.30		9.12	10.46	12.25		4.47		7.32			8.00 6.51
Arr. Smeeth	6.40		..	10.59	..		4.55		7.41			8.09 7.06
Arr. Ashford	6.48		9.26	11.08	12.42		5.03		7.50			8.18 7.15
WEEKDAYS: DOWN												**SUNDAYS**
Dep. Ashford	9.05					5.02	6.23					10.12 9.05
Arr. Smeeth	9.17					5.15	..					10.23 9.16
Arr. W'Hanger	9.25					5.23	6.45					10.32 9.26
Arr. Hythe	9.35	10.55	11.44	2.32	3.05	5.33	6.50	7.40	9.05			10.41 9.35
Arr. Sandgate	9.40	11.00	11.49	2.37	3.10	5.38	6.55	7.45	9.10			10.46 9.40

Francis Brady.

unable to accompany your Serene Highness, but we hope on some future occasion Her Highness may honour us with her presence.

We pray that, through life, every blessing and happiness may attend both Her Royal Highness and your Serene Highness.

Given under the corporate seal of the borough of Hythe this ninth day of October, eighteen-hundred and seventy-four.'

The Duke then replied:

'I beg you to accept my heartfelt thanks for the kind and cordial welcome you are pleased to give me on this my first visit to your ancient town. I am much gratified at having been able to assist at the opening of the Hythe and Sandgate Branch of the South Eastern Railway, an undertaking which helps to complete the coast system of the south of England, brings the Camp of Shorncliffe and the School of Musketry at Hythe in communication with all parts of the kingdom, and will, I trust, tend to promote the well doing of your town and neighbourhood.'

He then declared the line officially open, at which point the band of the 82nd Regiment struck up a well-known German air. Joining his waiting carriage, the procession rode down into the centre of town, the street crammed with folk from all walks of life cheering him on his way as they trundled along the High Street to Rampart Road and on to the corporation meadow where a huge marquee had been erected.

Close on 300 guests sat down to the appetising *déjeuner* served by Mr. Spencer of the City Terminus Hotel. After dining, numerous customary toasts were drunk before speeches of grati-

tude were made to the SER for constructing the line. The Mayor of Hythe proclaimed:

'I believe that the work which has been completed by the ceremony performed by His Highness this day will enhance the prosperity of our ancient town and that it will lead to it taking that proper rank among other towns from which it has been so long kept out by circumstances.' (hear, hear)

He went on:

'I have no doubt that when the energetic directors of the South Eastern Railway open another line in this part of Kent* that if we are honoured with yet another visit by your Highness, you will find our locality so progressed that the three towns of Folkestone, Sandgate and Hythe shall all be joined together in one unbroken line of houses.' (laughter and applause)

*The Folkestone harbour extension

It would have been interesting to have seen General Hankey's response to this remark as he was among the guests, but unfortunately it was not recorded. The Rt. Hon. Knatchbull-Hugessen then made his speech which included the following:

'If the Lords and Commons have passed one Act which is more creditable to them than another, it is that Act sanctioning the making of a branch railway to Hythe and Sandgate.' (loud cheers and laughter) 'I do not, however, think I ought call them entirely unselfish with regard to that Act, for jaded senators require relaxation when autumn's fading leaves release them from labour and I know no better thing they might do than come here to assist in opening up such a salubrious and pleasant watering place as Hythe will become when developed by the railway.' (laughter and much applause)

Throughout the afternoon threatening clouds returned to the skies and by the time the guests were ready to leave the marquee it was raining hard. The Duke departed at 4.37pm, to be driven up to Hythe station in order to board the 5.00pm train for London. In the evening the rain mercifully ceased, allowing a torchlight procession through the town to be enjoyed by the townsfolk. The trail of blazing beacons wound its way through the streets and up to the hillside adjacent to the station where a huge bonfire lit up the night sky. Finally, a display of fireworks rounded off the day's events with a bang.

Altogether, 1874 had been a good year for Watkin, not only the completion of the Sandgate branch had been realised, but he had become the Member of Parliament for Hythe when successfully returned on February 4th. He no doubt believed that this would add impetus to the SER's thrust to push the branch through to Folkestone.

SOUTH EASTERN RAILWAY.

HYTHE STATION
AND
GROVE PARK STATION.

The Public are hereby respectfully informed that the above Stations will be

OPENED
FOR
GOODS TRAFFIC

On FRIDAY, January 1st, 1875.

Inquiries regarding Rates, &c., to be made of the respective Station Masters; or of Mr. E. B. NODEN, Goods Manager, Bricklayers' Arms Station, London.

JOHN SHAW, Manager and Secretary.

McCorquodale & Co., Printers, "The Armonry," Southwark.—3876.

CHAPTER FOUR

Onward!

AFTER more than thirty years debate, the railway had, at long last, come to Hythe and Sandgate. On the first day of public operation, Saturday 10th October, trains were to be heard in the locality, whistling through the landscape. What a wonderful sight it must have been when driving in a carriage along the Seabrook Road to look across at the new embankment where a Cudworth engine would be sending up great billows of white steam and smoke as it departed from Sandgate station.

The initial weekday service commenced with eleven 'up' trains and nine 'down' trains. On Sundays there were just two trains each way. Goods traffic was not catered for until New Year's Day 1875.

Sandgate engine shed was a sub-shed of Ashford with one engine being stored here permanently in order to work the first and last train of the day. A few years later the first train of the morning was composed purely of 'Engine & Brakes', which ran non-stop to Westenhanger in preparation for the day's goods trips.

Regretfully, no record appears to have survived to reveal what class of engine hauled the ceremonial train conveying HRH the Duke of Teck on that eventful day. If the print depicting this event can be relied on it may have been one of James Cudworth's 'Mail' class 2–2–2s. Passenger services at this time were, in all likelihood, ordinarily handled by the Cudworth '118s' which were the most ubiquitous on the South Eastern. The vast majority of these 2–4–0s were constructed in the SER's workshops at New Town, Ashford and handled everything from main line express trains to secondary branch and goods duties. Although generally good-runners and popular for performance, the lack of a cab roof, as with most engines at that time, meant that the South Eastern men had to be built of stern stuff. A tarpaulin was all that was provided for wet or wintry weather and bearing in mind that they performed many of their duties tender first, it must have been at times a test of endurance.

One of the more interesting classes of locomotives known to have handled traffic on the Sandgate branch was the 'Folkstone' (*sic*) class, built in 1851. Originally constructed as 4–2–0s by Robert Stephenson & Co., No. 136, named *Folkstone*, won a gold medal at the International Exhibition at Hyde Park in March 1851. These engines were reputedly difficult to get started, but once running they are said to have been free-running and fast, in fact No. 136 is logged as reaching 70 miles per hour on the stretch between Redhill and Tonbridge.

Rebuilt 'Folkestone' class No. 140 standing on the down road at Sandgate with driver Jesse Pearson on the footplate. This engine was one of the first to be fitted with the simple vacuum brake. The ejector, which can be seen by the smokebox, was controlled from the footplate by a rod passing underneath the handrail and alongside the boiler. *C. J. Barnard/Alex Todd*

Towards the end of the 1860s the ten members of the class were rebuilt by Cudworth into 2–4–0s whereupon it is said a better engine emerged. Ashford shed received No. 140 in due course which then regularly appeared on Sandgate services until its withdrawal for scrapping in October 1891.

Others likely rostered for Sandgate branch workings at this time were Cudworth's 'Standard Goods' engines. No. 127 almost certainly hauled freight over the line.

The business of tying up all the loose ends had begun now that the railway was open as far as Sandgate. The position of Philip Stiff after his contract with the SER was peremptorily ended was, or so it appears, not very enviable. Having been given back all his machinery and tools after the SER workmen had finished his job, he evidently had no further use for them. Whether railway building proved too much for him is not known but he offered everything that had been returned, back to the SER for the paltry sum of ten pounds, to which they readily agreed. In October 1874 his two locomotives were put up for sale but evidently his Manning-Wardle was not sold on this occasion as it was again offered for sale during 1876 when in store at Dover.

On the branch itself, everything was settling down well and was apparently proving popular with the townsfolk, the SER

17

Driver Gardner and fireman W. Holmes on the footplate with cleaner Oliver in the foreground and a resplendent Cudworth '118' No. 189 in the goods yard at Sandgate about 1890.
J. R. Minnis Collection

The new brick station at Westenhanger, photographed in 1879, five years after the Sandgate branch had opened. The station master, in his splendid top hat, stands nearest the camera, whilst his family can be seen peering from the first floor windows. On the left, workmen pause from securing lumber onto flat wagons and the signalman stands in the doorway of his box. The second bridge marks the summit of the bank; from there the line descends towards Sandling Park Junction.
Tonbridge Historical Society

Cudworth 'Standard Goods' No. 127 in the down sidings at Westenhanger about 1876.
D. L. Bradley Collection

In this view the photographer is standing precisely upon the proposed route of the Sandgate-Folkestone Harbour extension. The railway would have passed in the gap between Marine Parade on the left and the Harbour offices and clock tower on the right. The Leas tunnel would have been bored through the cliff upon which stands the parish church.   *Eamonn Rooney Collection*

noting that 'results have been satisfactory considering the late season of the year'. Improvements were sought wherever possible, the first of these being the provision of a goods shed at Hythe for which an estimate of £850 was given. For some reason or other this was deemed to be too expensive and a decision was postponed until May, when £250 was authorised to be spent on a much smaller wooden lock-up shed on the platform. A few months later a further £130 was given in order to build Hythe's carriage and horse dock. Improvements were also forthcoming at Sandgate. Mindful of the meagre receipts from passenger traffic, the SER concentrated on the conveyance of goods traffic and decided that all trains would normally be better worked from the 'up' platform only. A new crossover, just east of bridge 2140 was laid to facilitate this manoeuvre and, with the alteration to the signalling apparatus, the bill came to £120. Henceforth, the 'down' platform, and the short siding leading from it, could deal with goods traffic uninterrupted by the passenger service. The third road through the station enabled locomotives to run round their trains after taking on water and coal near the engine shed.

The winter of 1874–75, the first in the life of the branch, was extremely wet and brought about a slight disaster which portended similar occurrences in the years to follow. A minor landslip, just to the east of Hythe station, took place in the high embankment crossing the Saltwood valley, caused by the swollen streams. Francis Brady recommended the SER to tap the springs with an adit driven parallel with the strike of the Atherfield clay. He mentioned that Lord Radnor had, following his advice, successfully halted the slide of his land near the Lower Sandgate Road in Folkestone. Brady warned the SER that otherwise the land would be unfit for building, upon which the company hurriedly ordered the £1,000 to be spent on the work. More expenditure was to follow when a claim from a Mr. Andrews, who lived in nearby Cannongate House, was presented for landslip damage which he claimed was 'brought about by the construction of the railway'. Rather than pay compensation the SER offered to buy the house, for which they finally paid £2,700.

Living up to their motto 'Onward', the SER wasted no time in pursuing their ultimate goal and introduced a parliamentary bill for the 1875 session which provided for:

> 'A railway (No.2) to be wholly situate in the parish of Cheriton, to commence by a junction with the Hythe & Sandgate branch at the present termination of that branch and to terminate in the same parish at a point on the north side of the street called the Broadway, Sandgate, at or near the house and shop in the occupation of Thomas Woodman (butcher).'

The plans for this first section show a line of double-track railway running from the engine shed, continuing parallel with the road, on a falling gradient of 1 in 527 and tunnelling under Encombe for 107 yards before finishing behind Woodman's shop in the High Street. By proceeding with the line stage by stage, the SER obviously aspired to the belief that, once started, the line would have to be finished off and no one, however influential, would be able to block its progress.

Claims for damages for the recent landslip continued to arrive at the SER board's headquarters, the latest coming from Seabrook Constabulary, amounting to £2,000. With it came a suggestion that the SER should purchase the buildings for the use of their station master and staff, to which the railway agreed. The bills for these numerous claims had just been settled when another landslip took place, this time on the hillside east of Hythe station, on the 23rd November 1875. The area most affected concerned that either side of the overbridge where the 'up' line was damaged on either side, although the 'down' line suffered only on the Sandgate side. The most dramatic damage, however, involved the roadway to the bridge, the southern approach dropping several feet. The bridge itself remained intact but had to be fenced off for safety until repairs could be made. The havoc also extended to the station master's house, at the foot of the approach road, which was badly shaken and cracked. Serious faults also showed up at the new stable at Cannongate House. Trains to Sandgate were suspended for a while but it wasn't too long before the 'down' line was made good enough for single line running with the 'up' route eventually being restored on 3rd December. The recent heavy rainfall was, of course, the culprit as it had waterlogged the hillside, and the SER ordered a thorough inspection of all the culverts, drains and soakaways along the branch and, more importantly, in the immediate area.

Throughout 1875 the debate over the Folkestone extension hotted up, particularly when rumours began circulating that the railway wouldn't bother to build a station in the heart of Sandgate once they had opened the new line throughout. These were scotched by John Shaw, the secretary of the SER, who published a reply in the local paper, promising that Sandgate would have a new and central station once the line was completed. He added that if the bill to extend the branch failed then he believed that a golden opportunity would have been lost for bringing Sandgate into repute as a watering place as well as a great commercial highway. Mr. Pledge, of the Sandgate Local Board of Health, remarked that members of his board were fully alive to the immense gain to the town in having a proper station and 'not merely a siding'. He believed that all the trains would call at Sandgate, thus putting the town on an equal footing with Hythe. He added:

> 'The viaduct will clear away some of the most unsightly and dilapidated properties and open out sea views from the Broadway and at the same time afford means for ornamental shops similar to those at London Bridge and other railway approaches.
>
> Allusion is made in the Herald about the bathing near the castle being interfered with. This is akin to the *nonsense* and *trash* published in Folkestone about the foreshore. I rejoice at the prospect of a good swim with the diversion of a train arriving and departing, and a signal of recognition from Sir Edward Watkin from a saloon carriage.'

Hythe Town Council passed a resolution backing the Folkestone harbour extension but opposition soon came from those in Sandgate who had most to lose, notably General Hankey. In a strongly-worded attack, he warned of the 'ruin of Sandgate' and promptly launched into a tirade against the 'greedy railway company and its chairman'. Watkin was both insulted and angered by Hankey's comments and there followed a heated exchange of letters between the SER and the general.

Elsewhere in the locality the attitude towards the railway was more favourable, especially Hythe where a new and palatial hotel was being planned for the seafront. The SER ordered Brady to prepare the plans for the 'Seabrook Hotel'.

At Folkestone, the main cause for concern amongst the ordinary residents, as well as the corporation, was the loss of access to the beach. In the New Year of 1876 Folkestone Corporation wrote to the board, asking them not to interfere with the Lower Sandgate Road as a driveway, nor the Bathing Ground, nor to allow the railway to sever the town from the sea. They also enquired whether the proposed level crossing at Golder Street (now named Marine Terrace) would be protected by a crossing keeper and might not a footbridge be erected for the safety of pedestrians?

In response to an enquiry from the SER, the War Department sought £40,000 in lieu of Sandgate castle as well as a suitable replacement for defence purposes. Watkin poured scorn on this proposal and their 'unrealistic price', stating he was 'distinctly assured upon competent authority that the fort is valueless as a fortification for defence'. Accordingly, the SER suggested that £10,000 should be offered for a new fort elsewhere. In view of the original claim, it wasn't surprising that the War Department refused and promptly demanded the full value as they considered it.

A public meeting was called by the Mayor of Folkestone, John Sherwood, for Wednesday 2nd February 1876 at 7 p.m. Attending this meeting were advocates of the railway extension, although it was largely boycotted by the opposition whose posters, decrying the new railway as the 'ruination of Folkestone', had been pasted all about the town during the preceding weeks.

The new plans and surveys showed the entire route, in great detail, from Sandgate station right through to where the rails would join up with those at the present harbour station. Once the engine shed at Sandgate had been cleared away, the lines through Sandgate station could be slewed closer together to form the normal distance between double track. After 138 yards, the line would reach the western portal of a 'covered way' tunnel which extended for 310 yards whilst curving slightly inland. On leaving this tunnel, which would have a 55 ft. retaining wall on the southern side, the line entered a fairly deep cutting, extending for 210 yards before entering another tunnel which burrowed deep into the hillside. With a falling gradient of 1 in 718 and a length of 961 yards, it would be built on a right-hand curve, coincidentally running immediately beneath two martello towers. From the eastern portal the railway would reach the heart of Sandgate and then proceed to cross it upon a massive, sweeping viaduct of 36 arches of 396 yards in length, almost a quarter of a mile. The viaduct would have been longer than the structure spanning the Foord valley at Folkestone, although nowhere near as high. Dimensions for the arches were thus: 25 arches with a 20 ft. span and 14 ft. high, 10 arches with a 20 ft. span and 12 ft. high, the main arch, across the Broadway, 42 ft. span and 16 ft. high. The viaduct would, as previously mentioned, necessitate the demolition of numerous properties, including Sandgate castle, which it would strike directly through the centre. An alternative route, avoiding the castle, was allowed for by running further northwards, but this would have involved a far sharper curve as well as the necessity to put up a 40 ft. span across Military Road. From the viaduct the line was shown as

ROUTE OF EXTENSION TO FOLKESTONE HARBOUR

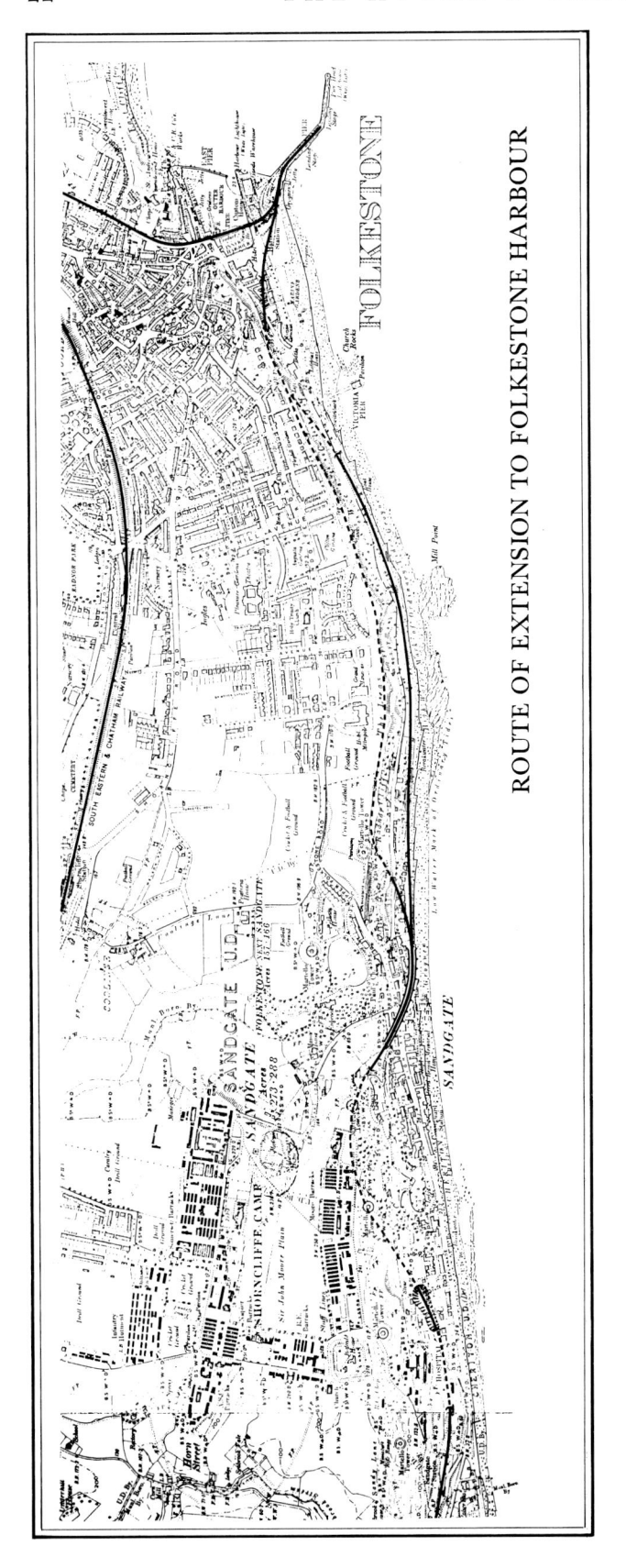

following either of two routes. The first, and infinitely less costly and therefore preferable to the SER, simply followed the coastline, running alongside the Lower Sandgate Road for just over a mile before swinging inland to enter another tunnel, of 608 yards, beneath the Leas. This route, on a falling 1 in 199 gradient would have involved the raising of the Lower Sandgate Road by almost 13 ft. to allow it to cross over the railway just before the line entered the tunnel. The 'inland route' would have been far more costly, requiring a tunnel underneath the entire Leas cliff for about 1½ miles on a gently descending gradient of 1 in 2900. Upon leaving the eastern portal of the Leas tunnel, the railway crossed Golder Street to run directly into the harbour station.

The Rt. Hon. E. H. Knatchbull-Hugessen, MP, then rose and spoke for almost a quarter of an hour, giving his whole-hearted support, not just because he happened to be a director of the SER, but also as 'a friend and admirer of Folkestone'. In his eloquent speech he assured the gathering that the last thing the SER wanted to do was injure the prospects or prosperity of Folkestone and stressed that the line would be of enormous benefit to the town, commercially and otherwise. He was greeted with rapturous applause.

Sir Edward Watkin then addressed the meeting, saying that since the railway to Sandgate had opened there was not one room or house unlet to a visitor during the season and that every bit of property had marvellously increased in value. He also pointed out that Folkestone had never been so full, nor the building trade so busy. Turning to the Leas, and those who feared its ruination, he told the audience of his recent early-morning stroll up Church Hill from the harbour to the top of the Leas. Ridiculing those who were concerned about the smoke from engines, Watkin related how he'd gazed down upon Mr. Tolputt's saw mill and timber yard where he saw 'the engine chimney puffing out smoke in a most *delightful* manner!' This drew loud laughter from the audience, as did his other remark about 'that most curious collection of cabbage gardens situated beyond the bathing machines!' He then suggested a clause be entered into the bill which would prevent the locomotive crews from stoking up before departing the new Folkestone Marine station, or that coke or smokeless fuel be substituted for the line between Folkestone and Sandgate. As for the destruction of the beach, Watkin assured them that this great asset of Folkestone's could be enlarged and improved by the groynes installed to protect the railway. Adopting an egalitarian stance, he declared that Folkestone meant *everyone*: 'The man who works with his hands or trades with his capital has as much right to be regarded and have his interests protected as those living in luxury and comfort.' (Loud cheers and applause.)

The resolution voicing support for the railway was, not surprisingly, carried with a large majority, accompanied by much applause and cheering, no doubt encouraging Watkin to hope that the prospect of the new railway route between London and Paris was that much nearer. However, augurs for its success were not good. It was, after all, the rich and powerful who invariably held all the trump cards and their own interests generally came before those of the town. Matters were only worsened when a local solicitor, Richard Hart, who in fact backed the railway scheme, let slip an incautious remark when dealing with the business of a mortgage on a house on the Leas. 'I'll have nothing to do with it,' he exclaimed. 'We shall have

ONWARD!

A view of Sandgate from Shorncliffe Camp showing the castle on the right, just where the viaduct would have been built. Further left the spire of the National Schools can be seen where the tramway later commenced, followed by the Sandgate Hill lift on the hillside. On the clifftop stand the plush hotels and villas of Folkestone.
Eamonn Rooney Collection

a new line soon and when the engines are puffing and smoking under your noses you'll soon see what will become of the value of your west end houses!' Gleefully, the opposition seized upon this remark which was subsequently placarded about the town, whilst in the corridors of power, those opposed to the railway gathered their forces in readiness.

While the wrangling over the extension rumbled on throughout that summer, life on the little branch continued much as always. Hythe was the busiest of the two stations but Sandgate was coming into its own as more and more troops were conveyed via the branch as it was nearer the military camp than Shorncliffe station on the main line. The first troops to use Sandgate station were the Coldstream Guards who departed early one morning in September 1876. The band of the 25th played them down the hill to the station whilst large numbers of the troops in camp turned out to bid them adieu. Later that day a troop train steamed in, bringing the 1st Battalion Scots Fusilier Guards, who took up the vacated quarters.

On 4th February 1877 there occurred a vacuum brake failure on the branch. Apart from a brief mention in the Board's minutes, no further details are known, but it must have been a minor incident, incurring no damage or injury.

By the summer the SER were no nearer seeing their dream fulfilled, in fact there was even speculation that the plan had been abandoned. This was reinforced by the announcement in the paper that extensive and costly alterations were to be made to Sandgate castle in order that it should be more suited to government needs. In spite of this, the SER instructed Brady in November to 'prepare plans and estimates for an extension of the Hythe & Sandgate Line to a further point in the direction of Sandgate'. Aware of the restrictions of Folkestone harbour, the SER was anxious to improve its facilities, for the future of the town as a channel port largely depended upon the outcome of this scheme. The route to Dover, through the Warren, was frequently under attack from natural causes, one of the most serious occurrences, up until then, having just taken place earlier in the year when the line was closed for three months.

Another minor slip on the Sandgate branch took place on 16th November 1878 in the embankment, just 100 yards west of Hythe station. The cause was found to be a choked culvert. Brady soon had the matter rectified for he was almost on call, having taken up residence in the town since the construction of the line, for which he was reimbursed £100 for accommodation. Another problem which he was requested to deal with concerned the overbridge a few hundred yards east of Hythe station which had now been fenced off for three years. Rather than reinstate the road, it was decided that the structure could be dispensed with, so Brady undertook its removal, noting that the material was to be stacked for use elsewhere.

The town of Hythe had prospered immeasurably with the arrival of the railway, despite the station being at the top of a steep hill on the outskirts. For those with a pony and trap the

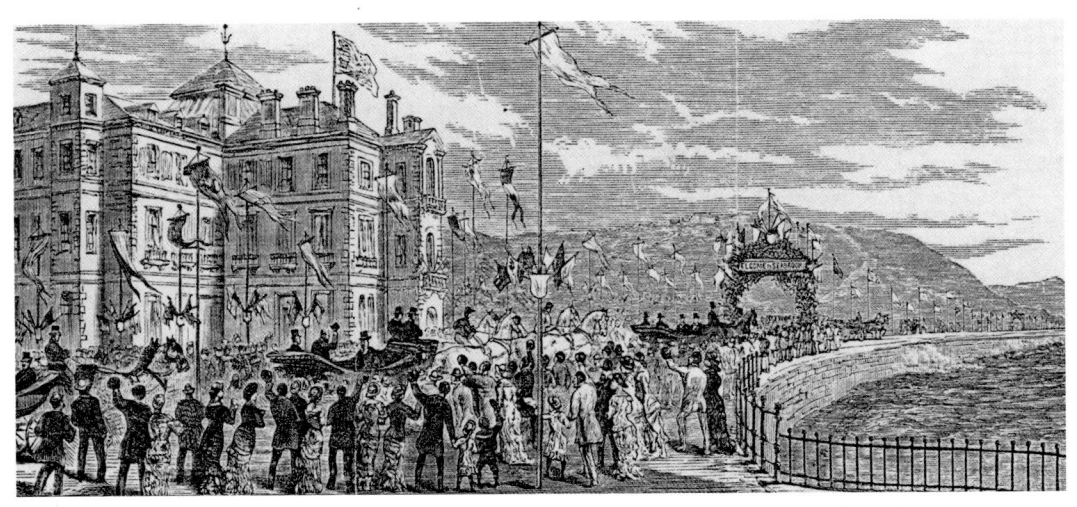

The Prince of Wales opening the Hythe Marine Parade and embankment from Hythe to Sandgate.

town offered a pleasant rest from the turmoil of London with cheap return tickets between the capital and Hythe, Westenhanger, Sandgate or Shorncliffe, offered at 21/- 1st class, 16s 6d 2nd class, or 9s 6d 3rd class. In addition, during July, August and September, monthly season tickets were available at £6 1st class or £5 2nd class. Unlike the Great Western Railway, which actively deterred the 'lower orders' from travelling in their trains, the SER couldn't afford such absurd pretentions and were keen for custom from whoever it came and money from the not so well-off was equally welcome. As railway fares were beyond the pocket of most ordinary people at that time, cheap excursion fares were introduced which helped fill up some of the empty trains. One of these first schemes constituted cheap pleasure trips from Hythe and Sandgate to Canterbury via Ashford, at 3/- for a 3rd class return, 4s 6d 2nd class or 6/- for 1st class comfort and luxury. Even so, remembering the wage levels at that time, it was a rare treat for ordinary people to travel by train, which had been the predominant preserve of the middle and upper classes.

On the 21st July 1880 the new Seabrook Hotel was opened to the public. Owned and managed by the SER, it seemed that before long Hythe would soon rival neighbouring Folkestone in attracting visitors. The sheer geographical position of the latter, not to mention better communication between its three stations and the town, as well as its express trains, meant that it was a tough rival. Realising this, Hythe Town Council wrote to the SER asking them to consider improvements by installing a tramway between the station and their new hotel. Initially, the SER were favourable to the scheme but apparently lost interest when the town declined to contribute towards the cost of building it.

The business of the harbour extension came to the fore once more in the late autumn of 1880 when Lord Brabourne, on behalf of the SER, promised to see the Secretary of State in the hope of getting the ball rolling. Meanwhile, John Shaw approached the War Office enquiring if they were still bound by the conditions in a letter from them which stated: 'SER must not enter upon WD grounds at all unless they accept all conditions imposed by WD as to hospital and castle.' If they weren't, he enquired, would they be allowed to enter upon WD land at the Shorncliffe end and begin building the line as far as the centre of Sandgate? He also hoped that the question of the castle could be settled, otherwise an application to parliament would be made for a deviation of the line. Finally, an offer of £20,000 was made for the castle. The War Office accepted the SER's offer and promptly sold the castle to them. At last the harbour extension came one step nearer and in the New Year the War Office let it be known that they had no objections to the SER proceeding with the building of the railway through their land. Inspired by fresh enthusiasm, Brady was summoned immediately and ordered to prepare new plans for an extension as far as Camp Road (now called Brewers Hill) 'in order that work can proceed as soon as possible'. A local paper commented in March 1881:

> 'An Engineer has been engaged in the past day or two stumping out the land for the extension of the Hythe & Sandgate Branch to Folkestone Harbour. Tenders for contracts will shortly be issued and the work commenced at once.
>
> There is also talk of extending the proposed Maidstone–Ashford Railway of the London, Chatham & Dover Railway Company. Parties have been observed surveying at Ruckinge where such line would be run from Ashford into the Romney Marsh with possibly an extension to Hythe.'

This last paragraph likely sent jitters through the Tooley Street headquarters of the SER!

The extension of railways was very much in mind, for at this time a new plan was born for a line from Hythe to Dymchurch and it is almost certain that this was in direct response to the threat from the LC & DR to extend from Maidstone. The precise route is unclear except that 'the line would be almost level after leaving Sandgate'. None other than that eminent Victorian engineer of railways, Thomas Walker, who later built the Elham Valley Line, was invited to tender for the cost of a cheap line and one, surprisingly, consisting of double track. Walker's tender of £62,000 was slightly cheaper than others received, and also revealed the extent of the grand schemes then being dreamt up: Hythe to Dymchurch £37,181, Dymchurch to Lydd £31,590 – the latter line joining up with the Appledore to Lydd railway already under construction and opened in the winter of 1881. While the engineering problems were minimal, the traffic potential was extremely dubious, even though the military establishments at Hythe and Lydd would be directly connected. The WD were invited to pay a moderate fixed rent for the use of the line but they declined and the scheme, like so many others, never came to fruition.

The completion of the sea wall and the parade at Hythe coincided with the new railway pier at Folkestone harbour with HRH The Prince of Wales being invited to perform the opening ceremonies. Once again, the houses in Hythe were bedecked with all manner of patriotic bunting as the great day dawned, Wednesday, 15th October 1881. At Charing Cross station His Royal Highness was received by Sir Edward Watkin, Myles Fenton, and J.G. Harris – Chief Superintendent of the SER. At 11 a.m. the train departed, arriving about an hour later at Ashford where more dignitaries boarded, before taking the branch at Sandling Park junction. By this time a large party had assembled at Hythe station to greet its arrival. Shortly before, the Mayor of Folkestone – J.B. Tolputt, the Mayor of Hythe – W. Mackeson and the aldermen, had gathered upon the 'down' platform. A local reporter noted that the 'station looked very pretty in its decorations of flowers and bunting while outside about 100 carriages were in waiting to receive the guests'. The train steamed in to the customary waving and cheering which was repeated as the entourage detrained and entered their waiting carriages. The Prince joined an open carriage pulled by four handsome horses, mounted by postilions. Watkin accompanied him, revelling in the usual fuss and pomp that was raining down upon the assembly. As the carriages moved off down Station Road, transformed with flags fluttering in the wind, a guard of honour, comprising the East Kent Rifles, waiting in the station yard, struck up the National Anthem. For the crowd lining the roads and patiently waiting, the excitement became too much and they soon 'gave expression to their pent-up feelings with vociferous cheers whilst the ladies waved their pocket handkerchiefs and everyone was in a flutter of excitement'. All wanted to see the future king of England. The grand procession made its way down into the town, passing underneath archways of evergreen, through streets lined with Venetian masts. Having driven along the newly-named 'Princes Parade' they made their way to Sandgate where the clouds thickened and the rain came down. At Folkestone the bells of the parish church were rung as the procession drove along the Leas and down Church Hill by which time the rain had ceased. At the harbour the Prince was introduced to Francis Brady who presented him with an ivory mallet with which to knock into place the ceremonial stone. In a cavity was placed a silver box containing local newspapers, coins and other mementoes of the day as well as a plan of the works. A marble block sealed the cavity. Mr. Sidney Weston then photographed the royal party who afterwards retired to the Pavilion Hotel where all and sundry partook in a sumptuous luncheon.

Afterwards, Watkin spoke of his burning ambition to 'make this part of the coast the most important in the country'. He

The down side waiting shelter at Hythe *en fête*. Believed to be on the occasion of the Prince of Wales' visit to Hythe in 1881.
Miss Eva Fright

The Folkestone Leas Estate photographed in 1893. The harbour pier can be seen in the distance and at the landward end the clock tower of the Harbour offices. In the foreground is the switchback railway and the Victoria Pleasure Pier opened in 1888.

Eamonn Rooney Collection

likely referred to the channel tunnel, the opiate of all political megalomaniacs, of which the first shaft had been sunk just ten months earlier. Watkin and Fenton had been to inspect it recently and witnessed the 'wonderful new drilling machine in action' which could cut through the chalk at 'half an inch per minute'! The spoil from this site in the Warren was trundled out in small trucks hauled by pit ponies.

At 3.30 p.m. the guests departed and drove to Shorncliffe station where the royal train was waiting. The Prince of Wales was the first royal personage to use the new station, opened just eight months earlier. This spacious, lavish and beautiful brick station was a joy to behold, with stained-glass windows bearing illustrations of the SER coat of arms and a Cudworth engine at Sandgate. Its ornate cast iron columns, glass canopies and decorative valancing reflected the importance which the SER attached to the area. The new station, replacing the rickety wooden structure situated a few hundred yards further west, became the subject of an expensive law suit. The SER classed Shorncliffe as outside Folkestone, therefore outside the agreement of pooled receipts with which it had foolishly entered into in 1865 with the LC & DR. The LC & DR took the SER to court and eventually won, much to the SER's chagrin and cost.

By 1882 the SER were still frustrated in their efforts to extend the Sandgate branch, but were busily buying up property all along the route as far as the Lower Sandgate Road whenever it became available. Some residents, either keen to 'make a bit extra', or fearful of losing out at a later date when notices would be served, were offering their houses quite readily. In April the War Office contacted the SER giving them permission to go ahead with the demolition of Sandgate castle.

The difficulties faced by the SER caused it to rescind its original agreement with the Seabrook Estate Co. leaving its aggrieved shareholders to, understandably, feel they'd lost out. Development and building could not take place until the railway extension had been completed, for it was planned to raise the level of the flood-prone land at Seabrook with the spoil from the Sandgate and Leas cliff tunnels. The shareholders' wrath was finally vented when they sharply reminded the SER that they had loyally supported them against any competing line, and went on to draw attention to the scheme currently being proposed by the rival LC & DR. This was the Alkham Valley line, promoted to run from Kearsney on the Victoria–Dover line, directly into Folkestone where one plan suggested the line should continue through the Seabrook Estate to Hythe and thence to Ashford to join up with their new branch under construction from Maidstone. Furthermore, the Seabrook Estate Co. threatened to sell off any land that the LC & DR might desire in order to build its extension to Hythe. It is not difficult to imagine the tense atmosphere pervading the SER Board meetings throughout that period.

Unable to proceed with the Sandgate extension and thereby satisfy the Seabrook shareholders, the only way the SER could alleviate the crisis was to hurriedly adopt the Elham Valley Railway scheme which would head off this latest threat from the 'Chatham'. Along with the Elham Valley bill went the whole Sandgate Extension bill for the 1883 session but the SER knew full well the latter stood little chance of success.

In the summer of 1884, Watkin paid an unofficial visit to Folkestone on 24th July to witness the guns from Sandgate castle being taken away by the WD. He toured around Folkestone, visiting the Sandgate branch as well as the route through to the harbour. On that day Watkin outlined three new schemes which were to be investigated and listed them thus:

1. To be prepared to deposit new line from New Romney to Seabrook.
2. An extension from Seabrook to Shorncliffe station by crossing Military Road.
3. Line from Folkestone harbour to Cheriton via Canterbury Road and the gasworks.

The first of these was nothing but a resurrection of the earlier scheme to lay rails across the marsh and was, no doubt, prompted by the opening of the new line from Ashford to New Romney station which had begun business four weeks earlier. The second and third schemes appear to be the actions of a desperate man. The line from Seabrook to Shorncliffe may well have been a vain attempt at finishing off the Sandgate branch whilst the third scheme, on the face of it, seems absurd. The re-introduction of this idea of the 1860s is curious and exactly what was in Watkin's mind will never be known. Needless to say, it was never mentioned again as the costs were prohibitive.

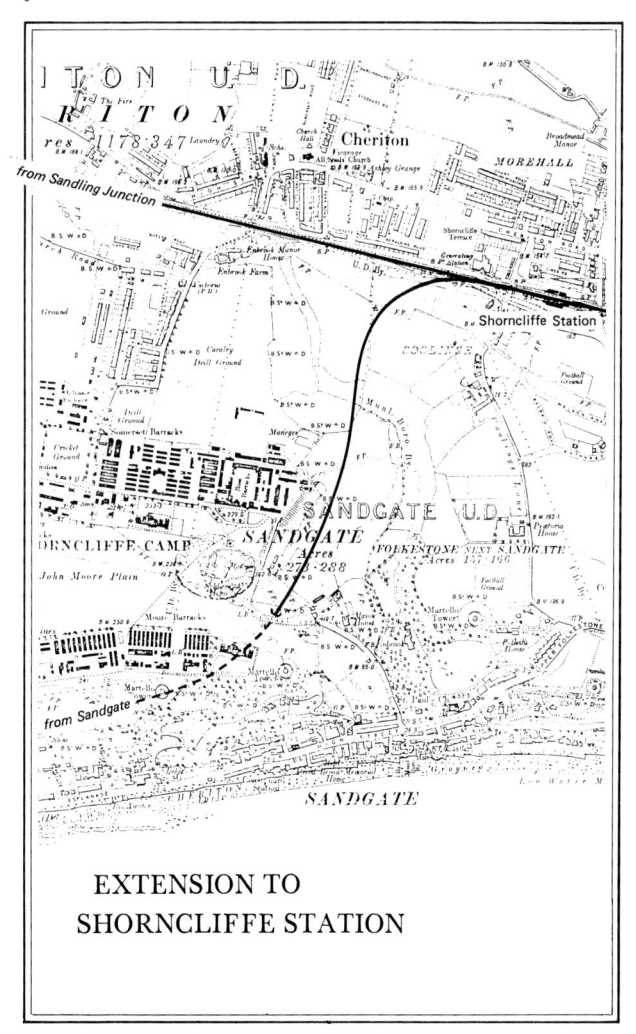

EXTENSION TO SHORNCLIFFE STATION

The Sandgate branch had been open for just over ten years now and life for the ordinary railway employees engaged on the line continued much as always in spite of the grand schemes and dreams of their masters. On October 24th the *Folkestone Express* reported:

> 'An entrance is being made on the western side at Sandgate station and when finished it will be a decided improvement and most convenient to the residents of Seabrook. The work is being carried out by J.J. Jeal.'

This refers to the flight of steps which led up from the Seabrook Road directly to the station, saving a circuitous walk.

The train service around this time remained virtually the same with ten weekday passenger trains in both directions although Sundays saw an improvement with four trains each way instead of two.

As each year passed so the feasibility of the Sandgate extension receded as property prices increased and land was used up for new buildings. The SER refused to let go of its dreams and persisted in holding on to its ambition which it held close to its heart.

In 1886 the SER began planning the buildings of a grand station at the junction between the Sandgate branch and the main line. The junction was situated amongst nothing but green fields and meadows, with only a few scattered farmsteads for company and even today the area is sparsely populated. At this new station, passengers would be able to interchange trains, although it was planned that the boat trains would run directly through Sandgate to the harbour. The plans for the station, as yet without a name, were submitted and approved, whilst the cost, over £4,000, was thought to be rather high, so it was recommended that efforts be made to reduce this.

In the meantime, Brady had been ordered to yet again prepare estimates for linking the Sandgate branch to the Ashford–Hastings line. This latest proposal ignored the direct route between Hythe and Lydd but instead followed the Royal Military Canal from Seabrook to Appledore. It was all a waste of time though, as events would prove, and for Brady it was time that he could well do with as he was being hard-pressed by Watkin and the Board in regard to the Elham Valley line. It had taken three years to reach Barham from Cheriton, which was far longer than expected, or necessary, in Watkin's view.

HYTHE & SANDGATE BRANCH.
SERVICE OF TRAINS BETWEEN WESTENHANGER, HYTHE, AND SANDGATE.

[Timetable, June 1883]

OVER THE BRIDGE FOR

The new station at Sandling Junction in 1890 with a train for Sandgate waiting in the down branch platform. Despite heavy retouching, there is much of interest in this photograph. No. 2 signal box can clearly be seen in the goods yard, and it is evident that work on roofing over the footbridge is in hand.
Tonbridge Historical Society

Another facet of railway development at this time had given Folkestone a fourth station, opened in 1884 and named Cheriton Arch. Two years later it was renamed Radnor Park, eventually becoming Folkestone Central in the summer of 1895.

Progress with the new station at Sandling Park was well under way by now, in the year that the nation paid homage to their beloved Queen who was celebrating her golden jubilee. The station buildings were beautifully designed and lovingly built by real craftsmen. Each of the three structures comprised exposed timber frames with red brick infill, high-hipped tiled roofs surmounted by huge brick chimney stacks, so reminiscent of Kentish farmhouses. They were almost identical to those at Nutfield, on the old main line from Redhill to Tonbridge, which had opened four years earlier in 1883. Tenders for the footbridge, planned to cross only the main line for the moment, were:

Joseph Westwood & Co., Millwall	– £255 0s 0d
Handyside's Iron Works, Derby	– £250 0s 0d
J. Shaw & Co., London	– £229 10s 0d (accepted)

With the new station nearing completion, a name had to be found and 'Westenhanger for Saltwood' was chosen. Confusion with Westenhanger for Hythe station, barely a mile to the west, would not be a problem as it was proposed to close it to passenger traffic. This decision had to be reversed a couple of months later, probably after complaints from the nearby village of Stanford, which meant that another name would have to be thought up. Eventually, someone suggested Sandling Junction as the obvious choice and this name suited everyone concerned. Having provided a station with four platforms, it was then realised that it might prove more convenient to passengers if the Sandgate branch trains could both arrive and depart from the 'down' branch platform. Accordingly, adjustments were made in the new pointwork and signalling to allow this to take place, and as the 'up' branch platform would then be used less frequently the SER decided that the footbridge need not be extended to link them. This decision, however, did not meet with the approval of the Board of Trade and General Hutchinson strongly recommended that a footbridge or a subway be constructed within six months of opening the station as he considered the simple wooden boarded crossing most dangerous. His recommendation was apparently not enforced and the bridge extension never materialised, the simple crossing remaining in use to this day even though the rails have gone.

Shortly before Sandling Junction station was declared open – on New Year's Day 1888 – Colonel Deedes wrote to the board

HYTHE & SANDGATE

A delightfully be-whiskered and bowler-hatted driver awaits the 'right away' in the down branch platform at Sandling Junction station. The locomotive is a Cudworth '118' No. 37.
*L & GRP
cty. David & Charles*

reminding them that he'd only agreed to the building of a single-storey structure for the station master to live in. Whether by deliberate action or oversight, the SER had given Mr. Lord, Sandling's first station master, a solid and handsome double-storey house, costing £403. The colonel then went on to state that the 'amenities of estate here are injuriously affected by the building'. He would, however, consent to it remaining *provided* the SER granted him a free pass between Sandling Junction and London for a period of eight years. In spite of being the season of goodwill, the SER declined, leaving the hapless colonel to dip into his pocket every time he desired to take the train to the city.

Hythe Town Council wrote to the board thanking them for the splendid new station at Sandling, adding that they hoped it would encourage more visitors to detrain and visit Hythe. At the same time Folkestone Town Council, probably nervous of losing its visitors to Hythe, wrote to ask whether more local trains between Sandling Junction and Shorncliffe might be provided.

Having improved the prospects of the branch at the northern end, the SER once again concentrated its efforts at Sandgate. An acre of land adjacent to the castle was snapped up at an auction for £300, whilst a house named 'The Hermitage' was bought for £1,350. Meanwhile, in an effort to stimulate development at Seabrook, a number of improvements were put in hand which included dredging the canal, tidying up the banks and prospects and planting a number of trees in an effort to alleviate the sparseness of the vista.

Even grander proposals were now coming forward for the development of the towns. Perhaps the most ambitious was the seaside pleasure pier at Hythe which, in typical Victorian flamboyance, was projected to run 250 ft. seawards from Princes Parade. On the plans the land immediately behind the pier is shown with tracings of wide avenues, imposing squares and terraces, much in the same fashion as Folkestone's elegant areas. Remarkable, although to a lesser degree, were the plans of the SER to develop the Scene Estate, just north of Hythe station, for housing with wide sweeping roads. They even bothered to name the individual roads, e.g. 'Saltwood Road', 'Avenue Road', 'Cliff Road' – in fact only the latter materialised – even then housing along this road was extremely slow in coming about. Commenting on the proposals a local paper wrote in August 1890:

'In an Ashford contemporary last week was a paragraph to the effect that a project was on foot to form a pier for Hythe and that the SER had offered £1,000 towards its cost. Origin of the idea came from Mr. Dan West, the Mayor, for in 1887 he wrote to the paper advocating a pier as the best memorial to Jubilee Year. Perhaps this will silence the critics of the SER, always publicly and privately abusing the company. Have we forgotten the enormous sums spent by the SER on the Seabrook Estate and the sea wall, preventing the flooding of lower Hythe, opening the Sandgate railway and relieving the town of the expense and upkeep of the canal?'

Almost two years after Sandling Junction station was opened it was found that some improvements to the sheltering arrangements for passengers and staff should be made. Accordingly, the sum of £1,100 was spent on lengthening the platform canopies and putting a corrugated-iron roof on the footbridge. Further expenditure was authorised in July 1890 when £250 was spent on a new siding for goods traffic at Sandgate. All these improvements didn't go unnoticed and were reported locally:

'The South Eastern Railway have recently expended a large sum of money on the improvement of their station at Sandling Junction. This has given rise to considerable amount of speculation on the part of the public as to the object the Company had in view. It is most probable that the following solution is not far from correct. When the compact was entered into between the South Eastern and the Chatham Companies, to pool the profits on the Folkestone and Dover traffic, the former Company never contemplated the extraordinary growth of Folkestone, and the corresponding increase

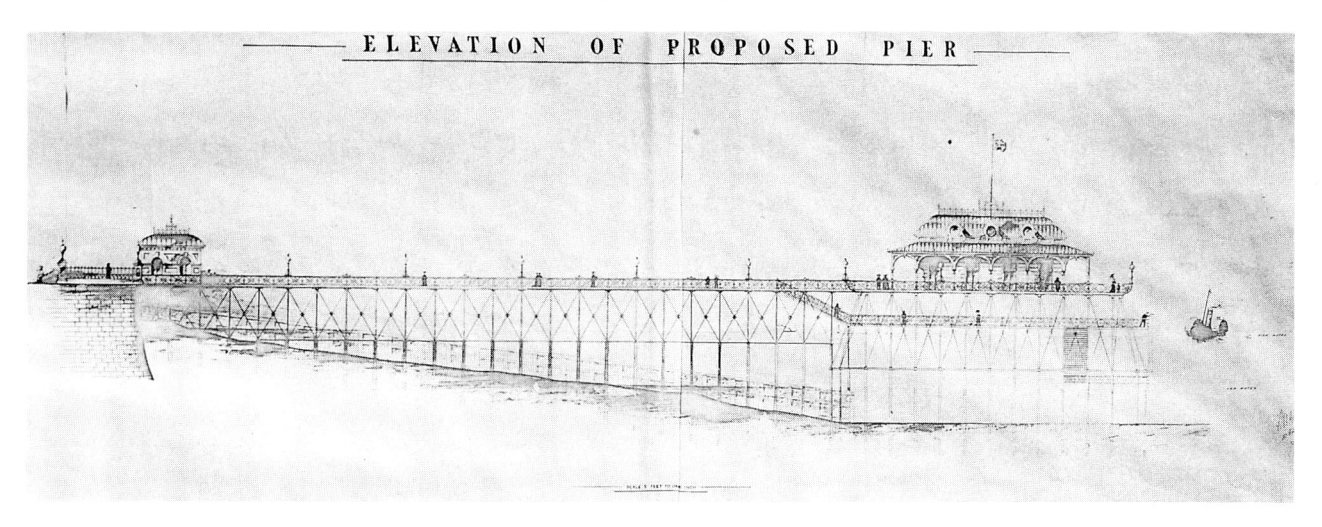

Proposed SER pier for Hythe.

The Marine Parade at Hythe. The line of defensive Martello Towers can be seen stretching into the distance. *Eamonn Rooney Collection*

Sandgate station in 1891 with station master Bertram Caudell standing proudly in his glossy top hat. The train has recently arrived and its engine, an unidentifiable Cudworth, can be seen near the shed.

Tonbridge Historical Society

ONWARD! 33

in the number of passengers to that town. The Shorncliffe scheme having proved abortive, the South Eastern naturally seek to find another solution to the enigma, and we suggest that they are making an effort to induce visitors to select Hythe, in preference to Folkestone, for their marine resort.

The Chatham Company cannot share in the Hythe traffic; they do in the Folkestone traffic.

We ought to feel grateful to the Company for issuing return tickets from London to Hythe every Monday for 3/6 (6d less than Folkestone). Does not this afford another instance of the desire of the South Eastern to place Hythe more in the foreground? And does not the offer of the Company to take over the canal, point to the same conclusion? It is with much satisfaction that we notice that the low excursion fare is taken advantage of by the Londoners, as the presence of strangers in the town every Monday testifies. Many more would do so if it were more widely known.

If we are correct in our surmise, we may safely repeat the proverb "It is an ill wind that blows nobody good".'

The fact that Sandling Junction station was a successful venture was verified by an editorial in the *Hythe Reporter* which appeared on 9th August 1890:

'The general opinion abroad is that 'Hythe is looking up'. People seem to be aroused from their lethargy and are anxious to bring the old Cinque Port into prominence. Visitors are pouring in in shoals. Sandling Park Station has been all activity during the last fortnight, last Friday being the heaviest day ever experienced at that Junction. To quote the station-master's words "there were tons and tons of stuff" brought into the station.'

Further comment was made:

'Now that Sandling Junction has superseded Westenhanger for Hythe traffic, we have practically the same advantages as towns upon the main line; and there is no reason, now that trains reach here in less than two hours from Charing Cross, why Hythe should not be as well known, and in time become as popular as Hastings and Eastbourne. We would like to see Hythe brought into closer communication with Shorncliffe by rail, as we should thus be better able to avail ourselves of the Elham Valley Line, and visitors to Canterbury would no doubt more often come over here. If this were remedied, we should have a capital service, comparing favourably with any towns upon the south coast.'

Direct access into Shorncliffe camp was being sought by the SER, especially since all stores and supplies, as well as the troops themselves, had to be transported or marched a mile or so to either Sandgate or Shorncliffe stations. In September 1890 Watkin suggested building a branch line from Shorncliffe, along Risborough Lane and into the camp. This plan was later modified when the 'Elham Valley Extension Railway' was proposed along with its bill for the 1891 session. This new line was to begin from the main 'up' line, 11 chains on the eastern

An enlargement of the previous photograph allows the engine shed to be seen in greater detail, despite retouching on the glass negative.

An up train waits at Sandgate in August 1898. Odd carriages can be seen in the down and up sidings, whilst two road wagons stand in the approach road.
C. J. Barnard/Alex Todd Collection

Cudworth '118' class No. 246 blows off excess steam at Hythe with a train from Sandgate in the 1890s. *National Railway Museum*

ONWARD!

No. 154 shunting at Folkestone Junction. *Author's Collection*

side of Cheriton Junction, where it would run southwards to terminate in the camp.

Throughout all these years when so many schemes had been put forward and lost, the daily business upon the Sandgate branch went on much as always. Train services had improved remarkably. There were now sixteen weekday trains departing from the little terminus whilst fifteen trains ran down the branch. Two goods trips per day catered most adequately for the traders in the area. On Sundays the train service had doubled from four to eight which may have upset one or two 'gentlemen of the cloth'.

Two particularly interesting locomotives were to be seen running up and down the branch during this period. One was No. 147, one of Richard Mansell's 'Gunboat' class, built in 1878, which had recently been employed with its sister engines on London suburban duties. When James Stirling's more powerful 'Q' class 0–4–4Ts came along as replacements, No. 147 was sent south to become the Sandgate branch engine. For a couple of years old 147 pottered about on this short stretch of the South Eastern's empire until it was finally laid up in the autumn of 1890 before being cut up for scrap in November. The other engine of note was No. 154, one of three engines from Cudworth's design begun in 1877 for working the steep Folkestone Harbour branch. After spending some time at Tonbridge on shunting duties during the late 1880s, No. 154 set off across the Weald for Ashford where repairs were carried out in 1890 before being sent for trials over the line to Sandgate. How it performed is not known but it was eventually withdrawn in July 1892.

The age of the excursion ticket was now really beginning. For instance, it was possible to walk into Hythe booking office and ask for a 1s 6d cheap return to Canterbury via the Elham Valley. Perhaps the necessity to change trains at both Sandling Junction and Shorncliffe stations was not viewed so much as inconvenience but more as an adventure. Mondays-only excursions continued to be popular, especially during the Christmas and New Year holidays when the London pantomimes enchanted folk of all ages and walks of life.

Support for westwards communication from Hythe was still surprisingly forthcoming. Whereas there were no serious obstacles in the way, as there were east of Sandgate, the SER were reluctant to spend money wherever there was a risk of insufficient returns. Far too much money had already been spent guarding and consolidating 'their' territory from the LC & DR, as the Elham Valley Line bore witness. Even so, the pressure for a connection to the marsh was maintained, for example:

'Possibly, in the near future, Lydd will supersede Shoeburyness as the locality selected for the School of Gunnery, and a railway from Hythe to Lydd will then be a necessity, to which the South Eastern Railway Company will no doubt willingly respond. We cannot too strongly impress upon our representatives, whether Municipal or Parliamentary, that every encouragement should be given for the concentration of troops in this district; since a military station contributes, more than anything else, to the attractions of a watering place.'

The winter of 1891 was notoriously severe with blizzards and snowdrifts, even as late as March, which brought chaos to East Kent. The last train from Charing Cross for Sandgate became stuck in a snow drift near Saltwood Castle and apparently the weather was so bad that the passengers dared not leave the comparative safety of the train. After spending the night in the unheated compartments, described as 'fearfully cold and dreadful in the extreme', they were 'rescued' at 8 o'clock the following morning by a friendly farmer who arrived with food and drink. A gang of railway workers eventually managed to extricate the train which went on to arrive at Sandgate over eleven hours late. Another train had a similar experience when a tree was blown down blocking both lines. Watchmen on duty managed to warn the driver of the danger but the train had to remain in the tunnel overnight. Elsewhere, parts of the Whitstable branch were blocked as was the Elham Valley Line at Bishopsbourne.

We shall probably never know what this young lady is handing the Sandgate signalman in this charming snapshot! Of interest is the original handwritten nameboard 'Sandgate Station Signals'.
Author's Collection

The railway companies were well accustomed to dealing with relatively minor occurrences such as these, but when Mother Nature really flexed her muscles, as often happened in the Warren, the problems truly began. One major disaster directly affecting Sandgate would have been extremely serious for the SER had they succeeded in building the railway through to Folkestone harbour. This was the great landslide at Sandgate which took place on the 4th March 1893. At about 6 p.m. on that Saturday evening a low rumbling noise heralded the event, the ground cracking up and shaking 'much as if a horse was kicking up underneath'. Remarkably, not one single person was injured or killed although, understandably, many were deeply shocked and distressed by the incident which cracked walls like egg shells and brought down ceilings. Almost a hundred houses were affected as terror-striken inhabitants rushed into the streets. The soldiers from Shorncliffe gave assistance and helped transport people to the safety of Folkestone and Hythe as the residents were fearful of spending the night in their damaged houses. The local press had a field day in reporting the incident in great detail:

> 'Amid the stories of personal calamity which have reached us, we think that none surpasses that of a poor fellow in the employ of the SER Co. who had invested all his savings in the purchase of a house at the west end, and who has lost everything in this terrible catastrophe.
>
> During the day the town has been thronged by thousands of people who flocked in from all the adjacent parts to see the results of the subsidence. The trams and omnibuses were loaded during the whole time they were running.
>
> All Hythe seems to have come to Sandgate with people arriving by every packed-out train. Although there are some deflections in the tramlines the trams have been running as fast as they could.'

A relief fund was organised to which Watkin personally donated a hundred pounds. Some locals blamed the railway company for disturbing the land, others, the recent blowing-up of two offshore wrecks, the 'Benvenue' and the 'Calypso'. In fact neither were to blame. One influential tradesman castigated the SER, blaming them for the East Cliff and Warren landslips by constructing Folkestone harbour. He claimed ruefully: 'They aimed the Seabrook wall too far seawards. They (the residents) welcomed the SER with open arms, they accepted Watkin's dinners, his excursions, and everything was fine in the extreme.' The newspapers adopted a more cool-headed approach and restricted themselves to commenting on the loose nature of the soil when the Sandgate branch was built, twenty years before. They remarked: 'In the case of Sandgate station, the building sank considerably after it was erected'. Whether there is any truth in this remark is highly unlikely for no reference is made in the meticulous records of the SER. It was probably this remark that gave rise to the myth, published in Charles Igglesden's delightful 'Saunters through Kent with Pen and Pencil' when referring to the Sandgate landslide, that reads: 'When the Directors arrived at the station they found the platforms level with the track!' This is quite untrue, however, for the railway was indeed fortunate in being quite unaffected in this instance.

The fact that the whole area, by reason of its very geological nature, had been periodically moving and crumbling for centuries seems to have been overlooked and it was only when the SER commissioned a report from two eminent geologists that the recriminations were stilled. Sir Benjamin Baker, KCMG, FRS and Robert Etheridge, FRS, accompanied Myles Fenton and Francis Brady by train to Sandgate where, on 15th March, just eleven days after the disaster, they inspected the area to assess the cause and whether future occurrences might be avoided so as to protect the existing railway as well as the harbour extension scheme. It was noted that although the same blue gault clay was to be found in the railway cutting near Hythe as that which caused so much trouble in the Warren, it was not aggravated by the actions of marine erosion. Myles Fenton pointed out that the slips in the cuttings and embankments when the Sandgate branch was first opened, had been successfully dealt with by Brady so that little trouble had been experienced since. The cause was simply put down to the waterlogging of the beds of brown sandstone and greensand which rest upon the deep layers of Wealden clay. All that could be done was to ensure that the land was adequately drained and, in the railway's case, that regular inspection of gulleys and culverts was maintained.

As twenty years had now elapsed without the trains running further than Seabrook, the inhabitants of Sandgate could be forgiven for thinking that the SER had now abandoned the grand scheme and it was not surprising that the board began

Courtesy Harry Moore

HYTHE & SANDGATE BRANCH.
SERVICE OF TRAINS BETWEEN SANDLING JUNCTION, HYTHE, AND SANDGATE.

DOWN TRAINS—WEEK DAYS.

STATIONS	Goods		Goods																
	arr	dep	arr	dep	arr	dep	arr	dep	arr	dep	arr	dep	arr	dep	arr	dep	arr	dep	...
Sandling Jun.	7 15	7 23	..	8 5	..	8 33	..	9 10	9 7	9 20	..	10 6	..	11 4	..	11 58	..	12 50	...
Hythe	7 27	7 35	8 8	9 3	8 41	8 42	9 13	9 14	9 25	9 30	10 11	10 12	11 7	11 8	12 1	12 2	12 53	12 54	...
Sandgate	7 42	..	8 13	..	8 46	..	9 18	..	9 35	..	10 16	..	11 12	..	12 6	..	12 58	..	...

(continued: 1 19 / 1 20 | 2 41 / 2 43 | 4 43 / 4 44 | 5 38 / 5 39 | 6 33 / 6 34 | 7 13 / 7 14 | 8 3 / 8 4; Sandgate: 1 24, 2 46, 4 48, 5 43, 6 38, 7 18, 8 8)

DOWN TRAINS—SUNDAYS.

STATIONS	WEEK DAYS—con.			Goods									
	P M arr	dep		A M arr	dep	arr	dep	arr	dep	P M arr	dep	P M arr	dep
Sandling Jun.	..	9 11		..	7 50	..	10 45	11 44	11 50	..	12 33	..	4 5	.. 5 45	.. 7 10	.. 9 18	.. 10 5
Hythe	9 14	9 15		7 53	7 54	10 48	10 49	11 55	12 5	12 36	12 37	4 8	4 9	5 48 / 5 49	7 13 / 7 14	9 21 / 9 22	10 8 / 10 9
Sandgate	9 19	..		7 58	..	10 53	..	12 12	..	12 41	..	4 13	..	5 53	7 18	9 26	10 13

UP TRAINS—WEEK DAYS.

STATIONS	Bks.		Goods							
Sandgate	.. 6 45	.. 7 48	.. 8 20	.. 8 55	.. 9 40	.. 10 0	.. 10 45	.. 11 45	.. 12 15	...
Hythe	.. ..	7 52 / 7 53	8 24 / 8 25	8 58 / 8 59	9 44 / 9 45	10 5 / 10 15	10 49 / 10 50	11 49 / 11 50	12 19 / 12 20	...
Sandling Jun.	6 55 / 6 58 See notes	7 57	8 29	..	9 49	10 18	10 54	11 54	12 24	...

(continued P M: 1 3 / 1 7 / 1 8 | 2 0 / 2 4 / 2 5 | 3 50 / 3 54 / 3 55 | 4 25 / 4 28 / 4 29 | 5 15 / 5 19 / 5 23 | 6 12 / 6 15 / 6 20 | 6 55 / 6 59 / 7 3)

UP TRAINS—SUNDAYS.

STATIONS	WEEK DAYS—con. Goods.					Eng. & Bks.									
	P M arr	dep	P M arr	dep	arr	dep	A M arr	dep	arr	dep	A M arr	dep	P M arr	dep	...
Sandgate	.. 7 35	.. 8 0	.. 8 45	..	.. 7 30	.. 9 40	B 11 10	.. 12 15	.. 3 50	.. 5 32	.. 6 25	.. 9 0	.. 9 42
Hythe	7 38 / 7 39	8 5 / 8 15	8 49 / 8 50	..	7 34 / 7 35	9 44 / 9 45	..	12 19 / 12 20	3 54 / 3 55	5 36 / 5 37	6 29 / 6 30	9 4 / 9 5	..
Sandling Jun.	7 43	8 20	8 30 / 8 54 A	..	7 38	9 49	11 18	12 24	3 59	5 41	6 33	9 8	9 50 Empty

All Trains are 1, 2 and 3 Class. **A** On Saturdays only this Train runs forward to Westenhanger—*See* Main Line Pages. **B** Engine and Brakes to Westenhanger, to work Goods trip from Sandling Junction—*see* Main Line Pages.
Sandling Junction will arrange for an Engine to fetch any Trucks from Westenhanger that may arrive there after the 7.10 a.m. Down Branch Goods Train has left.
Goods for Sandling Junction and Hythe and Sandgate Branch will be worked to Westenhanger, and be conveyed thence by the Sandgate Branch Goods Train, which will work through to Westenhanger.
An Engine, with Guards, will, every Week-day, leave Westenhanger at 7.35 p.m., for Sandgate. Returning with Trucks from Sandgate, Hythe and Sandling Junction to Westenhanger at 8.0 p.m. See times in above Tables.

October, 1891.

The Swan Hotel horse-bus, under the proprietorship of Mr. T. Elliott, pauses on Blackhouse Hill, Hythe, before driving down into the town.
British Railways

to receive the first of many enquiries about the future of the castle. The initial inquiry came from Mr. M. H. Judge, recently elected to the Sandgate Local Board, requesting that the castle be sold to the council as it was of interest to visitors. The SER replied that no permanent tenure was possible because they still had every intention of pushing ahead with the new line. Five weeks later, the Rev. Russell Wakefield wrote, seeking the tenancy. The Victorian railway builders held little or no respect for ancient monuments, particularly if they stood in the path of their routes, and Henry VIII's edifice was no exception. Prompted probably by the persistent requests to buy the castle, it was suggested that the SER directors consider getting rid of this nuisance by demolishing the building and using the stones for building work at Folkestone harbour. Three weeks later, Watkin paid a visit to Sandgate, looked over the castle, was evidently quite unimpressed by it and recommended it should be pulled down immediately! What happened in the next few weeks is a mystery for the SER had a change of heart and let the castle at £10 per annum to the Rev. Wakefield. A clause, giving three months notice to quit, was inserted, just in case the railway should find itself ready to begin laying down rails through Sandgate. In the meantime the Rev. Wakefield went about planning his 'Town Museum & Public Reading Room' within the premises.

In 1894 some minor building work took place in the vicinity of the line including four railway cottages next to the station master's house at Hythe amounting to £860. Authorisation for four similar dwellings at Sandgate was also given at that time. Grateful for the services of their secretary, who had given up much of his spare time in the interests of the SER, and in particular the new Hythe & Sandgate Tramway, the board granted him rent free accommodation at nearby Cannongate House.

Across the other side of the railway, the company agreed to build a club house for the golf links, which they just happened to own. This cost around £2,000 and was likely considered money well spent if the golfers would patronise the company's trains over the ensuing years.

The year 1894 also brought the retirement of Sir Edward Watkin, thus removing at a stroke the impetus of personal esteem and pride which he undoubtedly displayed in regard to the Sandgate branch. Of all his grand projects this little, and seemingly insignificant, branch was perhaps dearest of all and it must have been a bitter and persistent personal disappointment to him not to have been able to sink into the first class moquette at Sandgate and hear the porter shout 'Next stop Folkestone Harbour'. Whether he was an asset or a liability to the South Eastern Railway Company is a moot point. Evidently the stock exchange felt it was the latter for on his departure the SER shares immediately increased in value.

In the summer of 1895 sixteen more houses were built beneath Hythe station, on Blackhouse Hill, specifically intended for railway employees. In November Mr. Lord left Sandling Junction to take over from station master William Cheeseman who had just retired, leaving Edward Hilder to step into the vacancy at Sandling.

With the abundance of water in the vicinity, which periodically interfered with the railway, it is somewhat surprising that not until 1896 did the SER set aside £230 for mains fittings to enable both Hythe and Sandgate stations to draw upon the plentiful supply from the Honeywood spring.

In the town of Sandgate itself, the benevolent plans of the Rev. Wakefield came to nought for in July 1896 a Mr. J.J. Jones of the London Samaritan Society applied to the SER to rent the empty castle as well as 'The Hermitage'. Intending to spend £300 on sanitation and structural improvements, he explained he planned to cater for large excursion parties which, as he stressed, 'would be of great benefit to the railway company'. Incredibly, the SER adopted a disgraceful and thoroughly disdainful attitude and contemptuously replied in a fit of pique: 'It is a question however whether this sort of traffic would not keep away the better class of visitors and do more harm than good to Sandgate as a seaside resort.' Such a reaction might not come as a surprise from one of the large railway companies such as the pompous GWR, but coming from the ignoble SER, the butt of many a music hall joke, it was inept and, moreover, it is incomprehensible how they could afford to discourage business from any strata of society.

The Sandgate branch certainly didn't receive preferential treatment from the SER, even though some of its directors were under the impression that its patrons were better than the general 'riff-raff' who kept the company solvent. Sandgate was, after all, just at the end of a branch line and whilst crack expresses roared straight through Sandling Junction on their way to imperious Folkestone, the visitors to Hythe and Sandgate had to put up with second best. Apart from the through services to and from London, this essentially meant the shabbiest rake of carriages hauled by whatever worn-out engines could cope with the 1 in 54 gradient at Saltwood. It is probable that some members of the Ramsbottom 'Ironclad' 2–4–0s stationed in the area at this time helped out with the Sandgate locals, whereas Cudworth's increasingly asthmatic '118's are known to have been in evidence during this period, creaking up and down the line. Numbers 45, 90, 102, 132, 218, 227 and 246, all members of that once illustrious class, were frequent visitors. Absolutely nothing was wasted on the SER. The older engines took on the less demanding work of the branch lines as, in their turn, would the newer engines now hauling the prestigious expresses. Even when the days of hauling the humblest of goods trains were over, some locomotives had the ignominious task of supplying steam for workshops and heating. Bereft of wheels, fittings and shiny paintwork such survivors, if they could dream, would surely ponder upon those far off days when people stopped and stared in admiration as they dashed proudly through stations with the 'Tidal'.

The year 1899 was a landmark in the history of Kent's railways, when the union between the rival South Eastern and the London, Chatham and Dover Companies came about. The petty squabbles and vociferous hate campaigns that local people had become so accustomed to, were now left behind. Instead, the two companies formed the South Eastern & Chatham Railway Companies Managing Committee, to eventually emerge as one of the finest of Britain's railways. Soon, the locomotives pulling in to Sandgate would have 'S.E. & C.R.' emblazoned in gold upon their sides, whilst the new company name would appear at the top of the station billboards and on everything from posters to the humble platform ticket. It was a new era of hope and prosperity for the railways in general but what of the Sandgate branch? With Watkin now departed from the scene, the forces of opposition were stronger than ever. The eclipse of the Sandgate branch was just beginning.

CHAPTER FIVE

The Dream Fades

RE-ORGANISED under the SE & CR, the Sandgate branch enjoyed numerous improvements and alterations, many of which had already been planned and sanctioned by the SER.

Shortly before the emotional brink of the twentieth century was reached, two fatal accidents took place at Sandling Junction. The first happened on Midsummer's Day 1899 and was as spectacular as it was tragic, when a traction engine crashed over the parapet of the overbridge on the London side of the station. The engine, which belonged to a Mr. Padgham of Kingsnorth, near Ashford, was on its way with three truckloads of bricks to Saltwood where new almshouses were under construction. The road leading down to the station is very steep, and at that time unmade. Shortly after the engine had begun to descend the hill the driver, Henry Abbott, lost control of it. He shouted to his mate 'Look out, George!' as the weight of the 8,000 bricks in the wagons began pushing the engine, which had lost its grip, towards the bridge but George Bingham, the steersman, remained on the engine in a vain attempt to correct its course. As Henry Abbott jumped clear he saw his mate disappear over the parapet with the engine, followed by the trucks, onto the railway below. Signalman James Friend was standing outside his cabin at the time and was first alerted by the rumbling sound before he witnessed the engine plummet down the retaining wall on the opposite side of the bridge. The engine fell on its side but mercifully the boiler didn't rupture, otherwise a dreadful explosion would have followed. Luckily the safety valves were free to allow the steam to escape which roared out amidst the dust and debris spewed out across both lines. A pointsman working nearby dashed over to assist, whilst signalman Friend raced into his signal box as the Folkestone 'Tidal' express was signalled and due at any moment. Hurriedly sending the 'Line blocked' message to his colleague, 6 consecutive rings, he then slammed over the levers which bounced the semaphores back to 'danger'. By this time, Edward Hilder, the station master, and the rest of the staff had come across from the station to help clear the rails of wreckage. Poor Henry Abbott, enquiring after his mate, burst into tears when the unfortunate man's body was seen crushed beneath the wheels of the engine.

The 'down' express was brought to a sudden halt at Westenhanger where, after a short delay, it was worked 'wrong line' through Sandling with all heads peering from the compartments as the disaster was passed by. Soon after, Mr. Harlow and his breakdown gang from Ashford arrived and within two hours the line was cleared although it was some time before the wreckage was removed from the trackside.

At the inquest the character and behaviour of the men was questioned when it was revealed that the driver and his colleague had stopped a couple of miles further back at New Inn Green for a pint of beer and some bread and cheese. The coroner commented: 'You must recollect, these men are taken from a rough kind of class.' Mr. Padgham, their employer, would have none of it, however, and vouched for the crew's good conduct and insisted that his employees were as respectable as any other men. He mentioned that since the terrible accident poor Abbott had 'lost' his head. After a thorough investigation into possible mechanical failure, the cause was blamed on the slippery condition of the road. A verdict of accidental death was therefore subsequently recorded.

The traction engine incident exemplifies how all railwaymen had to remain alert and be prepared to deal with accidents of a particulary gruesome nature. It was doubly distressing when employees of the company were involved, for friendships were invariably struck up between the men and seeing a mate killed or terribly mutilated was a horrible experience. Fate played such a trick when, just ten months later, on 2nd April 1900, Sandling Junction's well-known and respected station master Edward Hilder was run down by an 'up' express just a few yards from his home. At the inquest Thomas Wellard, the district travelling inspector, replied that it was usual for the station master to visit the main line signal box, cabin no. 1, with messages shortly before the train from Sandgate had arrived and the express passed through. On the previous day, Hilder had complained of giddiness but otherwise seemed in good health. The driver of the train, Alfred Newman, was understandably upset, particularly as he knew Hilder well and thought of him as a good friend. He stated that he took his train out of Folkestone promptly at 8.55 a.m. keeping to the scheduled time to reach Sandling Junction at approximately 9.04. On leaving Saltwood tunnel on the approach to the station he gave one long whistle in the usual way and on rounding the curve saw a figure standing in the 'four foot way'. He slammed the regulator shut, whilst his mate screwed down the brakes, and gave several short sharp blows upon the locomotive's whistle. By this time, however, he was only about thirty yards away and his train, being heavily loaded, could not be stopped in such a short distance. The unfortunate Hilder, who showed no signs of realising that the express was

The wreckage of the traction engine which crashed over the parapet at Sandling Junction. *The British Library*

bearing down upon him, was struck by the engine and carried almost fifty yards to where the train stopped. Alfred Newman, his fireman, and the guard, had the unenviable task of inspecting the scene. Although the body was shockingly mutilated they could see that death had been mercifully instantaneous for he'd been struck in the back of the head by the centre lamp iron on the engine's buffer beam. Aged 43, Edward Hilder had been station master at Sandling Junction for little more than five years, having transferred from Smeeth in 1895. He left a widow and seven children aged from 2 to 21 years. A verdict of accidental death was recorded whilst it was stressed that the engine crew were entirely blameless and had done everything that could have possibly been expected of them.

On a more cheerful note, the year 1900 was set to bring many changes to the railways of Kent as the SE & CR gradually established itself. Slowly the liveries of the SER and LC & DR disappeared but some older engines, not long for the scrap road, retained the old company colours and it must have been interesting seeing them run over former 'enemy' territory. One of the first known instances concerning the Sandgate branch was the appearance of No. 133, named *Huz*. This was one of two 0-6-0 goods engines built by Sharp Stewart in 1873 for the LC & DR. The sister engine carried an equally enigmatic and rather comical name – *Buz*. At the union, both were stationed in London but shortly before they were withdrawn in 1901, it is interesting to know that *Huz* spent a brief period running about up and down the Sandgate branch.

Even though the gradients of this branch might at times have taxed these venerable machines to the limit of their ability, the timetable was sufficiently lax to allow a breather at either end. However, once on the main line, their performance had to be smarter in order not to delay the faster trains. Services over the Sandgate branch were altered only marginally by the SE & CR, mainly where the summer timetable was augmented with a couple of extra trains as well as a Wednesday-only excursion. On summer Sundays the service was quite remarkable, with a dozen trains in each direction. Clearly, the locality was popular with holidaymakers and day-trippers of the period.

Apart from handling a fair amount of tourist trade, the line earned a regular income with ordinary local passenger and goods traffic. There was extra revenue too from military trains since nearby Shorncliffe camp brought Sandgate into the affairs of protecting the Empire. The district which the line served was, with its military associations, always involved with the affairs of empire. Stores, supplies, horses, soldiers and so on, all frequently passed over the branch and occasionally events of an outwardly patriotic nature took place. One of the most memorable and well-recorded was the return of the Buffs, or the 'Ladysmith heroes' as they were dubbed. Their exploits in the Boer War were cited as 'thrilling, plucky and splendidly daring', and these deeds likely filled boys' journals and books of the day. On 23rd April 1900, news came through on the telegraph that the troop vessel had berthed at Southampton whereby the wounded and invalided men would arrive at Sandgate station by teatime. Appropriately enough it was St. George's Day thus providing a good excuse to unfurl whatever banner or flag that could be found. It wasn't very long before the neighbourhood took on the atmosphere of a jamboree. At the coastguard station, just across the road from Sandgate station, signal flags reading 'Welcome' in semaphore were to be seen fluttering in the sea breeze. Local children were given the afternoon off from school in order that they might 'witness this stirring event'. By mid-afternoon many hordes of locals were packing into every available tram and bus to make their way to the goods yard and station approaches at Sandgate. There was quite a crush in the immediate station area, whilst the road leading up from the goods yard to the camp was solid with spectators. Charabancs continued to arrive on the main road below, discharging their loads before returning to Hythe and Folkestone to pick up more eager passengers. On the station platforms were assembled civic and military officials.

LC & DR No. 133 *Huz* **which spent a brief period on Sandgate services.** *Ken Nunn/LCGB*

The 'Ladysmith Heroes' being transported by horse and cart out of Sandgate goods yard. *The Army & Navy Illustrated*

Wounded Boer War survivors are taken away, watched by onlookers, some of whom are waving hats and handkerchiefs.
Folkestone Public Library

Horse-buses line up to assist in transporting the detrained soldiers. *Author's Collection*

Reception committee on the down side approach of Hythe station awaiting the arrival of General Sir Ian Hamilton, 'the hero of the hour who had fought so valiantly in England's cause'. *Hythe Public Library*

A Stirling 'R' class 0–6–0T, believed to be No. 154, with full-length chimney and Stirling round cab, waits at Sandgate. Note the re-sited 'gents'.
C. J. Barnard/Alex Todd Collection

Shortly before the appointed time of arrival, some eighty stretcher bearers arrived from the camp, causing some consternation amongst the crowd. Across at the station, Major-General Hallam-Parr, the Commander-in-Chief at Shorncliffe, accompanied by his aide-de-camp, paced the worn waiting room floorboards where he received his guests. These included Alderman J. J. Jeal who had thoughtfully brought along several boxes of cigars to distribute among the soldiers. At about 4 p.m. the bell sounded in the signal box as the Hythe signalman tapped out his message, thus causing a flurry of excitement to sweep through the crowd. Moments later the sounds of an approaching train greeted straining ears before familiar clouds of white steam were seen curling round the hillside. The crowd stirred into activity as the train rolled in conveying its sad cargo. Some portions of the train were marked with bright red crosses which bore the more seriously injured and these were the first to be attended. The chairman of Sandgate council then read an address. There was a noticeable lack of music as strict instructions had been given that no band should play. Instead, as reported, 'the music of three hearty cheers as can only proceed from British throats'. A total of 115 men, rank and file, came off the train, wearied after a 6,000-mile journey across the globe. Some were assisted by helpers, others made their own way, hobbling with sticks. Many had heads and limbs swathed in bandages whilst everyone bore some evidence of the campaign. It appears that the crowd were somewhat taken aback, expecting perhaps smiling faces and tales of heroism. Instead, these sad men with their 'deep yellow complexions and sunken, glassy eyes', simply made their way silently to the goods yard and waiting horse buses which would carry them into kind hands at the Beach Rocks Convalescent Home in Sandgate.

The handling of such trains highlighted difficulties of manoeuvrability at Sandgate to the SE & CR which it sought to rectify a couple of months later. Trains arriving at the 'down' platform either had to be reversed towards Hythe, thence shunted into the 'up' platform, or run 'wrong line' to Hythe before gaining the 'up' road. In July a new crossover was laid at the western end of Sandgate station, between bridges 2138 and 2140, which eliminated this problem. Because extra levers were needed at the signal box to operate the new crossover and its signals, it appears that the 17 lever frame was re-designated accordingly. From then onwards certain functions at the eastern end of the station, previously carried out by the signalman, were transferred to a shunter by the addition of a 13-lever ground frame positioned near the water tower. Simultaneous improvements were forthcoming at Hythe when £620 was authorised to be spent on alterations. To deal more effectively with the increasing parcels traffic, the 'gents' at the Sandling end of the building was converted into a parcels office. A new convenience was provided at the Sandgate end. The main works, however, involved the installation of a crossover at the western end of the station near Blackhouse Hill bridge. An additional crossover was also sanctioned for Sandling Junction which would allow through trains from Sandgate to be despatched from the 'down' branch platform. This eradicated the need for Sandgate branch passengers having to use the foot crossing at Sandling when transferring to the 'up' London expresses and meant that their change of trains was not only safer but a great deal drier in wet weather. Once the express had departed, the branch train would leave the 'down' platform but, although fouling the 'down' main line, would soon regain the 'up' main via the new crossover just west of the station.

Whilst new works such as these improved the fabric of the branch, thereby enabling it to earn its keep more effectively, its *raison d'être* remained unfulfilled. Close on thirty years had elapsed since the first train had steamed into Sandgate and there was little hope left in anyone's mind that the rails would ever proceed beyond the engine shed. Unrelenting opposition from powerful quarters, rising land values, ever-increasing costs of construction – all tallied against Watkin's cherished dream. Recognition of this fact came from the SE & CR's secretary who, when referring to the proposed sale of 'The Hermitage',

SOUTH EASTERN AND CHATHAM RAILWAY.

A DAY AT THE SEASIDE.

EXCURSIONS TO SANDGATE.

RAIL & TEA, 3/9

Beanfeast Parties, Societies, School and Other Parties.

INCLUSIVE RATES.

THOS. COOK & SON have made arrangements with the Proprietors of the Grosvenor Hotel, Sandgate, for the accommodation of parties and individuals on

SATURDAYS, SUNDAYS, & MONDAYS,
(OTHER DAYS BY ARRANGEMENT).

AS UNDER:—	ADULTS.	Children under 12 years.
RAIL and Tea	3/9 each	2/-
" Cold Luncheon and Tea	5/- "	2/9
" FIRST CLASS Cold Luncheon & Tea	6/6 "	Full details of Bill of Fare and Departure Times upon application.
" SUPERIOR " "	8/6 "	
" VERY SUPERIOR BREAKFAST on arrival, LUNCHEON & TEA	10/6 "	

The Fare on Whit-Monday, June 4th, will be increased by 1s. per Adult.

THE ABOVE PRICES INCLUDE RAILWAY TICKET LONDON TO SANDGATE AND BACK.

The Bookings are limited, and THOS. COOK & SON reserve the right to refuse any application.

Sandgate is an ideal spot for a Day's Outing, there being excellent facilities for Boating, Bathing, and Driving. Folkestone, Hythe, and Shorncliffe Military Camp, with over 7,000 troops stationed there, are within easy walking Distances of Sandgate, and a frequent service of Omnibuses works between the places.

EARLY BOOKING IS NECESSARY FOR PARTIES, AND IN ALL CASES TICKETS MUST BE OBTAINED IN ADVANCE FROM—

THOS. COOK & SON,
EXCURSION BOOKING OFFICE,
(ST. BRIDE STREET ENTRANCE)
LUDGATE CIRCUS, E.C., or following Branches—

City Office—99, Gracechurch Street, E.C.

West End Offices {
33, Piccadilly (opposite St. James's Church), W.
21, High Street, Kensington, W.
13, Cockspur Street, Pall Mall, S.W.
82, Oxford Street, W.
}

Strand Office—Forecourt, Charing Cross Terminus, W.C.
Blackfriars—Royal Hotel Buildings.
Euston Road Office—In front of St. Pancras Station, N.W.

D. 348/1900.   Thos. Cook & Son, Printers, &c., Ludgate Circus, London.   (6604)

Courtesy David Banks

THE DREAM FADES

Sir Edward William Watkin 1819-1901.

told the board it was 'now improbable that the house would be required for railway purposes'. Nonetheless, perhaps cautious and hopeful to the last, the SE & CR insisted that only the lease be sold.

The aspirations of the Sandgate branch it could be argued, finally expired with the last breath of Edward Watkin who departed this earth, aged 82, at his home in Cheshire on the 14th April 1901. Appropriately, the life of one of the most colourful and representative Victorians connected with the pursuit of railways, along with the esteem and power it commanded, came to a close with the end of Victoria's reign.

It was in 1845 that the young Watkin, aged 26, had begun as secretary to the Trent Valley Line which was subsequently swallowed up into the London & North Western Railway. It was also in that year that he married his first wife, Mary Mellor. His parliamentary career began in 1857 when he stood as a Liberal for Great Yarmouth and in 1864 became the member for Stockport where he remained for three years until losing his seat. In 1874 his political ambition was galvanised by his railway pursuits when he succeeded in being elected member for Hythe, a position held for 21 years. Throughout his life he served as director, chairman, and general manager at various times on the Great Western, Great Eastern, and Metropolitan railways, yet it is with the South Eastern that he is best remembered. His crowning achievement in the development of the English railway system is stated to be the establishment of the last great trunk route of the 19th century – the Great Central Line. His exploits were not just confined to these shores either, for his name is given as the man who brought to successful issue the Canadian Grand Trunk Railway. He was a keen promoter of the Channel Tunnel and all matters relating to cross-channel traffic. Under his leadership improvements to the harbours at Boulogne and Calais were carried out which enabled the journey time between London and Paris to be brought down to seven hours. His energy and drive was abundant in other fields too, from the humble to the grand. He was not only instrumental in adding a fifth pathway up Snowdon but added to the gaiety of the nation in the construction of the abortive Wembley Tower. This structure, which naturally had to be taller than its counterpart designed by Monsieur Eiffel, never managed to go beyond the first stage and this 'monument to Watkin' was eventually dismantled. Always one who loved pomp and adoration, he achieved a knighthood in 1867 and received his baronetcy in 1880. Age evidently neither wearied nor worried him for, following the death of his wife Mary in 1888, he remarried in 1893 at the age of 74. His 82-year-old bride was the widow of Mr. Ingram, MP, the founder of the *Illustrated London News*. The irrepressible Watkin outlived her by five years.

With Watkin and the old SER now fading from memory, the SE & CR sought to improve its image. Yet real change was slow in coming and a sceptical public were quick to reprimand the railways for their shortcomings. Complaints concerning the railways have continued to appear in newspapers for almost as long as both have existed, be it late running of trains, dirty carriages, or lack of staff. 1901 was no exception, as reported by a columnist who signed himself 'Pei-li-khan':

'One occasionally hears murmurs about the inconvenience of the ticket office at Sandling Junction station. This inconvenience is sometimes felt in an unpleasant manner. A friend of mine, a working man, was coming home the other week and arrived at the station some time before the train was due. Of course the ticket office was not open then. He hung about the station for a while and then went over for his ticket, telling the guard of the train his intention. The office was not then open although the time of the train's departure was very close. A boy, at length, sauntered in and when asked for a ticket replied that the train was just off and there was no time to issue one. My friend rushed round at once just as the train was moving out. He essayed to enter it but, although the guard had not taken his place, he was stopped by the Station Master. As there was not another train to Hythe for an hour and a half he was compelled to walk home.'

Nonetheless, this was a time for optimism, when the emphasis was apparently on looking towards an even brighter future. On a national scale the coronation of King Edward VII in 1902 was an event to thrill the country, despite its postponement due to the King's ill-health. The SE & CR laid on special trains for London from all parts of its system with two being scheduled to leave Sandgate at the unearthly hours of 4 a.m. and 5 a.m. Evidently it would be the early bird who'd secure the best place along the route of the procession. It was certainly not a cheap trip though, for the 3rd class return fare was a substantial nine shillings.

Locally, prospects seemed very bright too with the re-opening of the Imperial Hotel on Monday 7th July. The need for renovations and improvements had brought about the temporary closure. A special train left Charing Cross at 11 a.m. to run non-stop to Hythe where it pulled in ninety minutes

THE HYTHE & SANDGATE RAILWAY

HYTHE & SANDGATE BRANCH.

SERVICE OF TRAINS BETWEEN SANDLING JUNCTION, HYTHE, AND SANDGATE.

DOWN TRAINS—WEEK DAYS.

[Timetable showing arrival and departure times for Sandling Junction, Hythe, and Sandgate stations. Column headers include N M Goods, M Goods, N M Goods, and numerous AM/PM columns.]

DOWN TRAINS—WEEK DAYS—continued

[Continuation of timetable with additional PM columns, including one marked W (Wednesdays only).]

DOWN TRAINS—SUNDAYS.

[Sunday timetable with AM and PM columns.]

All Trains are 1, 2 and 3 Class. N M Not on Mondays. M Mondays only. W Wednesdays only. X 5.15 p.m. Goods from Ashford.

Sandling Junction will arrange for an Engine to fetch any Trucks from Westenhanger that may arrive there after the 6.45 a.m. Down Branch Goods Train has left. Goods for Sandling Junction and Hythe and Sandgate Branch will be worked to Westenhanger, and be conveyed thence by the Sandgate Branch Goods Train, which will work through to Westenhanger.

A Special Trip over the Sandgate Branch will be run when required from Westenhanger at about Mid-day, when the 8.35 a.m. Ashford to Canterbury Goods is late starting from Ashford. Ashford to advise Westenhanger in good time when the latter cannot start before mid-day, and Westenhanger to arrange with Shorncliffe to send the Shunting Engine to work the trip. The Engine to run first to Sandgate to pick up Guard and Brake. Shorncliffe to advise Dover when this arrangement is made. (X 15,646).

HYTHE & SANDGATE BRANCH.

SERVICE OF TRAINS BETWEEN SANDLING JUNCTION, HYTHE AND SANDGATE.

UP TRAINS—WEEK DAYS.

[Timetable showing arrival and departure times for Sandgate, Hythe, and Sandling Junction stations. Column headers include B N M Eng. Bke., M Goods, N M Goods, Empty, Empty.]

UP TRAINS—WEEK DAYS—continued.

[Continuation with columns including Z Goods, Empty, Weds. only Excursion.]

UP TRAINS—SUNDAYS.

[Sunday timetable with AM and PM columns, one marked T.]

All Trains are 1, 2 and 3 Class. B Engine to Westenhanger, to work Goodstrip to Sandgate Branch—see Main Line Pages.

T Through to Ashford. Z Goods to Ashford. N M Not on Mondays. M Mondays only.

July, August and September, 1901.

later bearing the directors, officials and invited shareholders of the SE & CR as well as members of the press who accompanied them on this particular 'gravy train' special. A procession of horse-drawn carriages clattered its way down from Hythe station to the seafront where a grand reception awaited the 500 guests. On the surrounding lawns a military band filled the drowsy summer air with its brassy strains whilst inside the hotel's own orchestra played during luncheon. Quite likely the guests were treated to such popular contemporary salon pieces as Elgar's 'Salut d'amour', 'Chanson de matin', and 'Sevillana'. Afterwards, a grand tour of the railway-owned hotel took place, at which the assembly were invited to inspect the rooms and furnishings which might tempt the well-to-do to this corner of Kent. From the windows though the prospect was less inviting for the view stretched out across a bleak and empty landscape. Where, oh where, were the elegant mansions of the rich, the exclusive garden squares, the porticoed emporiums – the great and gracious London-super-Mare?

In spite of this unfulfilled prophecy, business on the branch was flourishing. Goods traffic had evidently increased and not merely small parcels, for a new 30 cwt. crane was installed in the goods yard at Hythe for the sum of £90. A 5 cwt. crane, from Messrs Jessop & Appleby Bros., costing £145, appeared at Sandgate. This arrived by rail once the SE & CR engineering department had finished the foundations. Traffic began each weekday with preparations for the first 'down' train which comprised a goods trip. At 6.00 a.m. Sandling Junction No. 2 and Sandgate signal boxes were opened, although Hythe box remained closed unless specifically required for goods workings at that time in the morning. Both Sandling No. 2 and Sandgate signal boxes were shut at 9.30 p.m. on weekdays, whilst on Sundays the signalmen could enjoy an extra hour in bed since neither opened until 7.15 a.m.; however they didn't shut until 11 p.m. At 6.15 a.m. the 'Engine & Brakes', as it was referred to, left Sandgate to run direct to Sandling Junction and, after a pause of two minutes, it continued on to Westenhanger, arriving at 6.28 a.m. Once the Sandgate branch goods had been shunted and prepared, it returned, arriving back at Sandgate at 7.17 a.m. On Mondays the 'up' goods ran only as far as Sandling Junction and, when not required for work at Westenhanger, the engine ran round to proceed 'light' to Shorncliffe to work the 'up' Elham Valley branch goods.

In 1904 William Fright, the station master at Hythe, wrote to the board concerning the poor condition of his house which stood at the bottom of the approach road. The SE & CR sent a surveyor to look over it and he agreed it would be pointless spending any further amounts of money on repairs as it had been quite seriously damaged in the landslips of the 1870s. Messrs. Scott Bros. duly provided a splendid new house with a large garden for £305 on the northern side of the station, it was also in a much more convenient position. A few months later William Fright, his wife, daughter Eva and son Harold, as well as Rufus, their terrier, moved into their comfortable new home. Rufus was a firm favourite with the station staff on the line. Often they'd open a compartment door for him to board the train where he'd travel all by himself to Sandgate, where out he'd trot to visit the Frights' aunt who owned a local china shop.

The provision of such cheap housing was a boon to the employees of the railway for whom the company would offer financial assistance by way of loans to enable them to find accommodation near their work. With this in mind, one of the Sandgate signalmen applied for an advance of £200 for the purchase of a house. However, not every applicant received a favourable response, and as the employee concerned had already received an advance in 1893, it was refused. A Mr. Leney of Seabrook had more success in connection with a different matter when he wrote to the SE & CR asking for 'a private access by gate to the up platform at Sandgate'. This was granted provided that an annual payment of twenty shillings was received.

Efforts to stimulate more passenger business for the branch came in 1905 when, for the first time, Hythe enjoyed the prestige of having through trains to the north of England. Co-operation between the SE & CR and the Midland Railway meant they were able to organise a weekdays-only service departing from Hythe at 11.09 to reach Manchester at 6.10 p.m. and Bradford at 7.28 p.m. Ventures such as these were closely monitored to ascertain profitability, but the railways were fortunate at this time for even short-distance motorised road travel had yet to make its impact. This is perhaps borne out by the fact that in July of that year the 'Hythe Trades Protection Society' decided that the venue of their annual outing should be the charming Wealden town of Tenterden. Boarding the train at Hythe, they journeyed to Headcorn where they changed trains before travelling over the newly-opened portion of the Kent & East Sussex Railway owned by the indomitable Colonel Holman Fred Stephens. Perhaps though there were some railway enthusiasts in the HTPS to have opted for such a circuitous route rather than hire a charabanc via the more direct way through Ham Street.

Throughout this decade excursions were very popular, either those organised by the railway companies themselves or by private arrangement. One example was the Final Tie of the English Football Cup 1906 for which the SE & CR laid on a 3s 6d return football special departing from Hythe at 7.27 a.m. and returning from London at 9.45 p.m. Private entrepreneurs also had a hand in the running of excursions:

> 'An excursion train for London for tomorrow has been arranged by that enterprising pioneer of cheap travelling, Mr. A. K. Baldwin. He has been successful in obtaining power from the SE & CR to reduce the fare for the whole day excursions from Hythe to 3/6 (normal fare 4/6). The train departs Sandgate at 10.09 a.m., Hythe 10.14 a.m. and returns from Victoria at 9.30 p.m.'

If railway excursions were popular, so too were jaunts in the ever-increasing number of charabancs. In many ways the dawn of the age of the combustion engine would soon start to affect not only the receipts of the railway companies but also their plans and decisions. With almost all hope gone of laying rails east of Sandgate, it was the turn of the New Romney extension scheme to fade away. The parliamentary powers to construct the line were left to expire in August 1905, but efforts were forthcoming to improve local transport. Perhaps intending to take advantage of the Light Railways Act 1896, the engineer was instructed to prepare an estimate for a light railway between Hythe and New Romney. In the meantime it was recommended that two railway-owned motor omnibuses be ordered for the 1906 season in order that an assessment of the traffic potential might be made.

The plan to develop the Seabrook Estate, as already mentioned, was pinned entirely upon the railway extension to Folkestone harbour, the success of the former relying absolutely

Station master William Fright and his staff on the up platform at Hythe. Presumably the up starting signal heralds the imminent arrival of a train from Sandgate. Taken about 1904.
Miss Eva Fright

THE DREAM FADES

The station staff at Hythe pose for the photographer beneath the down side shelter with its marvellous array of advertisements. Station master William Fright sports a fine beard, whilst Herbert Buswell stands on the far right. Other faces sadly remain unidentified.

Miss Eva Fright

on the realisation of the latter. The wonders of new hotels, plush villas and maisonettes bordering tree-lined avenues and squares evaporated every bit into thin air as the steam from the nearby trains running to and fro. In a seemingly last desperate attempt to stimulate some sort of justification for the Sandgate branch, the SE & CR awarded J.J. Jeal over £200 for a new road which would hopefully pave the way for new buildings around Hythe station but, alas, it was all too little and too late.

Continuing to cut their coat according to their cloth, the SE & CR ensured that nothing was dispensed with before its time. In many ways this policy pleased those who nurtured an interest in railways during that period and one example of this was the appearance, in 1906, of another ex-LC & DR engine on the branch services. This time it was No. 477, an elderly 2–4–0 of 1861 vintage, formerly LC & DR No. 18 named *Leopard*. This quaint engine was the last survivor of its class, with over a million miles notched up during its lifetime. Shortly before it was sent on its final journey to the scrap heap, *Leopard* spent its last days pounding up and down the Sandgate branch as well as wandering out along the bleakest and loneliest part of Kent to that other dream, Port Victoria.

On a more personal level, William Fright and his family moved away from Hythe to the little country terminus of Westerham where the post of station master had become vacant. Hythe's position was filled by Mr. W. E. Harris who arrived on 9th November, transferring from Horsmonden station on the delightful Hawkhurst branch which penetrated the High Weald. Unfortunately, one of William Harris's first tasks was especially unpleasant for just a few days later another death occurred on the railway when Mr. William Worthington, one of three brothers of the well-known firm of coach builders at Hythe, was run down late one evening by a train. On arrival at Hythe the driver of the 9.34 p.m. to Sandgate reported feeling the engine bump at Saltwood, as well as hearing 'the ballast fly'. Although he could see nothing when

A moment captured at Sandling Junction about 1907 with a Stirling 'Q' class preparing to depart from the up main platform and a rebuilt 'Q1' letting off excess steam in the down branch platform. A large portmanteau awaits a porter whilst a stack of baggage for the Sandgate branch can be seen underneath the canopy. The woman draped in black from head to toe adds considerably to the period feel of this wonderful photograph.
Norman Wakeman

THE DREAM FADES

Railmotor No. 1 and crew at Dover. *Author's Collection*

peering out into the darkness, driver John Gardiner wanted to return to the spot so, accompanied by signalman David Gravener and other station staff, they made their way on foot to investigate. Close to Saltwood Castle, where a bridle path crossed the line, the light from their lamps confirmed their worst fears when they made their gruesome discovery. The local constabulary were duly summoned whereupon the wretched body of poor Worthington was carried to the nearby coach house. The mystery remained unsolved, for 52-year-old Worthington was said to lead a most exemplary life, being a 'pillar of the church'. The coroner was therefore obliged to record a verdict of accidental death.

On a lighter note, the introduction of steam railcars to the Sandgate branch in July 1907 proved favourable with the public by their frequency although their comfort, compared with ordinary trains, was another matter entirely. When running with the engine in the rear, the unit vibrated and oscillated rather badly at times, so efforts were later made to rectify this fault. Also, the speed of the diminutive locomotive and its combined carriage was limited when heavily loaded or on the very taxing gradients of the Sandgate branch. Bill Young, who later became Elham's most well-known signalman, did a spell of duty as a guard on the Dover Town–Sandgate railmotor service and he remembered how the pace would drastically slacken to about 4 m.p.h. when heavily laden on the Sandgate branch, and stretches of the Elham Valley line over which they were latterly introduced. Railcars Nos. 5 and 7 were stationed at Dover at the commencement of these services in July 1907 and, although apparently only originally planned to work up until the end of September, they continued through to the end of the year. A note in a working timetable of that period states: 'The Dover & Sandgate and Rye & Hastings Steam Railcars will be discontinued from January 1st to April 12th 1908 inclusive.'.

Improvements to the railcars followed which appear to have eliminated the worst problems and from thenceforward they continued to augment the summer services which were sometimes so well patronised that a second trailer car was added which hindered their speed even more! They were one class only, containing 24 smoking and 32 non-smoking compartments with two vestibules for luggage. Finished in the smart crimson lake livery of the SE & CR they were a delightful curiosity and a change from the norm. Even so, it is probable that those passengers familiar with their occasional poor performance likely groaned when they arrived at the station to see one merrily panting along into the platform. Six railcar journeys were made on weekdays, excepting Thursdays, and departures in 1907 were as follows:

Dover Town: 8.20, 10.10, 12.15, 2.45, 5.15, 7.46
Sandgate: 9.19, 11.19, 1.19, 3.59, 6.11, 8.41

There were five trips on Sundays. The single fare for the journey, which took about three-quarters of an hour, was a shilling and the only real bonus was that there was no need to change at Sandling Junction. Viewed from the top of the Warren cliffs these tiny contraptions were dwarfed even more by a landscape which already made the railway look like a toy. There must have been some people who, pausing in Foord Road, Folkestone, stared upwards when the railmotors first appeared, to watch them cross Cubitt's towering viaduct. A passing boat train in the opposite direction served only to emphasise the railmotor's exiguous proportions, yet their usefulness to the numerous railway companies is undeniable. It is a great pity that the exploits of these remarkable machines upon the Kentish branch lines were rarely recorded by the wandering photographer. Indeed, it must have been quite a sight to witness No. 5 or 7 disturbing the normally tranquil environs of Saltwood on a summer's day when, loaded to full capacity, it gasped its way towards Hayne tunnel, the summit of the bank from Hythe.

Adding to the complaints over the unsuitability of the railmotors, further grievances were aired when the SE & CR adamantly refused to extend season tickets to third class travellers from Hythe, or from anywhere else for that matter. The *Hythe Reporter* commented on the company's approach to the resort and printed a letter from 'A Regular Visitor' who remarked on the 'general run-down state of Hythe and its overall tattiness'. The correspondent went on to suggest that the railway company should do more to attract visitors to Hythe, then added insult to injury by proposing that the initials SE & CR might stand for 'Stifled Enterprise & Commercial Rust Company'!

Trade remained on the increase, however, certainly in goods traffic terms, for during 1908 the railway spent £450 on new

A broadside view of 'A' class No. 163. The identity of the gentleman wearing a straw boater and plus-fours is a mystery, but it certainly isn't the driver!
Author's Collection

stables at Hythe station which could accommodate six horses. The company also invested in new vans built in readiness for their own collection and delivery service between the town and the station. This service commenced on 12th October and enabled the SE & CR to dispense with the private operators.

In the spring of 1909 a stranger appeared on the Sandgate services in the form of No. 163, the last survivor of Stirling's graceful 'A' class 4–4–0s. There were only twelve members of the class so they weren't seen that often by Edwardian train spotters. These elegant engines were built around 1880 to supersede the old '118's on the main line services. With the influx of Wainwright's more powerful 'E' class 4–4–0 express engines they were transferred to lesser duties, such as secondary passenger and branch line services. By the end of June this dignified old lady of the South Eastern made her last appearance on this seaside branch before running to Ashford to be dismantled for spares and scrap. Her number went to one of Wainwright's new and equally stylish 'E' class locomotives recently completed in the workshops.

Throughout the summer of 1910 the SE & CR attempted to respond to its critics by undertaking numerous improvements at Hythe. On the 'down' side platform the original wooden partition fencing was removed to be replaced with more durable iron railings. A fresh coat of paint helped matters considerably, but undoubtedly the main transformation came with the installation of gas lighting. Gas was generally introduced wherever there was a convenient supply, the source for the Sandgate branch coming from Folkestone Gas & Coke Company whose works were situated beneath the Foord viaduct. At Sandling the main line platforms received 'swan-neck' lamps mounted upon the existing 'barley-twist' posts but the branch platforms, as well as Hythe and Sandgate stations, simply had their original oil lanterns converted to accommodate the gas mantles. Undoubtedly this was of equal benefit to the staff, cutting down on the laborious and time-consuming task of filling vessels, trimming wicks and tending each lamp. Perhaps the most welcome convenience of all though was the mains water supply at Sandling Junction, worth every penny of the £4 annual fee to the Elham Valley Water Company. The old water pump could be dispensed with from now onwards for as much water as could be desired would pour henceforth from the taps – a positive boon for the station master's early morning shave not to mention the staff's daily consumption of tea! Sewage disposal was another irksome problem, particularly at remote country stations where cess pools were the only alternative. Pausing at such stations on a warm summer's day could be quite unpleasant, nor hardly evocative of the romantic landscapes framed above the compartment seats. In spite of the fact that Sandgate station purported to serve the town of that name, the local authority adamantly refused to empty the station's cesspool – perhaps sour grapes at being so ill-served by the railway. Thankfully, for staff and passengers alike, Hythe Corporation agreed to lay a pipe from the station directly into their sewer and no one complained about the annual £5 fee!

For a change, the SE & CR were congratulated over their recent efforts at Hythe although the grumblings of discontent continued in respect of the distance between the station and the town. One of those 'shaggy-dog' stories appeared in the *Hythe Reporter* which could, and probably did, apply to most railway stations:

> Passenger: 'Porter! Why is it that the station is so far from the town?'
> Porter: 'Because, sir, the Company thought it more useful near the line'.

Another bone of contention concerned the train service to London. The Mayor of Hythe, Alderman F. W. Butler, called a public meeting in July 1910, pointing out that the great drawback for Hythe residents was that they weren't able to get to London before 10.45 a.m. Therefore they resolved to ask the SE & CR to stop the 8.34 corridor train from Folkestone at Sandling Junction, but this the railway refused to do. Eventually, an amicable solution was found when the railway

THE DREAM FADES

A Sunday school outing from Hythe awaiting the arrival of the train from Sandgate in 1910. Inset is the Reverend H. D. Dale.
Folkestone Herald

Some of Hythe station staff standing outside the booking office with the horse-bus in the approach. Photographed shortly before the outbreak of the Great War, from left to right are Herbert Banks, (unknown), T. Faircloth, and Arthur Batt.
Alex Todd

arranged for a train to leave Hythe at 8.04 a.m. which allowed passengers to arrive at Folkestone Central at 8.24 a.m. so that they could board the 8.34 a.m. express.

The summer season of trains was, as usual, augmented by the railcars although Nos. 1 and 6 took over from cars 5 and 7. Also at this time another interesting locomotive turned up where, along with a trailer car, it assisted with the duties performed by railcar No. 1. This locomotive, numbered 751 by the SE & CR, was bought from the LB & SCR in 1904. It was a member of the 'Terrier' class, previously numbered 54 and named *Waddon*; however, it was charmingly nick-named 'Little Titch' by the South Eastern men, after Harry Relph, a Man of Kent who was a famous music hall artist of the day. No. 751's career was certainly colourful and 'Little Titch' fortuitously managed to evade the scrap merchant's torch to be eventually restored to the full splendour of LB & SCR livery before being shipped to Canada in 1963 for permanent exhibition.

On the 6th November 1910 passengers on the Sunday morning 9.11 from Ashford to Hythe had a most interesting or frustrating journey depending on how it was viewed. Shortly after leaving Smeeth the engine failed at Grove bridge, Sellinge, whereupon the signalman at Herringe cabin sent a message through to Sandling Junction for a relief engine. On arrival, the relief hauled the entire train to Westenhanger where the failed locomotive was detached from the train and shunted into a siding. However, during this manoeuvre the Sandling engine was derailed, so Westenhanger were obliged to ring through to Folkestone Junction to ask if they had anything to spare! Throughout this time the carriages of the 9.11 Ashford–Hythe and its passengers were left stranded in the 'down' platform at Westenhanger, preventing the passing of the lordly Boat Train, by now left indignantly waiting at signals further up the line. When Folkestone's relief engine arrived, the signalman hurriedly arranged for it to shunt the Hythe train into the 'down' bay to allow the passage of the Boat Train – by then over an hour late. Once past, the Folkestone crew took the train to Sandling where another train was by this time waiting to take them on to Hythe. The travellers eventually arrived at their destination just after midday, their journey having taken nearly three hours in which they were hauled by four different locomotives!

No doubt to the relief of all, the 1911 summer service was worked by conventional trains instead of the railmotors which instead were tried out on the unfortunate inhabitants of Lyminge and Elham. Throughout those months the 3/6d returns from Hythe tempted the public to travel by train to a host of spectacular events such as the Festival of Empire Exhibition at the Crystal Palace, the Ancient Art Exhibition at Earls Court, or the topical Coronation Exhibition at White City. With the return booked at ten minutes past midnight, the entire trainload surely slept all the way to Hythe after such an eventful and wearying day.

Another popular amusement at that time was a pleasure steamer trip on the paddle-boats plying from resort to resort along the south coast. The pier, which the SER had planned for Hythe, would have proved a valuable asset as both the North British Railway Company's steamer the *Waverley* and the *Brighton Queen*, owned by the LB & SCR, regularly drifted past Hythe laden with merry visitors. 'A pity we don't have a pier' wrote one correspondent to the paper, who went on to suggest that perhaps small boats could be used to take parties out to the steamers as they passed within a hundred yards of the shore. Alas, Hythe was left out yet again in preference to Folkestone. Further discontent was felt at the end of the year when the excursions by rail from Sandgate and Hythe were withdrawn. In 'Notes by the Wayside' the *Hythe Reporter* commented:

> 'Hythe seems to have been neglected of late in regard to the cheap excursions to London. Both Hythe and Sandgate no longer appear on the list and those residents who wish to take advantage of cheap excursion tickets must travel to Shorncliffe station.
>
> The ordinary fare to London is about 11/- and is hardly within the working man's reach for himself and his wife to spend a day in London.'

Quite clearly the failure of the Sandgate branch to reach Folkestone was now having its effect on the prospects of Hythe. The railway meanwhile were anxious to make use of their apparently useless assets, so the plots of land between Sandgate and Folkestone, which the SER had bought up in the 1870s, were now being leased off to interested parties. Land adjoining Sandgate castle was let to the Territorial Force Association for £2 10s 0d per annum, whilst Lieut-Col. R.J. Fynmore, the tenant of the castle, sought to purchase the property. Surprisingly, the SE & CR still refused to sell, but did agree to a 99 year lease at £100 per annum when the Kent Archaeological Society approached them.

In the few years prior to the outbreak of the First World War, the SE & CR carried out a programme of major civil engineering works in the district. This involved the rebuilding and strengthening of bridges, which not only had to cope with heavier locomotives and trains, but also allow larger forms of road traffic to pass beneath. On the Sandgate branch there were no problems with underbridges as there were at Cheriton, where the small arch at Risborough Lane had to be replaced by a modern girder bridge. Altogether three bridges were replaced, one at Sandgate and two at Hythe, by Eastwood, Swingle & Company. Bridge 2128, carrying the line across a farm track near Saltwood castle, was found to be especially weak so £150 15s 0d had to be found for repairs. Station bridge, no. 2132, just to the east of Hythe station, was also replaced but at a cost of £318, whilst bridge 2140 across Hospital Hill was renewed for £547.

Apart from bridge renewals, the platforms at Sandling Junction were lengthened and raised throughout the summer of 1913 when £350 was spent in extending the main line platforms towards Folkestone in order that greater train lengths could be accommodated. The SE & CR also had plans at this time to finish off the footbridge by extending it across the branch to connect with the 'up' branch platform. Quite why they should have resurrected this idea remains a mystery; perhaps they intended making greater use of the 'up' branch platform or maybe it was merely a safety measure. Whatever it was, they once again decided not to carry it out and instead spent the estimated £445 on something else.

In June 1914 Sandgate Council wrote a letter seeking an improvement in the early morning service to London, but it met with little success. They simply reiterated the fact that the 8.30 a.m. express could be caught at Folkestone Central. In the summer a railcar service was reintroduced, but the solitary engine and carriage made only four weekday trips (except Thursdays) with three journeys on Sundays. Stabled at Dover shed, the first journey commenced at 9.38 a.m. calling all

Kitchener's (First) Army, after being billeted in Folkestone, march past Sandgate station on their way to Aldershot in February 1915. The disused tracks of the tramway can be seen in the foreground.
G. L. Gundry

stations, including the Warren and Cheriton halts, to arrive at Sandgate at 10.30. Throughout the day the service started and terminated at Dover Town station until the last one, the 6.40 p.m. from Sandgate, which returned to the Priory, arriving at 7.31. As events unfolded, this was to be the last summer in which to ride in these fascinating, but uncomfortable, machines.

The SE & CR finally relinquished its management of the former Seabrook Hotel when the 'Hythe Imperial Hotel Co. Ltd' was established to lease the premises from the railway at an annual rent of £775. A few weeks later the Great War began, whereby the effects upon the railway were felt almost immediately.

On a national scale the railways came under the control of the government, whereas on a local level all the horses owned by the SE & CR at Hythe were soon requisitioned for the war effort. By October the scene at Sandling Junction was one of furious activity with the erection of a wooden shanty town for military accommodation. The SE & CR ran special trains for workmen employed on this project as well as the neighbouring camp at Westenhanger and Lympne. Troop trains to Sandgate arrived one after another as thousands of young men detrained to form columns of four in preparation for the march to Folkestone harbour, ironically along the very route that was to have increased trade and cooperation between the countries of Europe. At times such as these, the little terminus took on the guise of a busy London station, echoing to the sound of studded boots and bawling officers. The amount of rail traffic increased further, forcing the SE & CR to withdraw all concessionary excursion, day and half-day, cheap tickets. On top of the problems already faced came the great landslide in the Warren in December 1915 which effectively severed all rail traffic between the two channel ports for the duration of the war. This meant that Sandgate, as well as Folkestone, was even more hard-pressed to handle the burden of troops, horses, supplies, ammunition and stores which arrived from all parts of the country.

Obliged to cope with the needs of the military, it wasn't surprising that the locals deserted the trains for the buses. When the British Automobile Traction Co. Ltd began a service in the New Year of 1916 between Hythe and Ashford, it proved a great success, with four journeys each way, even though their 'bone-shakers' took an uncomfortable hour to complete the 11 mile journey.

On 10th June 1916 a calamitous accident took place early in the morning at Sandling Junction when the 4.30 a.m. ex-Ashford goods train parted at Westenhanger. The engine and first wagon broke away from the remaining 39 on Westenhanger bank without the engine crew noticing. On reaching Sandling, the driver brought his engine to a halt in the normal way before looking round, where, to his surprise, he found only one wagon behind his tender. Within a moment, the remaining train came hurtling down the gradient to crash into his engine, derailing and blocking both lines. Station master James Charman, awoken from his slumbers by the noise, raced to the signal box and tapped out the 'line blocked' message. His prompt action won him praise for he undoubtedly averted a serious accident as an 'up' special was due, conveying General

At Sandling Camp

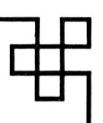

Imperial War Museum

An evening's entertainment in Hythe. *Imperial War Museum*

Joffre of France to London. The train was subsequently diverted via Canterbury, enabling the general to sample the rural charm of the Elham Valley. In the meantime the Ashford breakdown gang arrived but were unable to clear the line for normal running until well into the afternoon.

Some semblance of normal life went on as always when, in July, the annual Sunday school treat of Hythe Methodist Church comprised a day out by train. Over 130 youngsters crowded onto the platform at Hythe shortly before 12.40 p.m. in readiness for the arrival of the train from Sandgate. It steamed away to the accompaniment of loud cheering, waving handkerchiefs and arms, to Westenhanger where the children marched to Mr. Diver's tea gardens at New Inn Green, where a veritable feast, including fresh strawberries and cherries, awaited them. The 17th Battalion arrived to entertain the children who sang in accompaniment to contemporary favourites such as 'Keep the home fires burning'. A pipe band escorted them on their return to Westenhanger where a train had them safely back in Hythe at 7.45 p.m., no doubt weary and full of tales to tell once home.

In November another uncommon engine appeared running up and down the branch. This was one of Wainwright's smallest locomotives, a 'P' class 0–6–0, No. 555. Along with sister engine No. 325, it also worked the temporary Westenhanger–Lympne aerodrome branch which was laid to transport stores, fuel and aircraft supplies to the camp. Normal services on the branch were now being handled mainly by the 'Q' and 'Q1's, 'O' and 'O1's, with the occasional 'R' and 'R1's from Folkestone. An example of the stock is given in a working timetable of the period which reveals that set 253 was employed on the branch.

On the 1st January 1917 the Sunday service was withdrawn on numerous lines, the Sandgate branch included. Simultaneously a staggering 50% increase in fares was introduced, coinciding with a reduction in ordinary weekday trains. This was brought about by the need to lessen the burden of the railways as well as ensuring that the important military traffic was not hindered. In an attempt to cope with the severe staff shortages, a number of young lads were recruited to man the stations at Hythe and Sandgate as porters, goods handlers and clerks.

The air raid on Folkestone on 25th May 1917 caused heavy casualties, shock and outrage. Proposals to protect against a similar loss of life included a warning system whereby cones or flags could be hoisted to warn of enemy air attacks. Hythe station was one of the suggested sites since it was prominent on the hillside.

As the misery dragged on and on, the war effort lost much of its impetus, despite the daily newspapers' attempts to bolster the nation's spirit. The *Daily News*' campaign for more trains and cheaper fares made no impression for there was an acute shortage of coal, labour and rolling stock as well as an increase in running expenditure. Apart from people 'left limp by the war', the Grim Reaper scoured the land in the deathly form of the influenza epidemic when almost every family, my own no exception, lost cherished little ones. The blackout regulations affected the Sandgate branch from May 1918 when all blinds had to be tightly drawn as the line could be seen from the English Channel.

At last, on 11th November, the madness that had stalked the earth for over four years was brought to an end, allowing hope for the future to dawn at last even though there was much work to be done. Amongst all the railways the SE & CR had suffered in particular and it would be many months before normal working would again be achieved. This is borne out by the fact that perhaps Hythe suffered more than it should at the end of the war for in June 1919 the Mayor met the railway board to seek an improvement in the services to his town. The SE & CR agreed to provide a connection with the 3 p.m. from London whereby Hythe should be reached an hour and three

Entitled 'My first railway photograph', a young C. J. Barnard snapped this elderly 'O' class at Sandgate soon after the end of the Great War. *C. J. Barnard/Alex Todd Collection*

'O1' class No. 1 with rounded cab waits at Hythe station. *Kenn Nunn/LCGB*

Miss Mary Treacher and her dog pose for the camera outside Sandgate station. Miss Treacher was the first woman driver in Sandgate and delivered milk for her father's dairy.
Folkestone Public Library

quarters later. The 5 p.m. was also arranged to connect so that businessmen could be home in Hythe just after 7 p.m. In the reverse direction commuting was slightly better, with the fast 8.25 a.m. arriving at Cannon Street at 10.05 a.m.

The national rail strike in the autumn of 1919 caused widespread disruption across the country as well as the Sandgate branch, even so the local paper attempted to minimise the effect:

> 'As far as Hythe is concerned the railway strike has little affected the town up to the present. Most of the Hythe staff have come out. Mr. Harris, the stationmaster, has been driving engines assisted by Mr. Woodhams, an old railway employee, as stoker. Mr. Woodhams was also a former police constable in Hythe.'

The post-war depression seems to have played a part in a rather distressing suicide which took place on 4th December 1919. It seems that the Sandgate branch crews had more than their fair share of thoughtless individuals who selfishly chose the railway as a means of doing away with themselves. Only a few years before the war the hapless driver of the 5.58 p.m. from Sandgate had to witness his engine decapitate a man and now it was the turn of driver James Wells of Seabrook. As events later revealed, Lance-Corporal Shangenny of the Machine Gun Corps had been involved in a tiff with his young lady the preceding evening whereby he chose to deliberately walk in front of a train. Driver Wells, in charge of the 1.34 p.m. Sandgate train, told the inquest how he'd seen a man stroll out and lie down across the rails just as his train was approaching Waterworks crossing. Only a hundred yards separated them both and, despite blowing the whistle and bringing his engine to a 'shuddering halt', there was nothing more to be done and he and his fireman could only turn their heads before the inevitable happened. The train was eventually shunted back where guard Walter Clements accompanied Wells as they were duty bound to inspect the horrific scene. No wonder compassionate leave was granted on these occasions. The belongings of the deceased comprised a postcard, some photographs and a metal cigarette case. Recording a verdict of suicide whilst of unsound mind, it was a sad and pathetic end for someone who had managed to survive the five terrible years of war.

Fifteen months later another accident occurred at Sandgate although mercifully there was no loss of life or serious injury.

THE DREAM FADES

The Road of Remembrance, Folkestone.

Author's Collection

On the morning of Monday 14th March 1921, a motor lorry belonging to Ernest Clayson was being loaded with coal for the town delivery service when suddenly, without any warning, the lorry jumped the scotch block whereupon it ran onto the line. George Jarvis, a porter/signalman, was over at the ground frame engaged in shunting operations and had just allowed a wagon and goods brake into the siding which the lorry had fouled. Responding quickly, porter Wilfred Atherton attempted to pull them up by applying the brakes, assisted by Robert Clayson who tried to jam a wheel spoke. A collision was however unavoidable which left the wagon unscathed but completely wrecked the lorry!

An improvement in train services eventually came in 1921 when the new summer timetable replaced the previous emergency schedule consisting of ten trains each way. There were now seventeen 'up' trains, the first departing Sandgate at 7.05 a.m., the last 9.25 p.m., whilst sixteen trains travelled down the line, the first arriving at 7.34 a.m. and the last 10.07 p.m. In addition, a Sunday service of two trains each way was reinstated, but this was later increased to eight trains each way in 1923 although still only during the summer season. These improvements met with some favour although a Mr. Skelton, speaking for the 'city men' at a Hythe council meeting, complained they had no train to bring them home conveniently in the evening and asked the SE & CR to stop the 5.10 p.m. ex-Cannon Street at Sandling Junction. Surprisingly, the railway authorities agreed to this.

The need for economies wherever possible was apparent to the railway management with all expenditure being scrutinised. One example involved station masters taking charge of more than one station and this happened at Sandgate when George Wood retired, leaving it to come under the jurisdiction of Hythe. The engine shed at Sandgate was also surplus to requirements so it was officially closed on 31st December 1921, although the structure remained standing for another ten years.

More old veterans turned up on the Sandgate services around this time. James Stirling's rebuilt 'F1's occasionally appeared – the Ashford-based No. 172 being quite a regular. These 4–4–0s, known by the men as 'Jumbos', hauled in their heyday such crack trains as the 'Granville' express between London and Thanet as well as the Hastings Car Trains. They were almost certainly joined by some of the 'B1's which closely resembled the 'F1's, now displaced by Wainwright's engines which took over their main line duties.

Throughout the twenty-odd years in which the SE & CR had managed the branch, the changes which had taken place were generally for the better, be it improvements to the services, including speeding-up certain trains, or the very fabric of the little railway itself. During this time Watkin's great dream, of fast continental trains dashing above Sandgate on a viaduct before emerging from the Leas tunnel into the Folkestone Marine station, had been irrevocably laid to rest. Great changes were taking place in the travelling habits of the British public. The horse had given way to the motor bus or the electric tram and, alas, the railways were ill-suited to compete with such door to door convenience. The coming years would see the continuation of this process and would bring profound changes to the Sandgate branch. As the newly-formed Southern Railway Company took charge on New Year's Day 1923, the wind of change was already blowing hard.

AREA MAP OF HYTHE AND SANDGATE RAILWAY

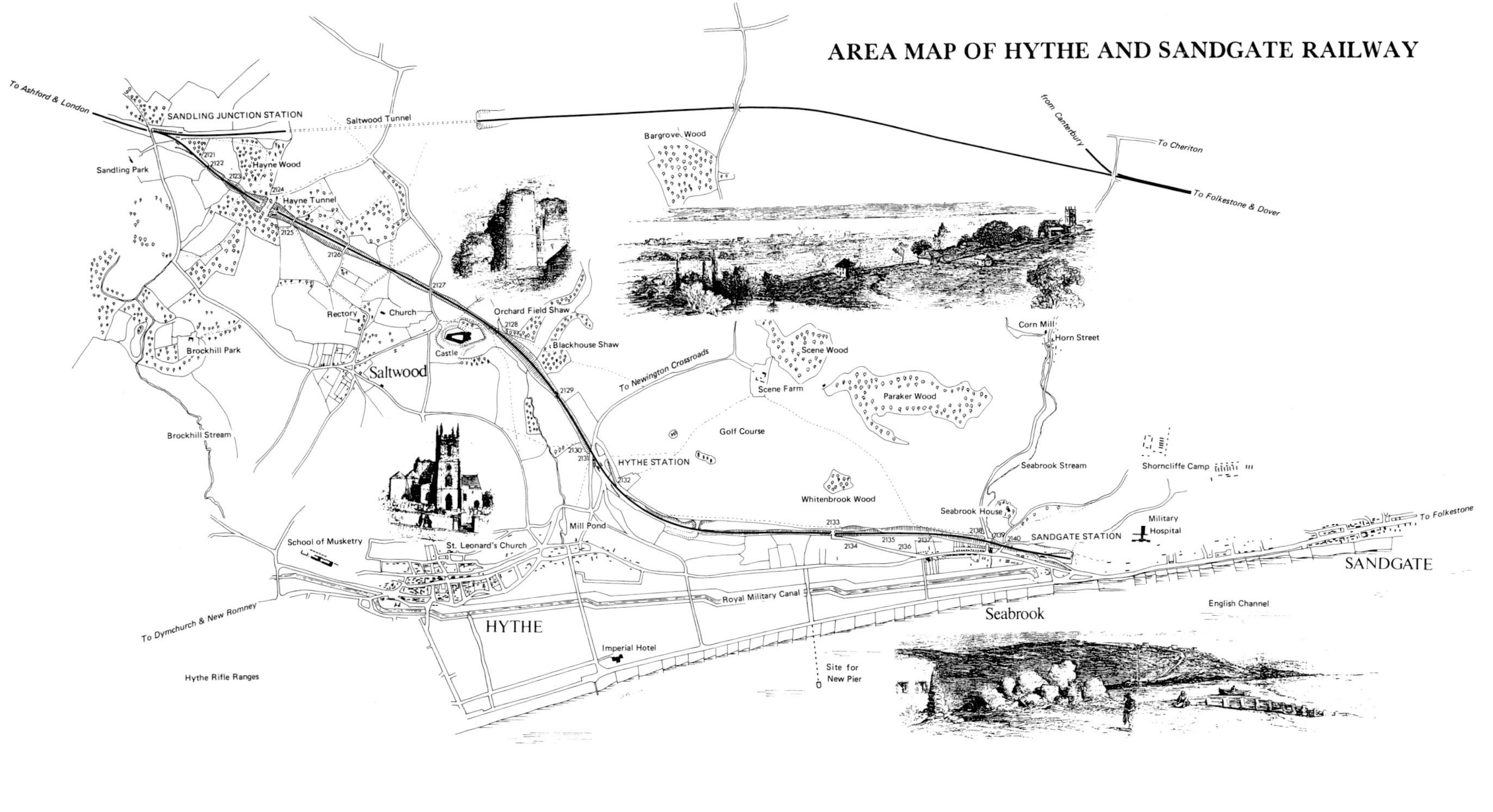

CHAPTER SIX

A Trip to the Seaside

Westenhanger in SE & CR days with a multitude of staff in evidence. Little has changed since the opening of the Sandgate branch, but perhaps the most notable feature is the much larger signal box, now on the down side. *Lens of Sutton*

DURING the first fourteen years of operating the Sandgate branch, anyone wishing to travel over the entire length of it would, until 1888, begin or finish their journey at Westenhanger. This was the station at which to alight when changing trains except of course for the through trains.

Westenhanger was laid out in typical South Eastern Railway fashion with staggered platforms, in this case either side of an overbridge carrying the ancient Roman Stone Street from Lympne to Canterbury. The importance of Stone Street as a main highway gradually diminished with the receding sea from Portus Lemanis, but it remained a useful road and was an obvious choice for a station site. The only village of any size is nearby Stanford, which never generated much business for the railway although sufficient traffic came from a wider area, especially places such as Hythe and Lyminge in the days before they had their own stations. The small wooden structure of 1844 was initially able to cope with the moderate needs of the locality. The design of this building remains a mystery for no photographs or prints have ever been discovered, but it likely mirrored the first Shorncliffe. The imposing and substantial brick structure, dating from 1861, gives an indication of the increasing importance with which it was viewed by the SER. The large goods shed, cattle pens, docks and sidings enabled the railway to efficiently manage the business of Hythe until the branch was opened. Even after Hythe station came into existence, Westenhanger remained an important station, especially with the business of freight. On certain days, the nearby racecourse brought forth crowds of people, so many in fact that special platforms were provided, a few hundred yards on the Ashford side, specifically for the race-goers.

Leaving Westenhanger, locomotives had to recommence their effort for the climb continues for a short section before the summit is reached where a descent, all the way to Dover, is begun. The line, on a falling gradient of 1 in 300, then passes underneath the main trunk road between London and Folkestone, through the short 100 yard Sandling tunnel, before levelling out on the approach to Sandling Junction. Meadows for grazing sheep stretch to the left whilst on the right the tamed countryside of Sandling Park reaches down into the valley. Ahead, the lofty signals warned of the junction, with the right hand signal arm lowered to allow the train to take the branch road. Immediately beyond the roadbridge, signal cabin no. 1 was passed on the right-hand side as the train clattered over the points before pulling into the 'down' branch platform.

At $65\frac{1}{2}$ miles from London, Sandling Junction station nestles in extremely pleasant and rural surroundings, bordered by wooded hills, gorse-strewn fields and pastures. It is not known whether the SER hoped for, or even anticipated, wide-scale development of the area but the station was well laid out with lavish facilities, certainly by South Eastern standards, and especially so, considering the sparseness of habitation. Perhaps it was intended that the station would be used mainly for an interchange point by passengers travelling on trains not running directly to Folkestone Harbour via Sandgate. Any other reason for its existence remains obscure although in later years it was often used in preference to Hythe as it enjoyed a more frequent train service.

The three main buildings were thoughtfully constructed in a harmonious and sympathetic manner, having warm red bricks framed by timber beams in the same fashion as nearby

The up side station buildings at Sandling Junction.

C. J. Barnard/Alex Todd Collection

A TRIP TO THE SEASIDE

One of Wainwright's elegant 'D' class 4–4–0s, No. 747, restarts from Sandling Junction with a train from Folkestone. A train bound for Sandgate is about to depart.
Lens of Sutton

'O1' class No. 65 (now preserved) waits in the down branch platform at Sandling Junction with a train for Sandgate in the 1920s.
C. J. Barnard/Alex Todd Collection

An 'O1' blowing off in the up branch platform at Sandling Junction, the steam obscuring the up branch splitting home signals in the background.
Lens of Sutton

houses. Their most striking feature, however, was the provision of high-hipped roofs and gables of an almost ludicrous yet delightfully pleasing character. Although open fires ensured a warm wait in all three waiting rooms, the trains were often very cold, so a footwarmer shed was built nearby to provide the ingenious contraptions for thawing out those frozen toes in railway carriage compartments. In summer, the soft wind through the surrounding trees was often all that would disturb the silence in this remote spot, until the sounds of the signalman busying himself with bells and levers drifted along from his little cabin by the bridge. In the periods between trains, and duties permitting, the staff were able to tend the flowerbeds and shrubs which were proudly cultivated here. In common with a good number of stations scattered throughout the British Isles, the name was laid out in the main flowerbed with stones or rocks, but in Sandling's case with lumps of local chalk. There

The entrance to Hayne tunnel (2124), looking towards Hythe in 1937.
R. F. Roberts

A TRIP TO THE SEASIDE

Saltwood cutting, looking towards Hayne tunnel in 1937. *R. F. Roberts*

can be little doubt that on a warm summery day, with the birds singing and bees fussing about with the orchids on the banks, Sandling Junction was one of the more pleasant places to miss a connection!

Departing from the 'down' branch platform, the train passed by no. 2 signal cabin on the right-hand side which not only controlled the coming and going of branch trains but also the adjacent goods yard. Once over an occupation crossing, a shallow cutting was entered as the line began gently curving leftwards, to run onto an embankment, pierced at the bottom by one of the many streams noisily gurgling and tumbling down from the chalk hills as it searched for the easiest path to the sea. The lush and leafy Hayne Wood embraced the train at this point, creating dappled shadows on the faded upholstery and where, after passing a platelayers' hut on the right, a public footpath crossed the railway on a boarded crossing. Stiles either side provided a welcome seat for weary walkers or ramblers who, if they were lucky, would be able to pause and watch the branch train drift by. A deep cutting begins at this point which leads a hundred yards further on to Hayne tunnel. Even though the length of the tunnel (numbered 2124) is a mere 94 yards, it remains more impressive and inspiring than its adjacent main line counterpart to the north. Saltwood tunnel, on the main line to Folkestone, may be many times longer yet its portals are plain and unremarkable. Hayne tunnel, on the other hand, stands proudly astride the railway, its brick piers supporting a decorative parapet, for is this not the way to the continent?!

From Sandling Junction to the eastern end of the tunnel, the line ran perfectly level, after which it began to descend sharply at 1 in 56. Once more into the daylight the line continued in a cutting to be crossed almost immediately by a graceful three-arched bridge, no. 2125, which carried a bridle-way from Saltwood village into the estate on the land above.

Looking back at Hayne tunnel from bridge 2125 in Saltwood Cutting. *Southern Railway Magazine*

Rebuilt Stirling 'O1' A390 passes Rectory crossing, Saltwood, with a train from Sandgate on 10th September 1926.

F. J. Agar/R. C. Riley Collection

Saltwood Village. *Author's Collection*

Part of that estate comprises the oddly-named American Gardens which are noted for their fine display of rhododendrons. All of this is, however, hidden from the railway leaving the gaze to fall upon the simpler delights of the common English primrose, floxglove and buttercup lining the grassy banks. 2126, another fine three-arched bridge, marked the end of the cutting whereupon a glance to the right caught the village of Saltwood and its church of St. Peter & St. Paul. A winding footpath from the rectory wandered up through meadows to cross the railway, protected by wicket gates and notices of a stern nature not to stray from the public right of way. Entering another, but shallower, cutting, the train ran under a brick and girder bridge (2127) carrying the road from Saltwood to Beachborough. Here the down gradient increased slightly to 1 in 54, the steepest on the entire branch. Another occupation crossing marked the end of this cutting which brought the railway to the western side of the Saltwood valley. On the right, perhaps the main attraction of the whole ride was seen. Surrounded by its dry moat, the ivy-clad twin turrets of Saltwood Castle grace the hillside where the best, if briefest, view was gained from the train. Here though are no grim, grey walls. Instead, this proud castle is positively welcoming and in autumn presents a most appealing and picturesque prospect. However, behind its innocent façade lie rumours of hidden, dark, secrets for it is believed that here one wintry night the murderers of Thomas à Becket plotted their wicked deed. With such fairytale features, however, the wide-eyed children on the trains could be forgiven for half expecting Sir Lancelot to appear on its battlements or a pretty Rapunzel to let down her golden hair.

Saltwood Castle from the railway. *Author's Collection*

Saltwood Castle From The Golf Links. Hythe. 47A.

View of Saltwood from Hythe. The railway line can be seen just to the right of the twin turrets of the castle. *Author's Collection*

Passing over bridge 2128, just a farm track to the adjacent field, the line ran onto the huge embankment which caused so much trouble with its slips in the 1870s. A wood, known as Blackhouse Shaw, lies beneath on the left, through which runs the mill stream, making its way beneath the railway through the troublesome culvert no. 2129. Having reached the bottom of the 1 in 54 incline, the railway levelled out, crossed culvert 2130, whereupon the train rumbled over Blackhouse Hill bridge (2131) to enter Hythe station, precisely 67 miles from London.

Being built high upon the hillside, the station provided a marvellous vista of the town below with its jumble of roofs peeping above the treetops. Beyond, stretched the sea wall and promenade with the English Channel on the horizon. Despite having such a spectacular vantage point, the station really was away from the centre of things, not such a problem to pedestrians arriving at Hythe, but those starting their journey here first had to walk the half a mile uphill. This exhausting climb evidently finished off one poor chap in June 1909. Henry Weston had just purchased his ticket, and spoken to a porter, when he collapsed on the 'up' platform from a heart attack. Horse drawn omnibuses were available for those with extra coppers to spare and there was usually a conveyance waiting to meet every train in the days before the Great War. Whereas the 'down' platform buildings met the road on the level, on the opposite side the land dropped sharply away just beyond the approach road. At this point the entire hillside had to be strengthened with a massive stone wall which remains to this

Underbridge 2128 at Saltwood, looking towards Sandling Junction in February 1939. *R. F. Roberts*

Hythe station, looking towards Sandling Junction in 1921. Iron railings have now replaced the original wooden panelling on the down side and gas mantles can be seen in the lamp housings. Both lines are set 'all clear' which probably denotes that Hythe box is 'switched out'.
National Railway Museum

'O1' No. 1 rumbles into Sandgate, past the signal box, with a rake of ancient six-wheelers in this unusual view taken about 1921.
G. L. Gundry

day, resembling a castle battlement. A fairly extensive goods yard was laid out beyond the station with sidings on both sides of the line.

Leaving Hythe, the line gently curved landwards, hugging the hillside, where it began to descend again. The 1 in 59 bank ran all the way down into Sandgate station. With a cutting, mostly on the left-hand side, the railway passed the site of the ill-fated overbridge which had to be removed by Francis Brady. Straightening out, the line continued, parallel with the Seabrook Road, following the coastline eastwards. Sandgate 'down' distant signal stood just before the Seabrook Estate overbridge (2133) which carries Cliff Road over the railway. Sandgate Urban District Waterworks passed by on the right, whilst 200 yards beyond, and situated in the 'up' line, the catch points were seen for derailing any runaways which would otherwise have careered into Sandgate station. As the hillside dips gently down, the line runs onto an embankment where, curving slightly seawards, it crossed the Seabrook valley. Horn Street, which leads from Seabrook northwards up hill to Cheriton, passes under the line through a very solid and substantial brick arch (2138). The little Seabrook stream, travelling all the way from Etchinghill in the Elham Valley and once powering a nearby corn mill, passes through a culvert to run behind the Seabrook Fountain Hotel, seen from the compartment window on the right. By now, steam was shut off as the junction signals notified which road was clear. Simultaneously clattering over the points and Hospital Hill bridge (2140), the train slowed down to pull into the 'up' platform at Sandgate. Here the engine was uncoupled, coaled and watered if need be, before running round via the middle road to join up to the other end of the train in preparation for the return trip.

Sandgate station, 68 miles and 33 chains from Charing Cross, stood on the hillside above the eastern end of Seabrook, yet almost a mile from the town with which it shared the name. In 1872 considerable earthworks had to be thrown up before the station could be mapped out. These embankments survive to this day and will live on as a permanent reminder of the railway. Passengers to Sandgate on leaving the station, walked down the approach road where, from 1892 until 1921, they might be lucky to find a horse-tram waiting to take them on into the town. Otherwise it meant waiting for an omnibus or walking.

The 'up' side goods yard comprised just two sidings, the southernmost of the two eventually being extended to run down the approach road to connect with the tramway. On the 'down' side most of the business of goods collection and delivery took place and this was without interference from, or hindrance to, passenger trains once the arrangement for the arrival and departure of passengers to the 'up' platform was carried out. The engine shed was a simple wooden structure of clapboard, tarred and creosoted. Somewhat surprisingly it never went up in smoke from stray cinders and lasted almost as long as the station buildings themselves.

If the line through to Folkestone harbour had come about then the station would have been altered accordingly and probably renamed Seabrook once the new Sandgate station was opened near the Broadway. However, a terminus it remained, much to the chagrin of those travellers deposited here on a wet and windy night and who, without means of transport, had to risk a thorough soaking by venturing along the esplanade when a vengeful high tide was lapping the wall.

An 'up' train waits hopefully for passengers at Sandgate in the summer of 1921. *National Railway Museum*

A turn of the century view of Sandgate signal box. The starting signal at the end of the down branch platform is interestingly of Messrs. Stevens' manufacture, not very common on the SER which was usually fitted out with Saxby & Farmer signalling.

Courtesy J. W. Sparrowe

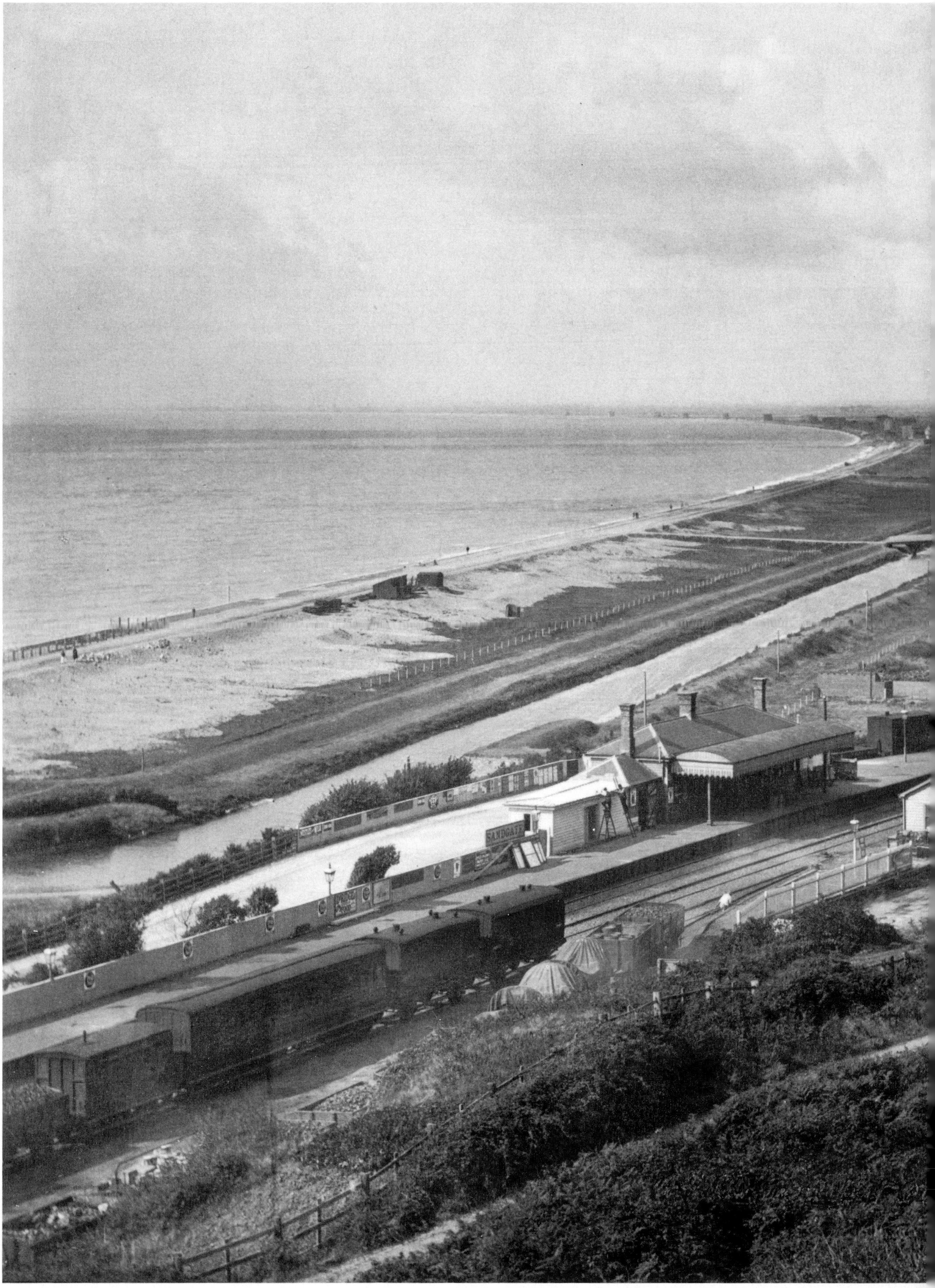
SANDGATE

Workmen busy at Sandgate station shortly before the alterations which involved moving the 'gents' from the western end of the main building to a new site halfway along the up platform. Note the billboards waiting to be erected, standing beneath the nameboard. *Francis Frith Collection*

The delightful poster depicting Hythe, designed by Kenneth Shoesmith (1891-1939).   *Victoria & Albert Museum*

CHAPTER SEVEN

The Pride of Kent

STRENUOUS efforts were made after the Great War to restore the area as a premier holiday retreat, but it had fallen from grace in the eyes of the rich who now only visited Folkestone on their way to European resorts. Holiday traffic was an important part of the annual income, particularly in the case of Hythe and Sandgate, and the line's fortunes were, to a great extent, linked to the ability of the towns to attract summer trade. Hythe, like Folkestone, was determined not to be left behind and beseeched the new Southern Railway Company to prominently display posters and adverts at Charing Cross and all other important stations in an effort to attract visitors.

Easter 1923 arrived with good weather, as did Whitsun when the *Hythe Reporter* announced 'Glorious weather and big crowds'. Boating on Hythe canal was a popular as ever, trains departed for the point-to-point races at Smeeth, whilst 'Luncheons *al fresco* were enjoyed by many'. The influx of visitors kept the porters busy with the quantities of luggage that arrived. The landladies were busy making their boarding houses spick and span, whilst the shops enjoyed a bonanza with tills ringing as people began to live a little better after the preceding years' misery.

The omnibuses were bustling with trade, especially now that the horse-drawn tramway was closed. Private charabancs and public conveyances were everywhere to be seen over the holiday period. One of these charabancs was involved in a most unusual accident, which now appears quite amusing although of course it didn't at the time. It happened on Easter Monday evening when a public service vehicle, belonging to Mr. W. Urwin of Belle Vue Street, Folkestone, suffered a mishap to the transmission which resulted in a total brake failure. The matter would not have been tremendously serious on a level stretch. Unfortunately, however, for the driver and his unlucky load of thirteen passengers, the vehicle had just begun descending Sandgate Hill. It soon gathered speed, with the driver, Robert Southern, desperately trying to halt its wild careering. He skilfully managed to negotiate the nasty corner at the bottom of the hill whilst his passengers likely prayed for deliverance and a clear road. What happened next resembled something akin to the silent films of the day when the back axle and wheels fell off, leaving the chassis to bump along, scraping the road until it came to a halt outside the Royal Norfolk Hotel. Thankfully no one was injured although most were badly shaken and quite probably in need of a stiff brandy in the adjacent saloon bar!

A minor accident involving a light engine took place in August 1923 at Sandling Junction. On this particular afternoon the engine arrived, as usual, to work the 2.30 p.m. train to

'Q1' No. 416 confidently breasts Saltwood bank with a train from Hythe, 17th June 1924.
F. J. Agar/R. C. Riley Collection

Sandgate. In order to clear the 'up' mainline for the 2.05 p.m. from Sandgate, it was necessary to move the light engine on to the 'down' line which was occupied at the time with the empty stock for the 2.30 p.m. train. The signalman at No. 1 cabin gave the bell signal to his colleague at No. 2 cabin for the light engine to proceed into the 'down' branch platform whereupon No. 2 reminded him of the empty stock, suggesting he warn the driver. The road was however already set, the shunt signal 'off' and away went the engine which merrily ploughed straight into the empty train, damaging two vehicles. A departmental enquiry blamed all concerned. Noting that the driver could not see the vehicles until he was just two yards away, the fireman, however, did have an unobstructed view and should have been keeping a look out. The signalman in No. 1 cabin was also found at fault for not halting the engine outside his box and telling the driver exactly what was required of him. Subsequently all three men were cautioned.

A month later, on the evening of 5th September, another minor accident happened but this time at Sandgate and involving the 5.55 p.m. from Ashford. The locomotive commenced running round in the normal way, via the middle road, before reversing onto the other end of its train left waiting in the 'up' platform for the 6.50 p.m. service. Both tender and engine were derailed on the points, consequently blocking the 'up' line. Single line operation had to be resorted to between Hythe and Sandgate for the rest of the evening. In the meantime the Ashford breakdown crane and its gang were summoned. Once the engine had been re-railed, the line was cleared, with normal working being restored at 4.15 the following morning. Several services had to be cancelled and there were also delays to other trains. The engine was slightly damaged as were a number of rail chairs which had to be replaced. It was concluded that the derailment was caused by the point blades not being properly closed. The driver said he believed the road was set ready with the shunt signal 'off', however, the enquiry were inclined to believe that the driver had started off before the signalman had had a chance to pull over the point blades.

A more serious accident took place at the end of the year when a Miss Mary Richards of Dover was knocked down by a Sandgate train at Sandling Junction. Had the footbridge spanning the branch platforms materialised, then it would have been avoided. The unlucky woman, having just purchased her

A rebuilt Stirling 'F1' takes on water in this rare glimpse of everyday life at Sandgate station. *C. J. Barnard/Alex Todd Collection*

ticket from the booking office on the 'up' branch platform, made her way over the foot crossing at the London end of the platforms. Although the 4.47 p.m. Sandgate train was approaching, she either didn't see it, or mistakenly assumed it was a main line train, so she continued, only to be struck by the engine. Even though she suffered a fractured leg, broken ribs and some internal injuries, she was extremely lucky not to have been killed.

At the start of 1924, Hythe Chamber of Commerce planned its strategy for promoting the town. A competition was organised whereby a suitable slogan might be found which would be 'catchy' and appropriate. Eventually they chose 'The Pride of Kent' which ultimately appeared upon the Southern Railway posters of the period. A further request to the SR sought to add the name 'Hythe' to the carriage destination boards on trains from the north. This was probably seen as taking Hythe's promotion a little too far.

On the first Sunday in September of that year, the booking office at Hythe was broken into overnight and cash and stamps to the value of 15s 2d were stolen. The goods office was also entered where a bag valued at £20 was taken. The police arrested two men who were subsequently dealt with at Seabrook Police Court, one was sentenced to 12 months hard labour whilst the other received three years imprisonment.

A rather miraculous event took place a few weeks later one Tuesday morning in October when a horse, attached to one of the Southern Railway's parcel vans, dashed unattended from one end of Hythe High Street to the other. It was thought the poor creature was startled by a noisy motor car, whereupon it took fright, scattering parcels *en route*. The runaway managed to negotiate the complete stretch without damage to the van, other vehicles, or any pedestrians, although it missed obstacles by a whisker. With the delivery man in hot pursuit, the horse ended its dash to pull up in Mackeson's Brewery yard, where both driver and horse probably needed a drink after that adventure!

In November the Sandgate booking clerk reported a deficiency of £1 1s 11d in his cash balance. Investigating the loss, the SR deduced that the money must have been taken by someone who obtained the keys to the booking office between Saturday night and Monday morning. The police were called in but were unable to detect the culprit or shed any further light on the matter. Normal practice involved the late porter locking up the till and the office before taking the keys across to the signal box. Subsequent arrangements were made which obviated the need to leave the keys unguarded throughout the weekend.

Mr. James Charman, the station master at Sandling Junction, retired in December 1924 to make way for Mr. Langford. He was a popular man with both staff and regular passengers, being noted for his kindness and civility. He was presented with a solid silver cigarette case, suitably inscribed from the staff, as well as a total of £58 in donations from local well-wishers and travellers. He recalled that he'd left school in 1874, incidentally the year in which the Sandgate branch had opened, to start as a telegraph learner on the LB & SCR at Three Bridges. Three years later he moved to Eastbourne as an excess luggage clerk before transferring to Clapham Junction as a ticket collector. After transferring to Polegate, he left the LB & SCR in 1879 to join the service of the LC & DR as a telegraph clerk at Victoria before moving to Faversham as a parcels clerk, later transferring to Canterbury in 1884. He remained there until 1898 when he was promoted to station master at nearby Selling before finally transferring to Sandling Junction in October 1908. He recalled that when he arrived there was no water or gas at the station, but to his mind the best improvement came with the raising of the platforms. The war years stuck vividly in his mind, a time of great stress and strain, with frequent weeks of hardly a proper night's rest. After leaving the railway's service, James Charman retired to a house in Somerset Road, Cheriton where, sadly, he died just four years later.

A landslip at Smeeth on 5th February 1925 indirectly affected the Sandgate branch when the early-morning 4.00 goods train from Ashford to Sandgate was involved. It took place about $\frac{1}{4}$ mile on the Ashford side of Smeeth station, derailing part of the train which was not brought to a standstill until it reached Smeeth. Consequently a total of 108 permanent way chairs were broken. All train services between Ashford and Sandling Junction were cancelled, with trains diverting over the Elham Valley Line. By 10 a.m. a single line was operable between Smeeth and Ashford 'E' signalbox, but with a speed restriction of 5 m.p.h. Normal working couldn't be resumed until five days later, causing considerable delays and cancellations.

In February 1926 there occurred another burglary at Sandgate when a window of the ladies' lavatory was forced to enable access into the general waiting room. From here the booking office window was then wrenched open. Oddly enough this was not the end of the matter for when station master Harris

District Inspector Bobby Burn with the SR's delivery wagon at Hythe. Horses eventually gave way to Scammel motor vehicles in 1933. Arthur Batt and Tommy Faircloth were both drivers.
Courtesy Sidney Burn

SANDGATE BRANCH.

SEPTEMBER 20th, 1926, and until further notice.

Distances.	DOWN TRAINS. WEEK-DAYS.	NS a.m.	SO p.m.	a.m.	a.m.	a.m.	11.0 a.m. ex Ashford. a.m. Q	a.m.	p.m.	p.m.
M. C.		arr. dep.	arr. dep.	arr. dep.	arr. dep.	arr. dep.	arr. dep.	arr. dep.	arr. dep.	arr. dep.
—	Sandling Junction...	. 7 40	. 7 48	. 8 24	. 9 0	. 10 5	11 13 11 16	§ . 11 45	. 12 45	. 1 20
1 34	Hythe	7 44 7 45	7 52 7 53	8 28 8 29	9 4 9 5	10 9 10 10	11 20 11 21	11 49 11 50	12 49 12 50	1 24 1 25
2 71	Sandgate	7 49 .	7 57 .	8 33 .	9 9 .	10 14 .	11 25 . Susp ended	11 54 .	12 54 .	1 29 .

§ To start at 11.52 a.m. when 10.5 a.m. Q (FO) Charing Cross is running.

	DOWN TRAINS. WEEK-DAYS.	2.5 p.m. Ashford. NS p.m.	2.10 p.m. Ashford. SO p.m.	SO p.m.	NS p.m.	NS p.m.	SO p.m.	p.m.	SO p.m.	NS p.m.
		arr. dep.	arr. dep.	arr. dep.	arr. dep.	arr. dep.	arr. dep.	arr. dep.	arr. dep.	arr. dep.
	Sandling Junction...	2 17 2 19	2 29 2 31	. 2 48	. 2 55	. 4 20	. 4 30	. 5 2	. 5 35	. 6 15	. 6 26
	Hythe	2 23 2 24	2 35 2 36	2 52 2 53	2 59 3 0	4 24 4 25	4 34 4 35	5 6 5 7	5 39 5 40	6 19 6 20	6 29 6 30
	Sandgate	2 28 .	2 40 .	2 58 .	3 4 .	4 29 .	4 39 .	5 11 .	5 44 .	6 24 .	6 34 .

‡—To start at 1.28 p.m. when 11.35 a.m. Q ex Charing Cross is running.

	DOWN TRAINS. WEEK-DAYS.	p.m.	p.m.	p.m.	MWThO Q p.m.	p.m.					
		arr. dep.	arr. dep.	arr. dep.	arr. dep.	arr. dep.					
	Sandling Junction...	. 7 2	. 7 46	. 8 30	. 8 45	. 10 5	.	.	.	.	.
	Hythe	7 6 7 7	7 50 7 51	8 34 8 35	8 49 8 50	10 9 10 10	...	...	...	...	...
	Sandgate	7 11 .	7 55 .	8 39 .	8 54 . Suspended	10 14 .					

Distances.	UP TRAINS. WEEK-DAYS.	NS a.m.	SO a.m.	a.m.	a.m.	a.m.	a.m.	p.m.	p.m.	p.m.
M. C.		arr. dep.	arr. dep.	arr. dep.	arr. dep.	arr. dep.	arr. dep.	arr. dep.	arr. dep.	arr. dep.
—	Sandgate	. 7 20	. 7 28	. 8 7	. 8 40	. 9 25	. 11 12	. 12 10	. 1 0
1 37	Hythe	7 24 7 25	7 32 7 33	8 11 8 12	8 44 8 45	9 29 9 30	11 16 11 17	12 14 12 15	1 4 1 5
2 71	Sandling Junction ...	7 30 .	7 38 .	8 17 .	8 50 .	9 35 .	11 22 .	12 20 .	1 10 .

	UP TRAINS. WEEK-DAYS.	SO p.m.	NS p.m.	NS p.m.	SO p.m.	NS p.m.	SO p.m.	p.m.	SO p.m.
		arr. dep.	arr. dep.	arr. dep.	arr. dep.	arr. dep.	arr. dep.	arr. dep.	arr. dep.
	Sandgate	. 2 22	. 2 30	. 2 55	. 3 55	. 4 5	. 4 40	. 4 45	. 5 16	. 5 50
	Hythe	2 26 2 27	2 34 2 35	2 59 3 0	3 59 4 0	4 9 4 10	4 44 4 45	4 49 4 50	5 20 5 21	5 54 5 55
	Sandling Junction ...	2 33 .	2 40 .	3 5 3 7 To Ashford.	4 5 .	4 15 .	4 50 .	4 55 .	5 26 .	6 0 .

	UP TRAINS. WEEK-DAYS.	NS p.m.	p.m.	p.m.	a.m.	MWThO Q p.m.	p.m.			
		arr. dep.	arr. dep.	arr. dep.	arr. dep.	arr. dep.	arr. dep.			
	Sandgate	. 6 5	. 6 42	. 7 30	. 8 5	. 8 25	. 9 35	.	.	.
	Hythe	6 9 6 10	6 46 6 47	7 34 7 35	8 9 8 11	8 29 8 30	9 39 9 40	...	...	...
	Sandling Junction ...	6 15 .	6 52 .	7 40 .	8 16 .	8 35 . Suspended	9 45 .			

	DOWN TRAINS. SUNDAYS.									
	Sandling Junction.......... Hythe.......... Sandgate..........	*Service Suspended on Sundays, Christmas Day and Good Friday.*

	UP TRAINS. SUNDAYS.									
	Sandgate.......... Hythe.......... Sandling Junction..........	*Service Suspended on Sundays, Christmas Day and Good Friday.*

EPSOM RACES
Southern Railway

DAY EXCURSION TO TATTENHAM CORNER
DERBY DAY,
WEDNESDAY, JUNE 4TH.

At a.m.	From	Fares s. d.
9.0 ...	Folkestone Junction ...	10 5
9.5 ...	Folkestone Central ...	10 3
9.15 ...	Shorncliffe ...	10 3
8.55 ...	Sandgate ...	10 1
8.59 ...	Hythe ...	9 11
9.24 ...	Sandling Junction ...	9 9

Returning same day only from Tattenham Corner 7.20 p.m. As the number of seats on this train is limited, passengers are recommended to purchase their tickets in advance. For full particulars, see bills.
H. A. WALKER,
General Manager.

arrived at 9.40 a.m. he found a soldier in his office. The soldier was brought before the courts and sentenced to seven days hard labour for breaking into the station, with a further seven days hard labour for wilful damage, even though nothing had been stolen.

A fortnight later yet another burglary took place at Sandgate when the signalbox and the porters' room were forcibly entered. The booty comprised two uniform overcoats, a carriage cushion and a carriage key. The following morning two soldiers were seen leaving a nearby platelayers' hut, further on towards Hythe, where the stolen property was recovered. One soldier was sentenced to two months hard labour whilst his colleague was bound over for 12 months.

The General Strike of 1926 affected the Sandgate branch as much as any other part of the railway network. By the middle of May it was reported that train services had improved, with the staff at Sandling Junction restored to normal strength whilst those at Hythe were considerably augmented enabling a skeleton service to be run. The *Hythe Reporter* commented:

> 'Mr. W. Harris, the station master at Hythe, showed a loyal example by undertaking all classes of work. His duties included signalling, shunting as well as some goods work.'

Normal staffing levels at that time consisted of nine employees at Sandling Junction – one station master class 4, two porters class 2, two porter/signalmen class 5 (nos. 1 & 2 boxes), and four signalmen class 5 (two for each box). At Hythe there was one station master class 2, one checker, two porters class 2, and two porter/signalmen class 5. Sandgate, now controlled by Hythe's station master, comprised one goods guard, two porters class 1, one porter class 2, and two signalmen class 5 (station box). For some years now, Hythe had been without permanent, full-time signalmen. Instead, the porter/signalman on duty opened up the box whenever there was shunting to be carried out, whereas during the day the 'up' and 'down' line signals remained 'off', with the block section operating as Sandling Junction–Sandgate.

It was about this period that young Wally Curtis, whose father was a goods guard at Sandgate, frequented the station, as the family lived in the former police station which had been bought and converted by the SER into dwellings. As with all small lads, he often sought to help out on occasions, one favourite job being the switching on of the carriage lights of the empty train left waiting in the 'up' platform. With time to kill before the next departure, the train crews often made their way down the steps to the road below and along to Seabrook's Fountain Hotel for a pint of Kent's best. On this particular occasion young Wally decided he'd prepare the train before the crew's return whereby, in leaning across to illuminate the compartments, he missed his footing and fell. Hitting his head upon a buffer, the little lad tumbled between the platform and the carriage, with his body slumped across the rail. Mercifully, he'd failed to switch on the lights which meant that the fireman had to and, in doing so, spotted young Wally thereby saving him from a gruesome death.

At the end of 1926 the Chamber of Commerce requested a covered goods shed for Hythe as they'd received many parcels

Guard Bill Curtis (on right) with other staff at Sandgate.
Courtesy Mr. & Mrs. W. Curtis

thoroughly saturated. It was felt that a proper shed would also enable goods to be dealt with more quickly – 'at the moment it takes five days for delivery of goods from London' they wrote in a letter to Waterloo. The SR was unhelpful and remarked that the relatively small amount of goods handled at Hythe didn't warrant a large shed and that the present office was quite sufficient.

More complaints followed in March when the town pressed for the reintroduction of Sunday trains as well as an improvement in the general weekday service. 'We are fed up with the poverty train' they complained. Some comfort was forthcoming in the middle of May when a round of applause was heard at a council meeting when the chairman announced that from the 5th June, a summer service of Sunday trains would commence. At this time there were 17 weekday trains each way throughout the year, although on summer Saturdays two extra trains were laid on. The Sunday service lasted until the end of September.

1927 is probably best remembered by most railway enthusiasts as the year in which Captain Howey's Romney, Hythe & Dymchurch Light Railway was opened. Rails across the Marsh at last, even though they were on a gauge of just 15", with miniature trains. It is worth mentioning here that in January 1928 it was proposed to extend the RH & DR to Red Lion Square, which incidentally had been rail-less for several years following the closure of the tramway. Another proposal, which likewise failed to come to fruition, was the extension to Hythe SR station. A number of people believe that had this been carried out then the branch line to Hythe would still be open.

On 16th April 1928 another landslide brought trouble to a branch train. The 4.14 p.m. from Sandgate had just left Hythe and was on its way through Saltwood cutting when about 100 tons of earth slipped on the southern side, clogging the wheels of the passing coaches and dragging them to a halt. After a preliminary inspection the driver managed to extricate his train, arriving at Sandling Junction only several minutes late. Single line working was in force soon after 5 p.m., but within two hours the permanent way gang had cleared the earth from the 'up' line thus allowing normal working to be reintroduced with the 7.50 p.m. from Sandgate.

The depletion of traffic from rail to road, which was actively encouraged by the Southern Railway Company, helped ensure that the Sandgate branch could not compete fairly and it became evident that the SR intended a run-down of services. For the staff, the line became something more akin to a rural branch line year by year and it was likely a pleasant enough job at that time. Meals were sometimes taken at the station; during quiet periods, for instance, porter Herbert Banks of Hythe would be brought his dinner by his two daughters who would pass their time at the station, returning home with the empty dishes. Herbert Banks began at Hythe in July 1913 at 16/- a week where he remained until being released for military service in Boulogne. After the war he returned to Hythe station where he stayed right up until 1951. When he retired he recalled his early days at Hythe – 'Those were the days of good tips. Ladies moved with huge hat-boxes and about nine trunks, and there was good money from tips. Nowadays, they have a couple of underclothes they can screw up in their hands, push into an attache case and travel light. It was the big old frilled petticoats and gowns that helped to make a porter's money in the old days.'

Easter 1929 brought into operation the usual timetable of extra trains for those wishing to get away from it all and enjoy a break from the seaside. As was customary, a limited service of approximately six trains ran each way on Good Friday, whereas on Easter Monday this increased to twenty 'up' trains and nineteen in the opposite direction.

Although the regular and much-favoured excursions were a thing of the past, the SR would provide them if the need was justified. One example was the Town Bands Contest at Tunbridge Wells on 14th May. The train left Hythe at 12.15 p.m., and presumably stopped at all stations, for it wasn't scheduled to arrive at the spa town until 2.15 p.m. Returning at 9.13 p.m. it ran on to Sandgate for the convenience of Seabrook residents, whilst the fare for the trip was just 4s 6d return.

Another minor derailment occurred at Sandgate in the summer, involving the 8.08 p.m. from Sandling Junction. Similar to the incident which took place a few years earlier, the driver failed to observe that the shunt signal controlling

Herbert Banks at Hythe. *Courtesy Mrs. E. Carter*

No. 1, still with its rounded cab, simmering away in the up branch platform.
Lens of Sutton

movements from the middle road to the 'up' line was still 'on'. His engine consequently ran through the trailing points, damaging the scotch block. For this mistake the driver was suspended from duty for one day.

The most spectacular and calamitous accident in the line's history took place on the evening of 14th June 1929. Shortly after the 10.05 p.m. goods train from Sandgate had arrived at Hythe, shunting operations began in charge of two guards. The train consisted of two brake vans and nine wagons. In order to carry out the necessary manoeuvres the engine and three wagons were detached, leaving the two brake vans and one wagon on the running line while the remaining wagons were sorted. As the line was on a falling gradient to Sandgate at 1 in 59, the brake was applied on the rear brake van by one guard who then asked his colleague to secure the other brake van, which he did. Both guards had experience of working at Hythe and judged that the brake vans would safely hold the wagons which would be shunted onto them. Not hearing the familiar metallic ring as the buffers met, they simply put it down to the fact that as the wind was blowing hard the sound had been carried away. Little did they realise that the brake vans were no longer there! As the remaining wagons were shunted, and in turn 'dropped off', they disappeared into the darkness to follow the others down the incline. These runaways would have continued their journey right into Sandgate station were it not for the precautionary catch points situated just to the east of Cliff Road overbridge. When the railway had been built, the land beyond the catch points was empty but since then two bungalows had been erected nearby. Inside, the residents of 'Belle Vue' and 'Holcombe' prepared themselves for bed as the clock approached 10.40 p.m. All of a sudden a distant rumbling announced the approach of the runaways as the leading brake van shot straight off the end of the catch points to topple over the embankment where it demolished a corner of 'Belle Vue'. A wagon loaded with ashes demolished the bathroom of 'Holcombe', filling the place with its contents.

The rest of the goods train followed bit by bit until they were all derailed, completely blocking the 'up' line. The occupants were unhurt but shocked and eventually settled for £175 damages as well as an assurance from the SR that the catch points would be resited. Back at Hythe station, the guards only realised their dreadful luck when they couldn't find the train where they'd left it. The breakdown gang was duly summoned at 11.18 p.m., arriving from Ashford at 1.32 a.m. The wagons were extricated and re-railed soon after midday, with temporary single line operation in effect from 2.18 a.m. till 2.05 p.m. on the next day. As for the unfortunate guards, both men were severely reprimanded and suspended from duty for a period of days.

With the number of people travelling by bus increasing year by year, the East Kent Road Car Co. (in which the SR held 49% of the shares) introduced the first double-decker buses on the Hythe–Sandgate–Folkestone route. This caused some consternation to those unfamiliar with such vehicles and voices were raised in protest. Sandgate Urban District Council thought them too dangerous to be used on Sandgate Hill, whilst the Rev. Chastel de Boinville, the vicar of St. Leonard's at Hythe, denounced them as 'utterly loathsome'!

As early as 1930 the Southern Railway was planning to bring electric trains to Folkestone which would, as they revealed, 'give Folkestone a twenty minute interval service'. The Board of Trade were unhappy with level crossings on electrified lines, urging the building of bridges. A local wag of the day asked whether farmers and their cows might have to undergo athletic training in order to cross the lines more quickly. With these proposals being sounded out there was every cause for optimism and it wasn't surprising that Hythe and Sandgate expected the live rail to one day penetrate their neck of the woods. Little did they realise then that plans of an entirely different nature had already been drawn up which would cause outrage and begin a battle for survival that would drag on for twenty years.

SOUTHERN RAILWAY

SANDGATE BRANCH

NOTICE IS HEREBY GIVEN that on and from Wednesday, April 1st, 1931, Sandgate Station **WILL BE CLOSED**, and the Train Service between Sandling Junction and Hythe (for Sandgate) and vice versa, together with a Service of Omnibuses operated by the East Kent Road Car Co., Ltd., will be as shown hereunder:—

WEEK-DAYS (commencing Wednesday, April 1st, 1931).

		a.m.	a.m.	a.m.	a.m.	a.m.	a.m.	a.m.	a.m.	a.m.	S p.m.	p.m.	E p.m.	p.m.
Sandling Junction	dep.	..	..	8 26	9 0	10 5	..	10 56	11 44	..	1 13	..	1 47
Hythe (for Sandgate)	arr.	..	..	8 30	9 4	10 9	..	11 0	11 48	..	1 17	..	1 51

Omnibus Service		a.m.	a.m.	a.m.	a.m.	a.m.	a.m.	a.m.	a.m.	a.m.	p.m.	p.m.	p.m.	p.m.
Hythe (Red Lion Square)	dep.	7 30	8 5	8 20	8 30	9 5	10 15	10 30	11 5	11 50	12 40	1 20	1 35	1 55
Hythe Station	"	..	..	..	8 35	..	10 20	..	10 11	11 55	..	1 25	..	2 0
Sandgate (Post Office) (see note A)	"	7 41	8 16	8 31	8 42	9 17	10 27	10 41	11 17	12 1	12 51	1 32	1 46	2 7
Folkestone (Westcliff Gardens)	"	7 54	8 29	8 44	8 55	9 30	10 40	10 54	11 30	12 15	1 4	1 45	1 59	2 20
Folkestone (Central Station)	"	7 58	8 33	8 48	..	..	..	10 58	..	..	1 8	..	2 3	..
Folkestone (Wood Avenue)	arr.	8 5	8 40	8 55	9 4	9 39	10 49	11 5	11 39	12 24	1 15	1 54	2 10	2 29

| Folkestone Central (for London) | dep. | 8 10 | 8 43 | 9 0 | .. | .. | .. | 11 10 | .. | .. | 1 17 | .. | 2 12 | .. |

		E p.m.	p.m.	E p.m.	E p.m.	S p.m.	E S p.m.	p.m.	p.m.	p.m.	p.m.	p.m.	p.m.
Sandling Junction	dep.	..	3 3	..	4 19	4 35	4 49	5 5	..	5 39	6 25	7 3	..	8 10
Hythe (for Sandgate)	arr.	..	3 7	..	4 23	4 39	4 53	5 9	..	5 43	6 29	7 7	..	8 14

Omnibus Service		p.m.	p.m.	p.m.	p.m.	p.m.	p.m.	p.m.	p.m.	p.m.	p.m.	p.m.	p.m.	p.m.
Hythe (Red Lion Square)	dep.	2 25	3 15	4 20	4 25	4 45	5 0	5 10	5 30	5 40	5 50	6 35	7 10	7 40	8 20
Hythe Station	"	..	3 20	..	4 30	4 50	5 5	5 15	..	5 55	6 40	7 15	..	8 25
Sandgate (Post Office) (see note A)	"	2 36	3 27	4 31	4 37	4 57	5 12	5 22	5 51	6 2	6 47	7 51	6 32	8 32
Folkestone (Westcliff Gardens)	"	2 49	3 40	4 44	4 50	5 10	5 25	5 35	6 4	6 15	7 0	7 35	8 4	8 45
Folkestone (Central Station)	"	2 53	..	4 48	..	..	..	5 39	..	6 8	..	..	8 8	..
Folkestone (Wood Avenue)	arr.	3 0	3 49	4 55	4 59	5 19	5 34	5 44	6 15	6 24	7 9	7 44	8 15	8 54

| Folkestone Central (for London) | dep. | 3 31 | .. | 5 0 | .. | .. | .. | 6 19 | .. | .. | .. | 8 15 | .. |

SUNDAYS (commencing May 3rd, 1931).

		a.m.	a.m.	a.m.	p.m.	p.m.	p.m.	p.m.	p.m.	p.m.	p.m.	p.m.	p.m.
Sandling Junction	dep.	..	10 4	10 54	..	1 5	2 50	4 25	..	..	..	..	7 30	..
Hythe (for Sandgate)	arr.	..	10 8	10 58	..	1 9	2 54	4 29	..	..	..	..	7 34	..

Omnibus Service		a.m.	a.m.	a.m.	a.m.	p.m.	p.m.	p.m.	p.m.	p.m.	p.m.	p.m.	p.m.	p.m.
Hythe (Red Lion Square)	dep.	8 40	10 16	11 0	12 8	1 20	3 0	4 35	4 0	5 25	5 50	6 45	7 35	7 40
Hythe Station	"	..	..	10 21	11 9	..	1 25	3 5	4 40	..	..	..	..	7 40	..
Sandgate (Post Office) (see note A)	"	8 51	10 28	11 10	12 19	1 32	3 12	4 47	4 11	5 36	5 51	6 56	7 51	7 51
Folkestone (Westcliff Gardens)	"	9 4	10 41	11 29	12 32	1 45	3 25	5 0	4 24	5 49	6 4	7 9	8 0	8 4
Folkestone (Central Station)	"	9 8	..	..	12 36	..	..	..	4 28	5 53	6 8	7 13	..	8 8
Folkestone (Wood Avenue)	arr.	9 15	10 50	11 38	12 43	1 54	3 34	5 9	4 35	6 0	6 15	7 20	8 9	8 15

| Folkestone Central (for London) | dep. | 9 14 | .. | .. | 12 44 | .. | .. | .. | 4 39 | 6 5 | 6 23 | 7 21 | .. | 8 22 |

WEEK-DAYS (commencing Wednesday, April 1st, 1931).

		a.m.	a.m.	a.m.	a.m.	a.m.	a.m.	S a.m.	E p.m.	S p.m.	E S p.m.	p.m.	E p.m.
Folkestone Central (from London)	arr.	..	..	..	..	10 58	11 14	..	12 58	1 12	..	2 21	2 43	2 58

Omnibus Service		a.m.	a.m.	a.m.	a.m.	a.m.	a.m.	a.m.	p.m.	p.m.	p.m.	p.m.	p.m.	p.m.	p.m.
Folkestone (Wood Avenue)	dep.	7 30	8 5	8 50	9 50	10 40	11 0	11 15	12 20	12 55	1 0	1 15	2 0	2 25	2 45	3 0	3 25
Folkestone (Central Station)	"	..	..	..	..	..	11 7	11 22	..	..	1 7	1 22	..	2 32	2 52	3 7	..
Folkestone (Westcliff Gardens)	"	7 39	8 14	8 59	9 59	10 49	11 11	11 26	12 29	1 4	1 11	1 26	2 9	2 19	2 36	2 56	3 11	3 34
Sandgate (Post Office) (see note A)	"	7 50	8 25	9 10	10 10	10 49	11 22	11 37	12 40	1 15	1 22	1 37	2 20	2 30	2 47	3 7	3 22	3 45
Hythe Station	"	7 59	8 34	9 19	10 19	11 9	..	..	12 49	1 24	..	1 50	2 29	2 39	..	..	..	3 54
Hythe (Red Lion Sq.)	arr.	8 4	8 39	9 24	10 24	11 14	11 35	11 50	12 54	1 29	1 35	1 50	2 34	2 44	3 0	3 20	3 35	3 59

| Hythe (for Sandgate) | dep. | 8 11 | 8 45 | 9 30 | 10 30 | 11 19 | .. | .. | 12 58 | 1 33 | .. | .. | 2 40 | 2 49 | .. | .. | .. | 4 4 |
| Sandling Junction | arr. | 8 16 | 8 50 | 9 35 | 10 35 | 11 24 | .. | .. | 1 3 | 1 38 | .. | .. | 2 45 | 2 54 | .. | .. | .. | 4 9 |

		S p.m.	E p.m.	S p.m.	S p.m.	E p.m.	S p.m.	E p.m.	p.m.	p.m.	p.m.	E S p.m.	p.m.
Folkestone Central (from London)	arr.	..	..	4 41	..	4 48	5 7	..	5 35	..	6 18	6 28	6 38	7 8	..	7 50	8 10	8 35

Omnibus Service		p.m.	p.m.	p.m.	p.m.	p.m.	p.m.	p.m.	p.m.	p.m.	p.m.	p.m.	p.m.	p.m.	p.m.	p.m.	p.m.
Folkestone (Wood Avenue)	dep.	3 40	3 55	4 15	4 40	4 45	4 50	5 10	5 30	5 40	6 20	6 30	6 40	7 10	7 15	7 55	8 10	8 40
Folkestone (Central Station)	"	..	..	4 47	..	4 57	5 17	..	5 47	..	6 27	6 37	6 47	7 17	..	8 2	8 17	8 47
Folkestone (Westcliff Gardens)	"	3 49	4 4	4 24	4 51	4 54	5 1	5 21	5 39	5 51	6 19	6 31	6 41	6 51	7 21	7 24	8 6	8 21	8 51
Sandgate (Post Office) (see note A)	"	4 0	4 15	4 35	5 2	5 5	5 12	5 32	5 50	6 2	6 30	6 42	6 52	7 2	7 32	7 35	8 17	8 32	9 2
Hythe Station	"	4 9	4 24	4 44	..	5 14	..	..	5 59	..	6 39	..	..	7 11	7 44	..	..	..	..
Hythe (Red Lion Sq.)	arr.	4 14	4 29	4 49	5 15	5 19	5 25	5 45	6 4	6 15	6 44	6 55	7 5	7 15	7 45	7 49	8 30	8 45	9 15

| Hythe (for Sandgate) | dep. | 4 20 | 4 34 | 4 50 | .. | 5 24 | .. | .. | 6 10 | .. | 6 48 | .. | .. | .. | 7 50 | .. | .. | .. | .. |
| Sandling Junction | arr. | 4 25 | 4 39 | 4 55 | .. | 5 29 | .. | .. | 6 15 | .. | 6 53 | .. | .. | .. | 7 55 | .. | .. | .. | .. |

SUNDAYS (commencing May 3rd, 1931).

		a.m.	a.m.	a.m.	a.m.	a.m.	p.m.	p.m.	p.m.	p.m.	p.m.	p.m.	p.m.	p.m.
Folkestone Central (from London)	arr.	9 46	..	10 10	10 35	10 59	..	12 12	..	..	4 32	7 38	..	9 47

Omnibus Service		a.m.	a.m.	a.m.	a.m.	a.m.	a.m.	p.m.	p.m.	p.m.	p.m.	p.m.	p.m.	p.m.	p.m.	p.m.
Folkestone (Wood Avenue)	dep.	9 48	9 56	10 12	10 36	11 0	12 4	12 12	1 45	3 25	4 5	4 35	7 40	7 45	9 50
Folkestone (Central Station)	"	9 55	..	..	10 10	10 43	11 7	12 19	..	..	4 42	..	7 47	..	9 57
Folkestone (Westcliff Gardens)	"	9 59	10 ..	10 16	10 23	10 47	11 11	12 13	12 23	1 54	3 34	4 14	4 46	7 51	7 54	10 1
Sandgate (Post Office) (see note A)	"	..	10 10	10 16	10 34	10 58	11 22	12 24	12 34	2 5	3 45	4 25	4 57	8 2	8 5	10 12
Hythe Station	"	..	..	10 25	..	..	..	12 33	..	2 14	3 54	4 34	..	8 14	..	..
Hythe (Red Lion Square)	arr.	10 23	10 18	10 30	10 47	11 11	11 35	12 38	12 47	2 19	3 59	4 39	5 10	8 15	8 19	10 25

| Hythe (for Sandgate) | dep. | .. | 10 39 | .. | .. | .. | .. | 12 50 | .. | 2 25 | 4 7 | 4 44 | .. | .. | 8 25 | .. |
| Sandling Junction | arr. | .. | 10 44 | .. | .. | .. | .. | 12 55 | .. | 2 30 | 4 12 | 4 49 | .. | .. | 8 30 | .. |

A. Omnibuses will also call at Sandgate (Seabrook Hotel).   S. Saturdays Only.   E. Saturdays Excepted.

Hand luggage only will be conveyed by the Omnibus Services, charges being made by the Omnibus Company for packages occupying floor, seat or roof space.

Passengers travelling to and from Sandgate via HYTHE.—Personal luggage, Dogs and Articles accompanying Passengers will be booked and labelled to and from HYTHE. Packages may be deposited in the Parcels Office at HYTHE for delivery to addresses in Sandgate at reasonable charges, or would be collected in Sandgate for conveyance to Hythe Station.

Passengers travelling to and from FOLKESTONE CENTRAL.—Personal luggage, etc., will be booked and labelled to and from FOLKESTONE CENTRAL. Owners must make their own arrangements for conveyance between Folkestone Central and Sandgate.

Arrangements have been made for Goods Train traffic to be dealt with at Hythe Station.

Waterloo Station, S.E.1.
February, 1931.

H. A. WALKER,
General Manager.

T.E. 6797/8,000/11331

Printed by McCorquodale & Co. Ltd., Ldn.—281365.

CHAPTER EIGHT

Gathering Clouds

ENDEAVOURING to improve the standing of the branch, in 1930 Sandgate Council approached the SR with a view to the introduction of excursion trains. Councillor Swain asserted that many tradesmen thought it would engender much prosperity as at other towns which enjoyed regular special trains. He then added that the SR had also been asked that two fast through trains between London and the Kent coast might connect with Sandgate. Finally, in order to promote Sandgate as a holiday resort, it was imperative that both Hythe and Sandgate should be linked into the local area seven-day season tickets, recently introduced, offering visitors unlimited travel within a specified area. In September the council received a reply from Mr. Whitworth, the SR's South Coast Commercial Representative, saying:

> 'I am now in a position to give you a reply upon the points raised in the interview with Mr. Swain.
> 1. Although there is every desire on the part of the Company to do all that is reasonable and possible in the interests of Sandgate, I am sorry that we cannot see our way to fall in with the proposal that the 11.30 a.m. Charing Cross to Folkestone should call at Sandling Junction, nor that the 7.15 p.m. Charing Cross to Folkestone should do so. I think that perhaps upon further consideration it will be obvious that there are very serious objections to both of these suggestions.
> 2. Since our 7-day season ticket programmes have already been issued some time it will not be possible to include Sandgate in the area No. 2 (also Hythe) but it will be borne in mind for next year.
> 3. As to including Hythe and Sandgate in the particular period ticket arrangements to which you allude in your letter of the 25th, this we shall be pleased to arrange.'

Clearly, one department knew nothing of another's plans, for exactly four weeks later, like a bolt out of the blue, the SR announced the impending closure of Sandgate station. Locally, a sense of bewilderment was coupled with outrage, for not only was Sandgate to lose its rail connection, but no prior consultation had been offered. The Mayor of Hythe, Alderman F. W. Butler, proclaimed 'We have got to fight this tooth and nail. I understand our own station might be closed – not yet of course but later perhaps'.

Whilst the forces against closure organised themselves, a spate of letters appeared in the local paper, including the habitual idiotic suggestion that the railway be turned into a road. Sandgate and Hythe councils decided to join forces in almost unanimous opposition to the SR's plans, although one councillor selfishly questioned why Hythe should support Sandgate as Hythe station wasn't threatened. A deputation, led by councillor E. C. Smith, met the Southern Railway Board in mid-January 1931, but they came away with precious little, as councillor Bayley revealed:

> 'When we arrived at the offices we found everything cut and dried. We were up against a brick wall. We were very courteously met but we felt right from the beginning that they had definitely made up their minds to close the station. The Southern Railway told us they'd received an offer from the East Kent Road Car Co. for Sandgate station and they couldn't neglect the opportunity. The Seabrook Estate was extended in consideration of the service at Sandgate station.'

Seemingly as a crumb of comfort, another councillor pointed out: 'There is one thing you might like to know – Sandgate will not be off the map entirely. On the Hythe platform there will be a big notice 'Hythe for Sandgate'!

The closure of Sandgate was therefore precipitated by the East Kent Bus Company's offer for the station site which it viewed as an ideal spot upon which to build a new bus garage. The SR needed precious little persuasion to part with it, quickly preparing figures which would justify its closure, arguing that the approximate annual passenger train earnings were £1,331 – about one third of this amount being traffic to and from Sandgate. The withdrawal of staff from Sandgate would save £679 per annum, added to which would be savings in train mileage. This amounted to a weekly figure of 252 passenger miles and 18 freight miles on Mondays to Saturdays, whilst on Sundays (May to September only) there were 18 passenger miles run.

As well as closing the Hythe–Sandgate portion of the line, it was planned to reduce to single-track the remaining section to Sandling Junction, arrangements for which were well in hand. The estimated cost of £2,841 for singling would be offset with a profit from recovered material worth £3,710 10s 6d. A saving of £436 a year in staffing Hythe was also calculated. There would also be £150 coming in annually from the lease of Sandgate station site, although this was eventually sold outright to the East Kent Bus Company.

It is often claimed that branch line closures before 1948 went ahead without the benefit of the Transport User's Consultative Committee, set up in that year to oppose closures. However, as its recommendations were, and still are, frequently ignored and over-ruled, the SR would likely have had its own way in much the same fashion as British Rail does today. Elsewhere, in 1931, the SR withdrew passenger services over the Canterbury–Whitstable branch and, more contentiously, singled the Elham Valley Line between Lyminge and Canterbury. This policy continued throughout the decade with many stations and lines being lost in other southern counties.

The end for Sandgate station came on Tuesday, 31st March 1931 after almost 57 years of use by holidaymakers, commuters, locals and soldiers. It was perhaps ironic that its official date of closure was April Fool's Day. The *Kentish Express* summed up the events on that Tuesday night:

> 'All change! For the last time Mr. T. Down, the porter who has been at Sandgate station for nine years, shouted this as the 8.19 p.m. train from Sandling Junction rumbled into the platform on Tuesday.
> As the train – two coaches and a van, came to a standstill its three passengers alighted. I turned to the booking clerk, Mr. J. Lusted, who had been at Sandgate for ten years and said: 'Quite a record freight isn't it?' 'Yes', he replied with a laugh. Without regard that they were at an historic event, the passengers gave up their tickets without a glance of regret. The engine, driven by Mr. Sam Hall, of Ashford, took back a cargo of goods on the return trip. In the signalbox Mr. George Jarvis, stationed there for over twenty years, kept watch and guards, Messrs C. Goldsmith and H. Phillips of Ashford said their goodbyes. As I went down the steps to the road, someone was turning out the station lights. Only ghost trains will run to Sandgate in future.'

THE HYTHE & SANDGATE RAILWAY

Sandgate signalbox remained open to deal with the last 'clear-up goods' which was run to take out all the station furniture and fittings and all re-usable material. Once this had been done the next train would be the demolition train. Without the need for working the points and signals, Sandgate signalbox was officially abolished on Tuesday, 19th May. The black & white enamel sign reading 'SANDGATE SIGNAL BOX' was removed and presented to Cecil Barnard, a local resident and railway enthusiast who was well-known to the staff. The closure was, as he recalled many years later, quite disgraceful. Soon after, the demolition gang arrived to begin pulling down the station buildings, but leaving most of the track which was temporarily treated as a siding from Hythe. On the weekend of the 4th/5th July, Hythe signal box was abolished, as was no. 2 cabin alongside the goods yard at Sandling Junction. From that date single-line operation between Hythe and Sandling Junction came into effect.

Mr. W. E. Harris, Hythe's station master, had retired on 2nd May 1931 and the fact that Hythe station from thence forward came under the jurisdiction of Sandling Junction, gave rise to rumours that Hythe would very soon share the fate of Sandgate. These were only quashed when the *Hythe Reporter* printed an assurance from Herbert Walker, the General Manager of the Southern Railway, that 'the SR has no present intention of closing Hythe Station'. The inclusion of the word 'present' brought little comfort to regular travellers or remaining staff at Hythe. By now, the only staff which Hythe could boast were two grade 1 porters and two lengthmen.

Hythe station, which had been renamed 'Hythe (Kent)' on 21st September 1925, had its name changed yet again in

"GOOD-BYE FRED."—The driver of the train from Sandgate bidding good-bye to his guard on Tuesday, when the Hythe-Sandgate line was closed.

Sandgate station, from the approach road, soon after the train service had been withdrawn. *C. J. Barnard/Alex Todd collection*

November 1931 when it became 'Hythe for Sandgate'. This lasted until the 5th July 1939 when it reverted simply to 'Hythe'.

With the alterations to the track and signalling, the Hythe branch, as it was known from then onwards, was worked by the Train Staff Instrument, which permitted only one engine in steam (or two coupled together) at any one time on the branch.

In a half-hearted attempt to alleviate the difficulties faced by Seabrook residents, the SR provided a bus service from Hythe station to Seabrook, as far as the site of the former Sandgate station. However, the heavy buses which were used not only caused considerable damage to the road surface but it was an awkward job turning them around at Hythe station. Those living at Seabrook found that after booking through to 'Sandgate' at London they were frequently left high and dry at Hythe station, with no bus, just a long walk home. The replacement bus was of course no substitute for, apart from all the extra inconvenience, it was unable to cope with luggage. It was a case of the time-honoured trick of making travel as awkward and impossible as ever, so that people would tire from using the service, thus enabling it to be withdrawn.

At the end of 1931 Hythe station was burgled on a couple of occasions. The first instance happened in October when the porters' tea and cigarettes were stolen by remorseless pilferers who also ransacked a number of parcels. Then, in December, an unsuccessful attempt was made to remove the safe. Having failed, the intruders stole articles from the goods office before making their getaway in a motor car which was later found abandoned nearby. The booty was evidently of little use for it was later recovered, washed up on the beach near Sandgate.

In the meantime the razing of Sandgate station was under way with the demolition of the main buildings, signal box and all other sundry structures. The engine shed had disappeared

Where the line ended after 1931. *R. F. Roberts*

Now reduced to a single track, looking towards Sandling Junction. *R. F. Roberts*

Hythe in the mid-1930s with the new nameboard on the right. D. Thompson

some time before but, strangely enough, the water tower remained intact, as did the gent's lavatory situated nearby on the former 'up' platform where it continued for a good many years serving the needs of the bus crews. The track to Hythe was subsequently removed, the severed ends being fitted with buffers. Gradually the land at Seabrook was sold off, the portion between the new bus garage and bridge 2140 across Hospital Hill going to Mr. Vant, a local builder, who erected a row of terraced houses upon the embankment.

Voices of discontent continued to be raised well into 1933, especially in connection with the replacement bus service. The SR solved the problem by simply withdrawing the facility entirely, justifying the action by claiming that it was not being used as much as it should be. Connections at Sandling Junction were also a bone of contention. A high-ranking BBC official found they weren't very good when he alighted from the Folkestone train at Sandling Junction only to be told that the next train for Hythe was four hours hence! Seemingly, even the Almighty struck a blow against the SR, for during a violent thunderstorm on the 19th June the booking office chimney was hit by lightning! The pot toppled off and, by a quirk of fate, snapped the telephone wires, thereby severing all station communications.

In the following month the *Hythe Reporter* remarked: 'Councillor Smith dropped a bombshell at a council meeting when he referred to the possibility of Hythe being closed.' A persistent rumour had recently swept Hythe whereby it was suggested that the town clerk should write immediately to the SR. 'A seaside town without a railway service was a very serious matter. Hythe is an important town and deserves an important train service!' The source of the rumours came from a newspaper piece which claimed that Sandling Junction was to be re-named 'Sandling for Hythe' and that a replacement bus would run between there and the town.

A public meeting was duly arranged where Mr. Dixon, representing the council, questioned the traffic figures quoted by the SR. He added: 'On the 3 o'clock train last Saturday over a hundred people went from Hythe, some had to stand in the guard's van and others were left at Sandling Junction, so crowded was the train.' He had carried out his own private survey, reckoning that an average of 1,700 passengers a week used Hythe. Almost 90 milk churns regularly went in and out, as did 250 pieces of luggage, 1,200 parcels, 30 cwt. of daily papers, 3 tons of fresh fish per day, plus three delivery vans. He commented: 'Sometimes the porters are at their wits end to cope with the goods.' He then referred to a letter he'd received from a vigilant regular visitor to Hythe which drew attention to the reduction in the number of trains in the peak summer period. 'This year there are five weekday trains to Hythe – last year there were eight. On Saturdays there are now just five – last year there were eleven. Up to London there are now six weekday trains compared with last year's ten, and eight compared to ten on Saturdays. Also, there is no train after the 5.28 a.m. until 1.15 p.m. on Saturdays, whereas last year there were intermediate trains at 9.10 a.m. and 11.18 a.m. Having closed Sandgate it seems they are intent on squeezing out passengers from the line so they can close it completely.' Many other people voiced their fears about the future of the Hythe branch as well as their hardship now that Sandgate had been shut:

A glimpse of Sandling Junction in September 1938. Interestingly enough, the tall down starting signal still survives, seen just to the left of the telegraph pole.
R. F. Roberts

'Seabrook has suffered heavily through the closing of Sandgate station and the number of visitors has dropped by an alarming 50%. Landladies now face a bleak time indeed.

The bus service, between Hythe and Sandgate stations, provided by the SR was a failure simply because of its inconvenience to passengers. It was a fiasco and there was no provision for luggage etc. Reading between the lines it seems it is their intention to close the line completely.'

Surprisingly, the SR responded favourably to the criticisms levelled at it by restoring the train service nearer its former level. The summer 1934 timetable contained nine new trains, four 'up' and five 'down', although the Sunday service remained at just four each way.

The Hythe railway was now, more than ever, a rural branch line and in time the locals became used to seeing the same tank engines with their two-coach sets plying up and down its 1½ mile length. Stirling's 'Q' class and 'Q1' rebuilds were once familiar sights hurrying up the bank from Hythe but by 1930 they had all been withdrawn. The 'O' and 'O1' classes, which seemingly monopolised the services in the 1920s were now less common, as were the 'R' class and their rebuilt counterparts. By the thirties the most common engines seen running between Sandling and Hythe were former LB & SCR tanks. Stroudley's 'D1' 0–4–2Ts were often rostered to run the two-coach motor trains as were Billinton's 'D3' 0–4–4Ts. These ran throughout the day although the first 'up' train in the morning was almost always taken out from Hythe by an 'O1' or 'C' class which brought down the early morning goods. Goods traffic continued to be the lifeblood of the branch. In 1938 for example the 'down' goods was worked as follows:

	arr.	dep.
ASHFORD	–	4.15 a.m.
SEVINGTON SIDING*	–	–
SMEETH	4.27	5.10
WESTENHANGER	5.20	5.55
SANDLING JUNCTION	6.00	6.05
HYTHE	6.15	

* Calls at Sevington Siding on request.

In the evening the last train 'down' to Hythe was worked by the goods engine, arriving at the little terminus at 7.12 p.m. where the stock was stabled in the station. The engine then shunted for an hour before departing with the 'up' goods of the day which ran thus:

	arr.	dep.
HYTHE	–	8.15 p.m.
SANDLING JUNCTION	8.25	8.46
WESTENHANGER	8.51	9.35
SMEETH	9.45	10.35
SEVINGTON SIDING		C. on R.
ASHFORD	10.50	

A curious incident took place in February 1938 when a great gale was blowing hard. Having just arrived at Hythe with his passenger train, driver Arthur Batt spotted a greyhound and a goat sheltering from the wind against a haystack. He thought no more of it until he happened to glance over in the same

Stills from a film shot in 1937 of a trip from Sandling Junction to Hythe, featuring the cameraman's young son.
Courtesy John Huntley Archives

Two views of push-pull unit No. 722, hauled by ex-LB & SCR 'D3' 0–4–4T No. 2365 waiting on a wet day in July 1938. Four years later this engine had the dubious honour of bringing down an enemy aircraft which shot it up on Romney Marsh, causing an immediate boiler explosion. No. 2365 was repaired and again handled Hythe branch services.

R. F. Roberts

Ex-LB & SCR 'D1' 0–4–2T No. 2239 shunts the loop, the former up line at Sandling Junction in April 1940. *V. R. Webster*

direction a few moments later, just as the haystack toppled, completely burying the animals. He swiftly rounded up a party of assorted helpers who began pulling the stack apart. Arthur Batt was obliged to return to his engine as it was due to depart, but the rest diligently continued until they eventually heard the plaintive cries of the animals. At last 'Paddy' the greyhound emerged, wagging his tail and gratefully licking the patting hands whilst the goat, forgetting his manners, promptly charged the band of rescuers!

Throughout the last few summers before the outbreak of the Second World War the Southern Railway gave Hythe its best train service for years. In spite of the decade being best remembered for its years of economic depression, this was largely confined, as always, to the industrial north of England and, generally speaking, the southern counties of Britain were prosperous and buzzing with activity. The Southern Railway was adept in promoting its resorts and, in contrast to the prevailing attitude towards Hythe at the start of the thirties, by the end of the decade it was advertised as never before. Once again the 'Pride of Kent' was seen displayed at London terminii south of the Thames. The number of trains provided must have pleased visitors and townsfolk alike. On weekdays there were twelve trains to Hythe with eleven in the opposite direction. On Saturdays this increased to fifteen 'down' and fourteen 'up', whilst on Sundays twelve trains ran each way. Alas though, these years soon came to an end. The gaily-painted metal toy buckets, with their motifs of starfish and yachts, were packed away, along with thermos flasks, into suitcases that would not again be opened for several years. The sandy beaches would lose their imprints of tiny feet, while the paper flags fluttering on top of castles would soon give way to barbed wire.

The declaration of war in 1939 brought with it the evacuation of many London children into the comparative safety of Kent. Pressure was put on the Hythe authorities to accept their quota of evacuees at Sandling Junction, rather than Hythe, owing to 'locomotive difficulties'. Presumably this referred to the limited axle weight on the branch which prohibited the larger main line engines from venturing down to Hythe station. Whatever it was, it caused some objections from Hythe people who had to travel to the junction station. Eventually the London evacuees were moved away from Kent and, with the threat of invasion increasing week by week, the military authorities began establishing defences all along the south coast. This brought about the cessation of passenger trains to Hythe. Rail-mounted guns were literally brought out of the cobwebs at sheds and depots around the country in preparation for stationing at sites all across England. In September 1940 a detachment of the Royal Engineers attached to the 4th Super Heavy Battery R.A. travelled down from Kirton, in Lincolnshire, to establish a base at Hythe. This unit comprised two 9.2 inch rail-mounted guns, an ex-GWR Dean 'Goods' 0–6–0, WD No. 195, along with some French ferry vans for sleeping purposes and all the necessary ammunition, stores and supplies.

Members of the 4th Super Heavy Battery R.A. pose with their WD engine, ex-GWR Dean 'Goods' 0–6–0 No. 195, in the goods yard at Hythe.
Charles Turner

One gun was soon secured in on the former 'down' line at the far eastern end of Hythe station, whilst the other went to sidings at Folkestone Junction.

As far as the crew were concerned it wasn't just the change of scenery which they'd have to get used to, in fact many of them had never before even heard an air-raid siren. As the Battle of Britain reached its climax, they witnessed daily the massed German bombers returning from raids upon London. On one of these days a gunner decided to man the Lewis gun, mounted on a tripod in the golf course bunker near Hythe station and even though the aircraft were almost certainly well out of range, he gave them a burst of fire. Whether the crew realised they were being fired at isn't known, but one plane did turn, probably because he had a couple of bombs left over, and these were dropped but they did little damage.

At about 7.30 on the evening of 28th August 1940 an enemy bomber was hit by the coastal defence guns at Folkestone whereupon it continued losing height until finally crashing near Sandling Junction. Although it missed the station, it severed the telegraph wires, causing a failure of the signalling block instruments and bells between Sandling Junction and Cheriton Junction signal boxes. This caused some disruption for a few hours until the S & T Dept had the lines repaired by 1.30 a.m.

In Hythe, the war brought the usual miseries of shortages, not to mention the evacuation of its own children to Wales and the West Country. Elsewhere in the town, life went on as best it could and only on the seafront were stark reminders of the conflict. The once-impressive Seabrook Hotel was steadily dilapidating, having been requisitioned by the army.

Charles Turner, who was a member of the RE Detachment at Hythe, clearly remembers his unforgettable Christmas Day

GATHERING CLOUDS

1940 which began when they were awoken at 5.00 a.m., not by Father Christmas, but their Commanding Officer who ordered them to dress in full battle order. Having done so, they were allowed to lie down again where they were served tea by NCOs, after which they had to stand until 8.00 a.m. As these were the days when invasion was expected at any time they had to be constantly prepared. Each daily order had written along the bottom the ominous message: 'You are the first line of defence. There will be no retreat!'

As in the Great War, the town was well-patronised by soldiers, being the nearest venue for entertainment where, for a few hours, an escape into fantasy could be had, thanks to the local cinemas. Even then they were obliged to wear their steel helmets and carry their rifles at all times.

The Hythe branch was never an important target for enemy aircraft and, unlike the Elham Valley Line which suffered a number of attempts to destroy it, no record of direct hits upon the track or the shooting-up of trains has been found. However, Hythe station did suffer a bomb from which the porter had a very lucky escape. During a raid he took shelter in the adjacent booking office chimney breast, which was just as well for it saved his life when the parcels office was hit. Although quite unhurt, he emerged looking more like a miller, being covered in white mortar dust from head to toe. The parcels office was wrecked beyond repair and was subsequently left for the common buddleia bush to invade.

The branch was never taken over completely by the military as was the Elham Valley Line. Instead, the SR continued to run its own daily goods train which, although listed 'emergency', ran approximately an hour later in the evening. Throughout the rest of the day the line was left to the army for whatever manoeuvres were necessary. Undoubtedly the high spot of the week was the Saturday trip to Ashford when the WD engine was taken to the works for boilerwashing and

The battery's 9.2 inch gun stabled in the siding at Hythe on the former down line to Sandgate. *Imperial War Museum*

THE HYTHE & SANDGATE RAILWAY

The rather beautiful buddleia bush that was quick to take advantage of the bombed-out parcels office at Hythe.
Gresley Society

cleaning. The 'bark' of an ex-Great Western engine echoing through Saltwood cutting as it breasted the 1 in 59 bank was certainly a different sound compared to the familiar beat from a South Eastern engine. Training was given to the army personnel by the SR enabling them to 'learn the road' between Sandling Junction and Ashford whereby they could operate without a railway pilotman. Two crews handled this duty alternately which understandably was a popular detail for, once the engine had been stabled, the men had the rest of the day to themselves in Ashford. Battledress, along with toilet requisites, were taken in a sandbag, whilst their hotel for the night was a Southern Railway Camping Coach parked alongside Ashford Railway Works. On Sunday mornings the engine was washed and thoroughly cleaned, with the firebox prepared and lit in readiness for the return to Hythe at around 2.00 p.m. These days hold pleasant memories for Charles Turner for it was on one of these weekend visits that he met a local girl who later became his wife.

The base at Hythe was soon fitted out with what home comforts were available. Although the French ferry vans had been provided with double bunks at each end, the detachment preferred to sleep in the nearby Scene Golf Club house which sufficed as a mess room.

On 10th February 1941 the battery left Hythe, transferring to Rolvenden and Wittersham Road stations on the Kent & East Sussex Railway. Charles Turner went on to serve with the 13th Battery at Sellinge before moving over the hills to Lyminge station to work on the Elham Valley units.

For a brief period the only trains over the short branch were the goods. However, in 1942 the SR was persuaded to reinstate the passenger service which came into effect as shown in the timetable at the foot of this page.

This service lasted up until the spring of the following year when the military authorities drew up further plans for the Hythe and Elham Valley branches. As a result, both Hythe and Lyminge stations were closed to passengers on Monday, 3rd May 1943 for the duration of the war. The WD were anxious to stable a 13.5 inch gun at Hythe and possibly an 18 inch howitzer. In December a meeting took place at Tonbridge station between representatives of the WD and the SR where the proposals were fully examined and discussed. Lt. Col. Hyde-Smith elaborated that he would like to house the 13.5 inch gun, as well as at a later date an 18 inch howitzer, in the 94 yard Hayne tunnel. The tunnel would simply be 'home' to these guns for no firing positions or facilities on the Hythe branch were envisaged. When needed, these guns would be shunted out via Sandling Junction to Cheriton Junction, thence up the Elham Valley Line to the military firing sites already established. Needless to say, the whole scheme rested on the availability of using the Kent coast main line between Sandling and Cheriton without interruption to other traffic as well as clearance and weight restrictions. Mr. Robarts, the SR's Eastern Section Divisional Engineer, expressed some doubt as to whether the machines could, at present, travel over this portion of the system, but he undertook to carry out a survey within the next few days. As to the request to run between Sandling Junction and Sellinge siding, the SR foresaw no problem. It was also discussed whether the WD might prefer to take over the entire Hythe branch, including the running of the goods service, in much the same way as the Elham Valley was operated. However, Capt. L. Smith R.E. pointed out certain difficulties, mainly locomotive power, in respect of their diesel engines being restricted from running as far as Hythe station. Finally, it was agreed that the best method would be to construct a loop in Hayne tunnel by relaying the former 'up' line, with the points at either end locked by the Train Staff Instrument. This would allow the WD's diesel engine to put in, or take out, the gun and vehicles but it would have to return to the stabling siding at Sandling in order to give up the Train Staff. The SR's goods trains could then be worked as normal. It was brought to the attention of the military that as the 'down' goods train occupied the line between 5.25 a.m.

HYTHE BRANCH. (Single Line.) NO SUNDAY SERVICE.

Distances	DOWN TRAINS. WEEK-DAYS.	* a.m.	* a.m.	* a.m.	* a.m.	a.m.	* S.O. a.m.	* p.m.	p.m.	* S.O. p.m.	* S.X. p.m.		* p.m.
m. c.	Sandling Junction .... (E) dep.	8 22 §	9 5	9 50	11 0		11 40	3 5	5 5	5 46	6 20	6 30		7 8
1 44	HYTHE .... (E) arr.	8 26	9 9	9 54	11 4		11 44	3 9	5 9	5 50	6 24	6 34		7 12

Distances	UP TRAINS. WEEK-DAYS.	a.m.	* a.m.	* a.m.	* a.m.	a.m.	* S.X. p.m.	* S.O. p.m.	* S.O. p.m.	* p.m.	* S.O. p.m.	* S.X. p.m.	* p.m.	
m. c.	HYTHE .... (E) dep.	7 48	8 55	9 20	10 35		11 15	12 40	2 40	4 20	5 30	6 7	6 12	6 50	
1 44	Sandling Junction .... (E) arr.	7 53 ‡	9 0	9 25	10 40		11 20	12 45	2 45	4 25	5 35	6 12	6 17	6 55	

‡—To Ashford.   §—From Ashford.

SR Passenger Timetable 1942

A wartime 'pill-box' disguised as a bus shelter, directly above the former Sandgate station. The 'gents' remains, as does the lamp room and the water tower. The ornate building, nicknamed the 'goose cathedral', was the former lifeboat station. *Imperial War Museum*

and 7.30 a.m., it would not be possible for the diesel to work to and from the loop during that time. The loop would need to be 300 ft. in length, with the connection on the Sandling side as far forward as possible without interfering with the points leading from the single line loop at the station. Mr. Robarts expressed concern about the weight restrictions on the bridges, both 2128 at Saltwood and 2131 across Blackhouse Hill, neither of which would likely allow the passage of the WD's diesel engine, let alone the guns. Precisely what the military authorities had in mind remains vague. For example, Lt. Col. Hyde-Smith commented that if they were prohibited from running across 2128 at Saltwood then their movements would be considerably restricted, yet 2128 stands over three-quarters of a mile away on the Hythe side of Hayne tunnel. Why they needed to run across 2128 remains a mystery especially considering it was clearly stated that the guns would merely be stabled and not deployed on the branch, nor were any arrangements proposed for strengthening the track or bridges as had been necessary at Canterbury, Bridge and Barham on the Elham Valley Line.

A week later the report from Mr. Robarts was forthcoming. As regards the Elham Valley Line, the WD would be permitted to run from Cheriton Junction to Elham with the Hythe guns but in the case of the 18 inch howitzer the speed would have to be reduced to a walking pace when passing beneath Beerforstal bridge, 2081, south of Elham. It was also stipulated that the howitzer should not pass over the crossover at the southern end of Lyminge station, but it was confirmed that no restrictions would be imposed between Cheriton Junction and Sellinge. The Hythe branch was a different matter. Whilst there were no clearance problems involving Hayne tunnel, as at first feared, bridge 2128 was deemed to be far too weak to even allow the WD diesel engines across. Fortunately, events on a much wider scale apparently changed in the course of the war whereby the military were able to relinquish all further use of the Hythe branch as part of their operations.

Comparative peace therefore returned to the little branch once more where unchecked foliage was opportune at taking a firmer hold of the banks along the line, reaching out across the cuttings. Ivy and moss crept into every cavity in the brick-work and the once glossy paintwork faded, blistered and peeled in the quiet, hot summer days. What would become of the branch, now thoroughly neglected and derelict? It was upon such a question that many locals had cause to ponder.

Sandling Junction from the up main platform, looking towards London in 1950. *Denis Cullum*

The branch platform in 1950. *Denis Cullum*

CHAPTER NINE

The End of a Dream

RESPONDING once more to local pressure, the Southern Railway reintroduced passenger trains to the Hythe branch on Monday, 1st October 1945, but it was a far worse service than any previously experienced. On weekdays there was only one 'up' train in the morning, departing at 7.50, whilst the first train into Hythe didn't arrive until 5.10 in the afternoon. This formed the only other 'up' train of the day, the 6.12 p.m. Matters were little better on Saturdays with just three 'up' trains, at 7.50 a.m., 2.55 p.m. and 4.10 p.m. and three 'down' trains, arriving at 2.16 p.m., 3.15 p.m., and 5.10 p.m. The pre-war summer Sunday service was never restored. From the SR's point of view the only traffic was likely to be those few early morning and evening travellers to and from Ashford, Tonbridge and London. There would be no visitors, certainly not for a few years anyway, so it would be pointless running empty mid-day trains.

Another thorn in the side of the SR was the derequisitioned Hotel Imperial. Over the years it had been necessary to assist the Hotel Company with allowances off the rent as well as loans to meet additional expenses. Once the hotel business had been liquidated, the furniture was sold off with the SR receiving £4,368 as creditor, whilst the building was put up for auction.

Not surprisingly, the paltry train service sparked off renewed criticism from Hythe Chamber of Commerce who complained that 'Hythe had been pushed into the background yet again'. They bemoaned the loss of the 8.45 a.m. fast train from Sandling Junction to Victoria via Maidstone and Bromley, as well as the fact that the 9.28 a.m. had been slowed-down, not reaching Charing Cross until 11.34 a.m. 'By the time the trader got to the warehouse it left little time before lunchtime closure, so half the day was wasted. On many of the trains, people had to change at Ashford – in fact it was quicker to go to Folkestone!'. Little did the chairman realise he'd hit the nail squarely on the head. Indeed, it was quicker to go to Folkestone and this was precisely what the SR intended encouraging.

A short time after, a post-war report was published, receiving wide coverage in the local press, outlining the SR's resumption of electrification schemes, part of which included a proposal to use diesel traction on the Hythe branch. This might have been held up as witness to the SR's good intentions but there was little substance behind the ambitious plans, simply because the finance was unavailable. Instead, the little branch train continued to steam up and down twice a day waiting for the inevitable visit from the dreaded 'time and motion' experts who would assess its case for closure.

The bus companies weren't slow at moving in at the railway's expense and taking away what few passengers were left. Apart from the East Kent buses which ran a frequent service between

'D3' No. 32380 gets ready to propel the 4.26 p.m. Ashford-Hythe train out of Sandling Junction on 31st August 1949. *S. C. Nash*

Hythe and Folkestone, Messrs Newmans' bus competed directly with the train by running from Hythe to Sandling Junction to meet the London arrivals. Although the bus operators were at liberty to compete with the railway, the station staff were understandably resentful when the bus driver habitually boarded the waiting train for Hythe where he'd announce to passengers he was just leaving and they'd be better off travelling with him.

The immediate post-war years were, as we all know, particular times of hardship and shortages. Coal was rationed, along with most other items, so occasionally the odd bag of coal chippings, scraped from the bottom of the engine's bunker or tender, would be exchanged for some local eggs or freshly-caught Hythe fish. Many a rabbit or straying pheasant *à la Saltwood cutting* was bagged by the fireman where it journeyed in the bunker on its way to the kitchen pot. In the autumn months the train crew would often leave Sandling Junction station to tramp the few hundred yards to Hayne tunnel, which was shrouded in beautiful chestnut trees. Quite often they'd be so engrossed in harvesting the nuts that they'd forget their train waiting in the bay until the station porter came panting along, shouting that the 'old man' was 'blowing his top' as it was well past the time of departure.

A variety of 'old wheezers' was sent to work the Hythe branch in its twilight years. Billinton's 'D3' 0–4–4Ts were consigned to spend their last days here, especially Nos. 2365, 2380 and 2388, as were ex-LC & DR 'R1' 0–4–4Ts nos. 671 and 660 although these two did manage to survive a little longer. Ordinarily, the Wainwright 'H' class 0–4–4Ts handled the passenger services whilst the 'C' class 0–6–0s ran the goods. In contrast to other Southern lines, the 'H's and 'C's were never that common on the Hythe branch, in fact it always seemed to end up with the most worn-out locomotives of all. One interesting visitor, but not until after the line had closed, was a Maunsell 'N' class 2–6–0 which Sid Nash remembers watching as it made uncommonly heavy going when moving out some wagons stored in Saltwood cutting.

Operating the Hythe branch was now a relatively simple affair with the pattern as follows. The first train of the day was the 4.45 a.m. freight from Ashford which, after calling at stations and sidings on the way, reached Hythe at 6.50 a.m. For an hour the engine shunted the goods before coupling up to the stock berthed in the former 'up' platform where it departed at 7.52 a.m. This train ran through to Ashford, arriving at 8.15 a.m. The station remained quiet throughout the day until the arrival of the early evening train from Ashford which pulled into the 'up' platform where the stock was berthed for the night. The engine proceeded into the yard to put together the 'up' goods, which had been prepared during the day, before leaving via the former 'down' line at 6.50 p.m.

The Hythe branch platforms, showing the long-disused up platform.

Lens of Sutton

THE END OF A DREAM

Ex-SE & CR 'H' class No. 31520 leaves Hayne tunnel on its way with the 2.55 p.m. ex Hythe train on 13th May 1950. *S. C. Nash*

bound for Ashford. On Saturdays only the service was augmented with a Sandling Junction–Hythe shuttle at the following times:

Down:
ASHFORD	1.30		
SANDLING JUNCTION	1.50	3.10	5.07
HYTHE	1.56	3.15	5.12

Up:
HYTHE	2.55	4.20	6.50*
SANDLING JUNCTION	3.00	4.25	
ASHFORD			

*Freight only

With the neighbouring Elham Valley Line now closed, the last to be axed by the Southern Railway Company, railwaymen and locals wondered for how much longer the small Hythe branch could last. Nationalisation in 1948 brought forth new hope for the future of the railway network as well as the chance to have a fully-integrated public transport system. In reality though, the new management differed little from the old private companies and eventually succumbed to become just another political football for successive governments.

In the summer of 1948 a deputation from Hythe met representatives of the newly-formed Southern Region of British Railways in the hope of persuading them that the town deserved better treatment. British Railways replied that it was their 'intention to restore the railway service to Hythe up to its pre-war standard at the earliest possible moment, but that coal and carriages were the limiting factor'. They were unable to give an assurance that Hythe would not be closed for goods items as their new policy was to concentrate merchandise from small stations to larger railhead centres. The deputation then suggested that Sandling Junction should be re-named 'Hythe Junction' in order that passengers should know to alight there to board either train or bus to Hythe. British Railways shunned this idea, stating they'd be 'extremely loath to alter the name'. A request that more trains stop at Sandling Junction, instead of Shorncliffe, was brushed aside simply because Shorncliffe dealt with far more passengers. Nor could the 9.17 a.m. ex-Charing Cross be stopped at Sandling Junction as it was closely followed by the prestigious 'Golden Arrow'. As for Sunday trains, BR promised to look into the matter before the start of the next season. The *Hythe Reporter* aptly summed it all up with a heading: 'Town gets little change from British Railways'.

BRITISH RAILWAYS

CLOSING
OF
HYTHE (KENT) BRANCH

The line from

SANDLING JCT. TO HYTHE

will be closed to all traffic on and from

MONDAY, 3rd DECEMBER, 1951

HYTHE station will be closed, and SANDLING JUNCTION will be renamed "SANDLING for HYTHE."

Omnibus services are operated between FOLKESTONE CENTRAL and HYTHE via Bouverie Square by the East Kent Road Car Co. Ltd. and between SANDLING and HYTHE by Messrs. Newman & Sons (Hythe) Ltd.

Parcels and freight traffic for cartage by the Railway Executive will be dealt with at FOLKESTONE and enquiries should be addressed to the Station Master FOLKESTONE JUNCTION telephone Folkestone 4077 (Parcels, Luggage in Advance, etc.) or the Goods Agent, telephone Folkestone 3154 (Freight train traffic).

Facilities for other traffic are available at SANDLING, SHORNCLIFFE and FOLKESTONE JUNCTION.

Further information may be obtained from:—

THE DISTRICT TRAFFIC SUPERINTENDENT,
BRITISH RAILWAYS,
ORPINGTON.

Telephone:- ORPINGTON 3940   Ext. 24 or 25

A.D.16327/B1

Printed Great Britain at THE BAYNARD PRESS

THE END OF A DREAM

Interesting visitors to the branch in its twilight were a couple of ex-LC & DR 'R1' class 0–4–4Ts. Here No. 31671 starts away from Sandling Junction on 4th August 1951.
Gresley Society

The warm and memorable summer of 1949 brought no Sunday trains to Hythe, in fact, behind the scenes, plans of an entirely different nature were being concocted. In December of that year the East Kent Road Car Co. inaugurated a new service between Hythe, Sandgate and Folkestone which should have left little doubt in anyone's mind what was beginning to take place. Whereas in 1949 there were 33 season ticket holders, within two years these had been sufficiently discouraged so that just half a dozen loyal travellers remained. One of the most friendly and respected members of these regular commuters was Mr. Rhodes who knew all the staff and train crews by name. A survivor of the terrible Sevenoaks train crash of 1927, he moved to Hythe where he journeyed regularly right through to the end. On some days he was the only passenger aboard the train. At Christmas he made a point of presenting gifts to his railway friends. Perhaps, though, his most charitable act involved a member of the station staff at Sandling Junction who could ill-afford a tricky and expensive operation. All the same, the operation was carried out soon after, paid for by an anonymous donor, although there was little doubt in anyone's mind who had picked up the bill.

In July 1950 a traffic census was carried out whilst a report on goods receipts was prepared. A couple of months later a meeting was held at Sandling Junction to discuss permanent way renewals at the station if the branch was closed but with the goods yard remaining open. If passenger trains were to continue then the facing connection from the 'down' main line would have to be maintained, whereas if access to the goods yard only was required then a trailing connection to the 'up' main line could be installed.

Train	From	To	Total Passengers Week ending 22/7/50	Average
1.30 p.m. SO	Ashford	Hythe	41 (2)	41 (2)
3.10 p.m. SO	Sandling	,,	11 (4)	11 (4)
4.18 p.m. SX	Ashford	,,	30 (20)	5 (3)
6.26 p.m. SX	Sandling	,,	52 (26)	10 (5)
7.52 a.m.	Hythe	Ashford	176 (52)	29 (9)
2.55 p.m. SO	,,	Sandling	– (–)	– (–)
4.20 p.m. SO	,,	,,	14 (1)	14 (1)
6.15 p.m. SX	,,	,,	4 (1)	$\frac{2}{3}$ (1/6)

Figures in brackets denote corresponding passenger statistics for week ending 18/2/50.

A comparison between the years 1937 and 1949 was made:

		1937	1949
Passenger tickets issued		5,110	971
Season tickets		78	33
Parcels, P.L.A.,D.L. Etc.	Forwarded	2,751	3,426
	Received	32,832	18,159
Gallons of milk	Received	17,608	–
Fish, Meat & other goods	Received	5,360 cwts	–
	Forwarded	37 cwts	–
General Merchandise	Forwarded	576 tons	652 tons
	Received	3,236 tons	2,591 tons
Coal, Coke & Patent Fuel	Received	8,298 tons	4,345 tons
Other minerals	Forwarded	172 tons	–
	Received	1,073 tons	351 tons
Livestock	Forwarded	4 truckloads	–
	Received	–	–
Loaded wagons –	Forwarded	1,000	892
(other than livestock)	Received	2,759	2,109

'H' class No. 31521, having brought its train from Sandling Junction, sets off for the goods yard to perform shunting duties on 25th August 1951.

R. C. Riley

Two views of 31521 shunting at Hythe on 25th August 1951. *R. C. Riley*

An up express roars through Sandling Junction whilst the Hythe branch train waits to follow on 25th August 1951.

R. C. Riley

No. 31521 and set 721 await the 'all-clear' in preparation for the trip to Ashford. *R. C. Riley*

The detailed report was studied, along with a brief from the Civil Engineering Department which revealed that if the line remained open, a repair bill in the region of £8,000 would soon be due. All milk, newspapers, and postal sacks now went by road into Hythe, with only household coal and stores for Mackeson's Brewery as the main inwards traffic. Outwards freight comprised mainly returned empties from the brewery as well as some small parcels traffic. It was felt that no great hardship would be felt by passengers in transferring to Sandling Junction or Folkestone Central stations as extra buses would be laid on or existing services extended. In conclusion, the British Railways Board could find no justification for the line's retention and therefore sanctioned its closure. Subsequently the presses began to roll off the customary closure notices which were duly pasted up.

Whereas the Elham Valley Line had slipped away quite unnoticed, the Hythe branch literally went out with a bang. On the last day, Saturday, 1st December 1951, a number of railway enthusiasts descended upon the branch, determined to make the passing of the line a memorable event. A Union Jack was flown half-mast from the parapet of Station bridge 2132, underneath which was a laurel wreath, a Hythe 'target' sign from one of the lamp posts, and a notice reading 'R.I.P.'. It was, however, far from being a peaceful departure. The booking office was a hive of activity with railwayman John Laker punching-out souvenir tickets in exchange for the handfuls of coppers thrust at him. At 3.15 p.m. the last train came rumbling in from Sandling Junction, hauled by 'C' class 31721

Farewell to the Hythe branch. *Gresley Society*

The end of a dream as the Hythe branch train heads for Hayne tunnel.

R. C. Riley

and driven by Victor Morgan and his mate Bob Hukins. A splendid wreath made from carrots, celery, Brussel sprouts, turnips, hops and laurel, was produced and fitted onto the engine's top lamp iron. A suitable motif indeed for the garden county of England.

For an hour No. 31271 and its train were treated like a film star with every feature captured on celluloid. Just before 4.20 p.m., guard Alex Anderson unfurled his green flag ready for the last wave, while District Inspector Bobby Burn fumbled for his silver whistle which would herald a rush for the seats. For a few seconds time seemed to stand still, until the death knell was sounded by 31271's shrill wail which echoed out across the Saltwood valley, harking back to that first happy day. Under Driver Morgan's careful guidance, 31271's regulator was opened, allowing her wheels to crush the first detonator. Further loud explosions followed in rapid succession, accompanied by the crew playing an obligato on the Wainwright whistle, as the last train steamed out of Hythe. Nearby an alarmed resident, thinking there'd been a terrible accident, telephoned the police who arrived to ruefully observe the half-masted flag, before resuming their duties.

The cold, grey, lowering day continued to darken as the beat of the Edwardian engine grew even fainter. The chilling evening air, pervaded by the pungent odours of dampness, decaying leaves and rotting wood, created mists which rose to enshroud the now deserted platforms. At one end, a lone gas lamp hissed and 'popped', its wan light vainly attempting to scatter the encroaching shadows until the porter's hook would reach up to extinguish its life forever.

It was now exactly a hundred years since Colonel Sandilands had, in those far distant days, first sat down at his desk, pondering awhile on what might be, before reaching out for his pen to instigate those wondrous dreams and schemes.

If the ghost of Sir Edward Watkin had been given grace to stroll along the lonely platform to witness the porter snuff out the last lamp, what would have been uppermost in his mind? Would it have been a fleeting impression of that final train disappearing towards Saltwood, its red tail light fading into the dusk as its merry band aboard looked forward to the brave new festive Britain of 1951? I fancy not. Instead, perhaps the spectral forms of so many events that had gone before would now be released as the spirit of the line vented its last gasp, unravelling before his eyes. The recent images of the battles fought in the sky would be followed by those of happier times when laughter filled the air as the excited children of the 1930s and 20s, armed with buckets and spades, jumped out of the trains gliding into the Pride of Kent. There would be heartbreaking images too of countless sad faces, peering from dirty, steamed-up compartment windows, destined for God knows where. Their last memories would not be the lush green fields of England but some alien, muddy battleground, filled with the cries of men and beasts, before the Hand that wipes away all tears might take them away. Edwardian youngsters in smocks and stockings crowded upon the platform – off on their annual Sunday school treat, hearts beating faster as an elderly engine wheezed into the station. Victorian lacy fripperies, glossy top hats and walking canes to humble shawls, frayed collars and cloth caps – the railway saw it all. Echoes of royal footsteps, of eloquent speeches and cries of 'God save the Queen!' would surely have rung in Watkin's ears while flooding into his mind would come the visions of those heady days and exuberant messages – 'Onward', 'Welcome Prince Arthur, Welcome Sir Edward', 'Success to the Hythe & Sandgate Railway' and, of course, 'Oh! What a day Hythe is having'!

Just as the last mantle was doused, plunging the station into its ultimate darkness, his frail form would be called back, disappearing into the all-enveloping mist and taking with him his hopes and aspirations for *his* railway, *his* new route to the continent. Alas, it really was the end of a dream.

For we are born at all adventure, and we shall be hereafter as though we have never been.

SANDLING JUNCTION

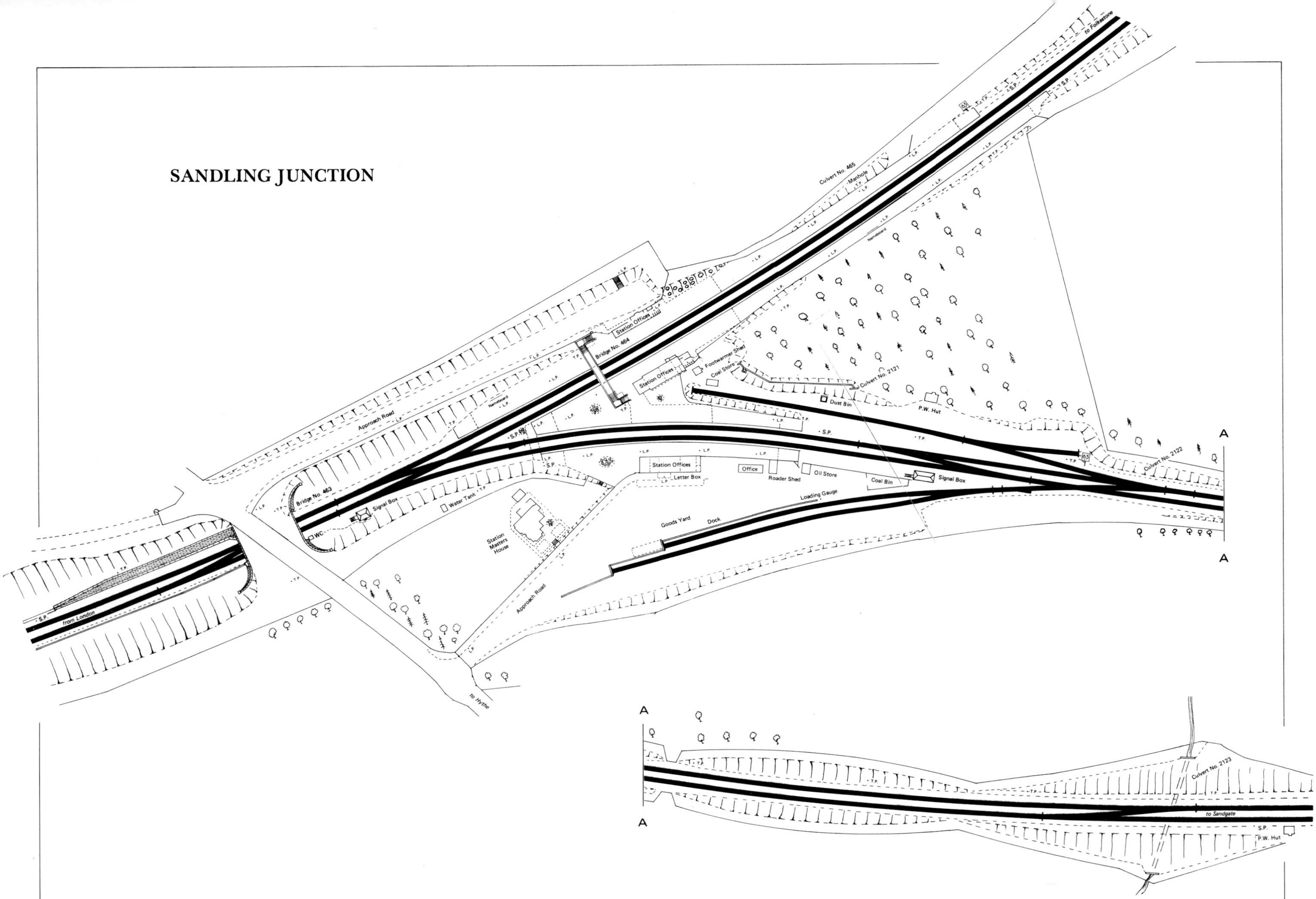

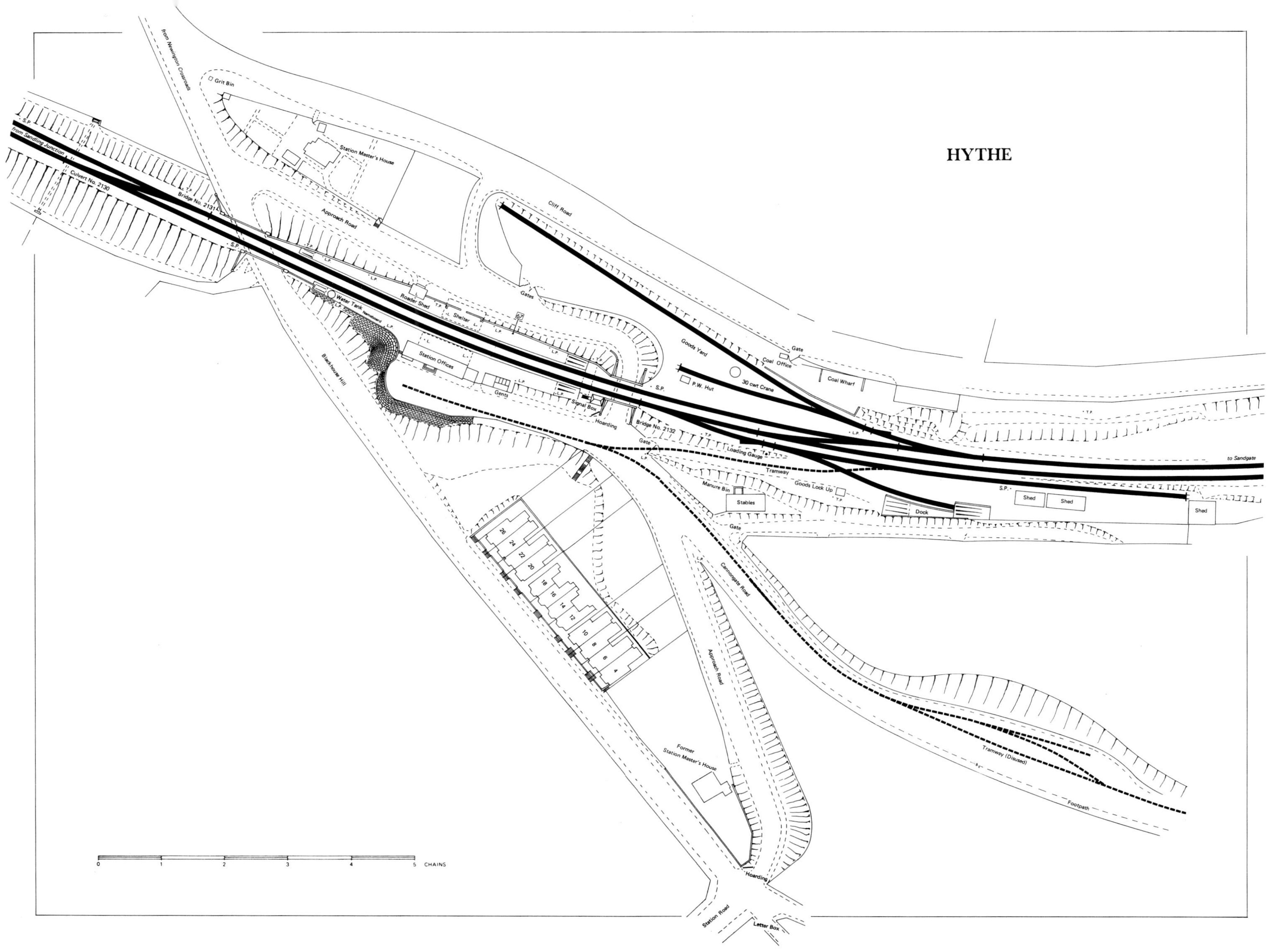

HYTHE

SE & CR HYTHE STATION   Alterations to existing station buildings – December 1899

Gents' lavatory moved to new site east of Station Master's Office and former Gents' converted into Parcels Office

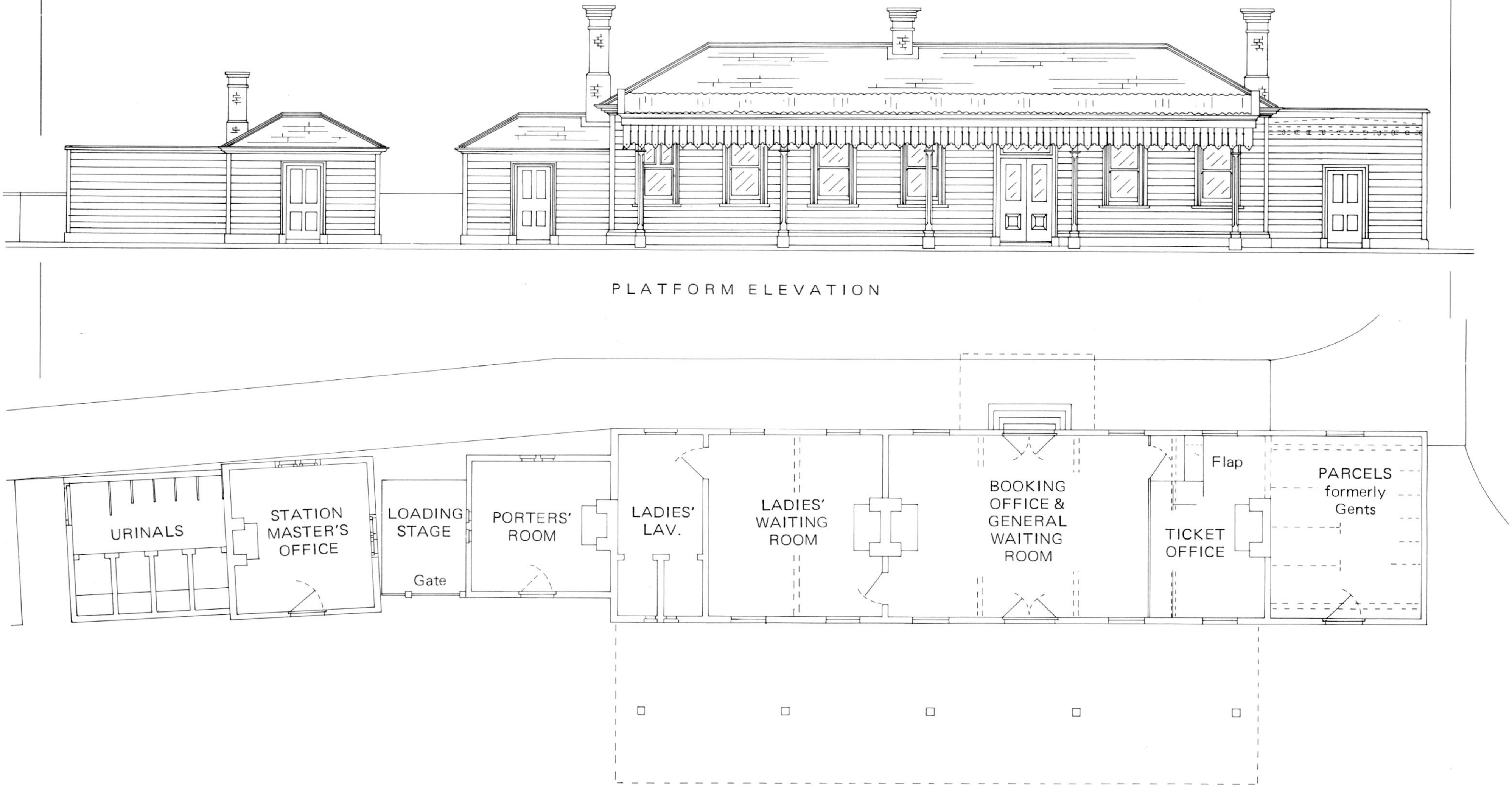

PLATFORM ELEVATION

APPROACH ROAD ELEVATION

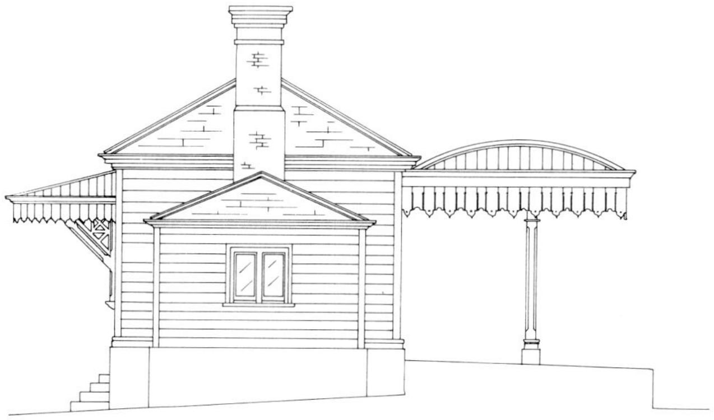

EAST ELEVATION

Scale: 2mm to 1 foot

SER WAITING SHELTER AT HYTHE

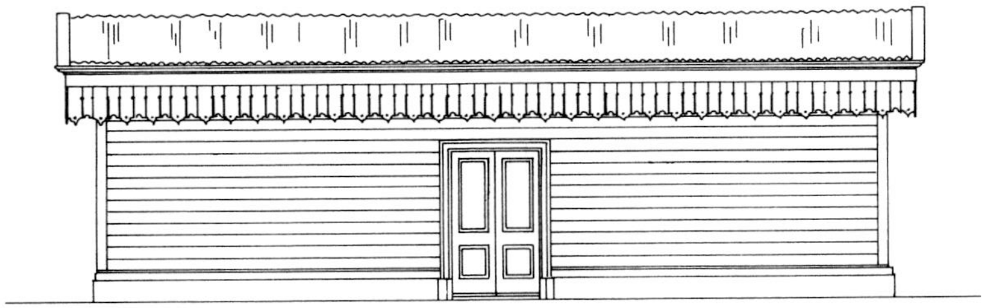

PLATFORM ELEVATION

PLAN

APPROACH ROAD ELEVATION

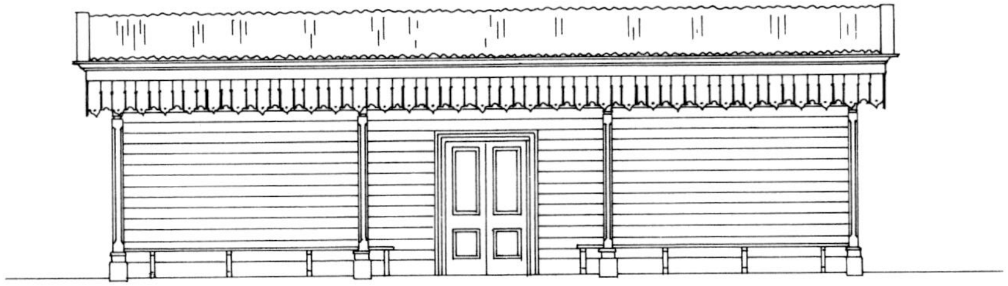

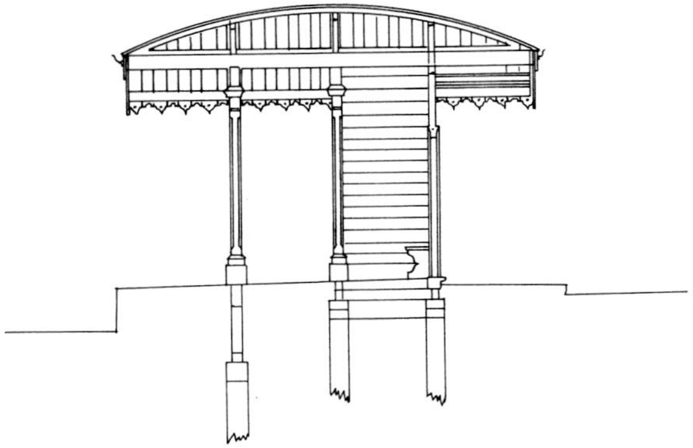

TRANSVERSE SECTION

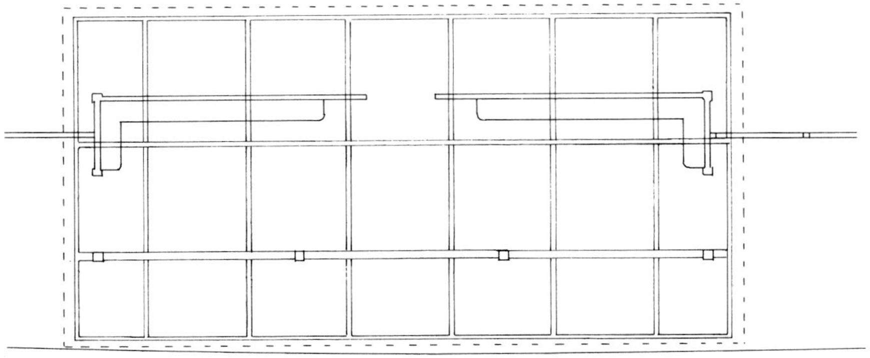

Scale: 2mm to 1 foot

SANDGATE

SER PROPOSED NEW STATION AT SANDGATE 1874

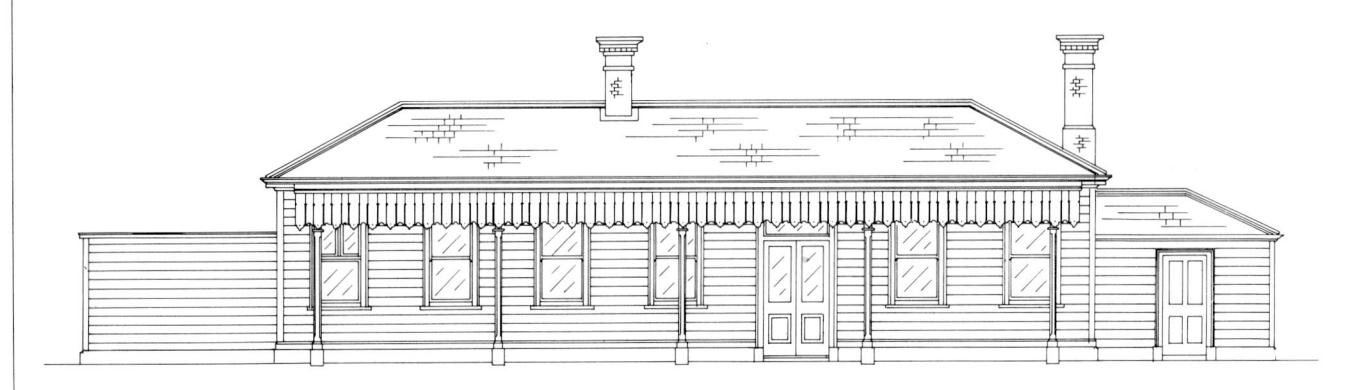

NORTH (PLATFORM) ELEVATION

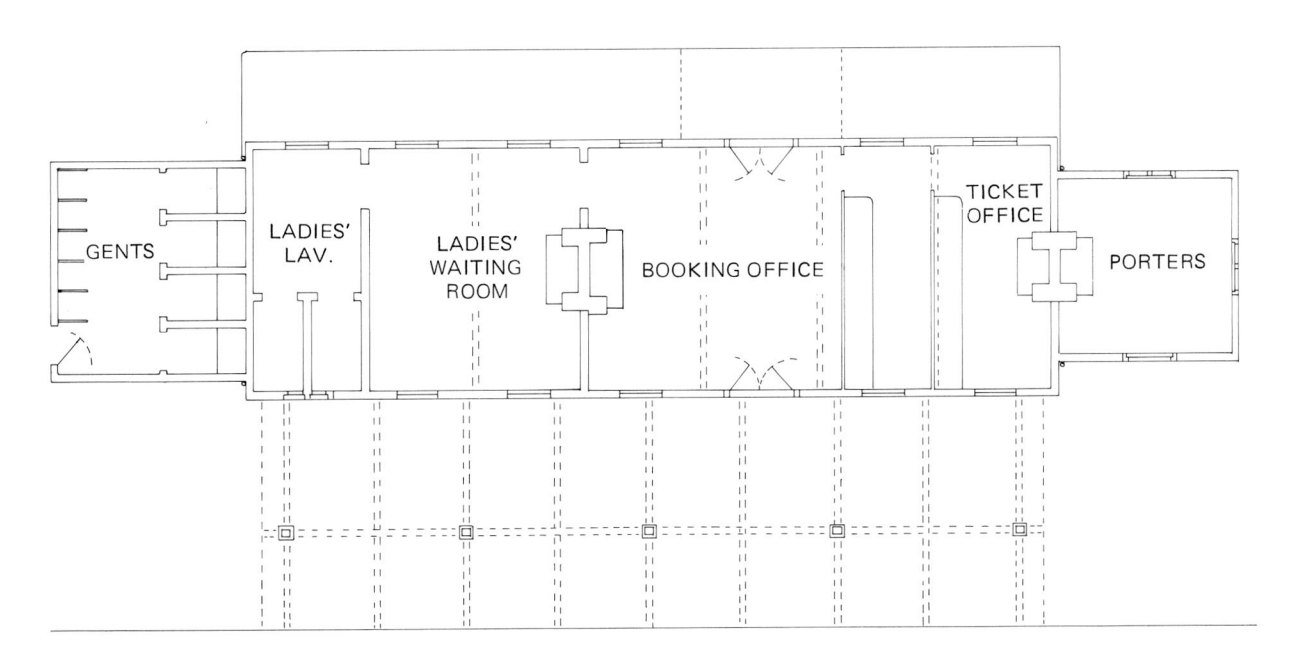

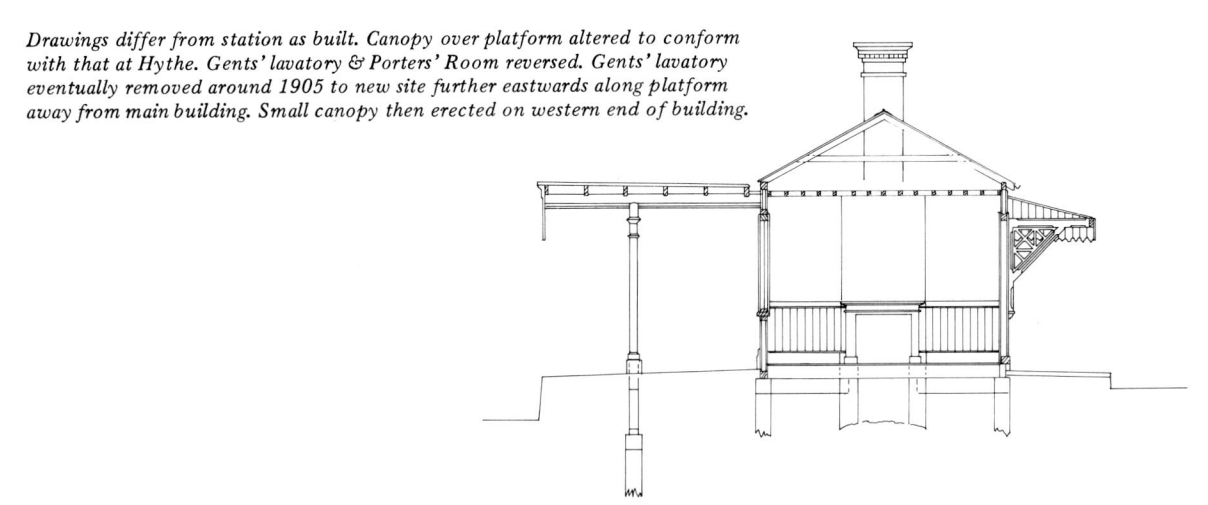

GENTS | LADIES' LAV. | LADIES' WAITING ROOM | BOOKING OFFICE | TICKET OFFICE | PORTERS

Drawings differ from station as built. Canopy over platform altered to conform with that at Hythe. Gents' lavatory & Porters' Room reversed. Gents' lavatory eventually removed around 1905 to new site further eastwards along platform away from main building. Small canopy then erected on western end of building.

TRANSVERSE SECTION THROUGH BOOKING OFFICE

SOUTH (APPROACH ROAD) ELEVATION

EAST ELEVATION & SECTION

WEST ELEVATION

Scale: 2mm to 1 foot

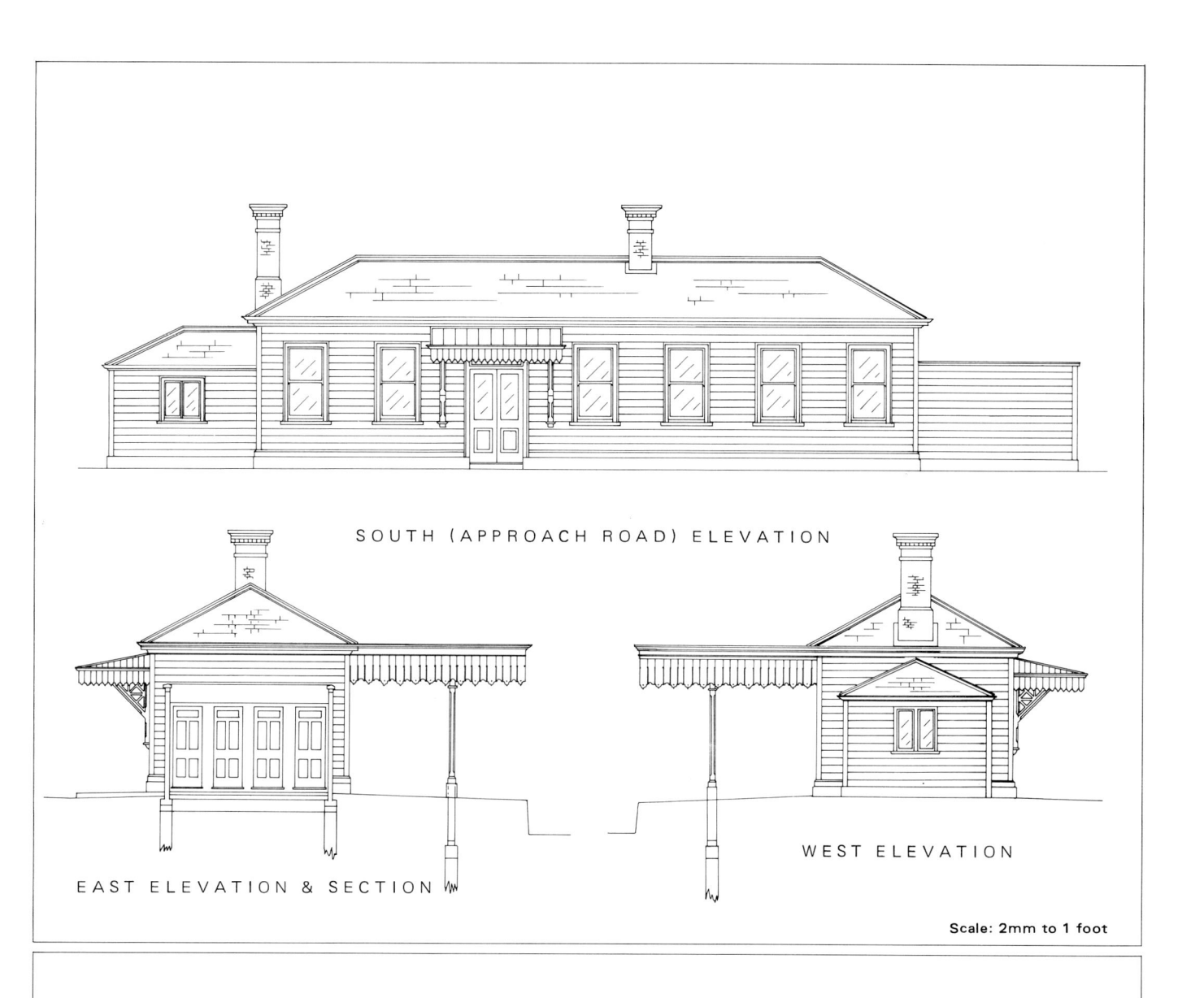

SANDGATE SIGNAL BOX

SANDGATE STATION SIGNALS.

The signal box is shown before front staging was provided.
Almost identical boxes provided at Hythe and Sandling Junction (1 & 2)

Scale: 2mm to 1 foot

SANDLING JUNCTION SIGNALLING PLAN

SANDLING JUNCTION: No. 1 CABIN
1. Down Branch Distant
2. Down Branch Stop Slot
3. Down Main Facing & Catch Points
4. Down Main Distant
5. Down Main Stop
6. Main Crossover Points
7. Down Main Starting
8. Up Branch Starting Slot
9. Up Branch Stop Releaser & Slot
10. Up Branch Trailing Points
11. Spare
12. Up Main Starting
13. Up Main Stop
14. Up Main Distant

SANDLING JUNCTION: No 2 CABIN
1. Down Stop Slot
2. Down Junction Releaser
3. Down Starting
4. Spare
5. Spare
6. Disc Shunt from Down to Up Line
7. Main Up Crossing Points
8. Disc Shunt from Up to Down Line
9. Disc Shunt from Down Siding
10. Down Siding Points
11. Disc Shunt from Down Line to Siding
12. Disc Shunt from Up Siding to Down Main
13. Points from Up Siding to Down Main
14. Disc Shunt from Main to Up Siding
15. Spare
16. Disc Shunt from Up Main to Down Main
17. Main Crossover Points
18. Disc Shunt from Down Main to Up Main
19. Up Starting Slot
20. Up Platform Stop Slot
21. Up Platform Distant
22. Spare
23. Up Stop to Down Platform
24. Up Distant to Down Platform
25. Spare
26. Spare

Note: Points and signals controlled by No. 2 Cabin are shown in italics on the diagram.

GRADIENT PROFILE

SANDLING JUNCTION 65m 35ch — 1 in 264 — Level — Hayne Tunnel — 1 in 56 — 1 in 54 — Level — HYTHE 66m 79ch — 1 in 59 — catchpoints — Level — SANDGATE 68m 33ch

Radius in chains

13 — 72 — 70 — 33 — 85 — 30

HYTHE SIGNALLING PLAN – *details unavailable*

SANDGATE SIGNALLING PLAN

SANDGATE SIGNAL BOX
A1. Ground Frame Release Lock
1. Up Starting
2. Up Starting from Down Platform
3. Crossover Points No. 1
4. Up Advanced Starting
5. Down Siding Points
6. Disc Shunt from Middle Road to Up Main
7. Middle Road Points & Scotch Block
8. Disc Shunt from Up Main to Middle Road & Up Platform Line
9. Up Siding Points & Scotch Block
10. Facing Point Lock on No. 3 Points Down Line
11. Facing Point Lock on No. 5 & 13 Points Down Line
12. Disc Shunt from Down to Up Main via Crossover Points No. 2
13. Crossover Points No. 2
14. Disc Shunt from Up to Down Main via Crossover Points No. 2
15. Down Platform Stop
16. Down Stop to Middle Road & Up Platform
17. Down Distant
* Selected by No. 7 points

SANDGATE GROUND FRAME
1. Point Releaser
2. Disc Shunt from Middle Road to Shed
3. Scotch Block on Middle Road
4. Down Siding Points
5. Crossover Points from Down Main to Middle Road
6. Middle Road Points
7. Disc Shunt from Up Main to Shed
8. Spare
9. Points from Up Main to Shed
10. Disc Shunt from Shed to Middle Road
11. Spare
12. Spare
13. Spare

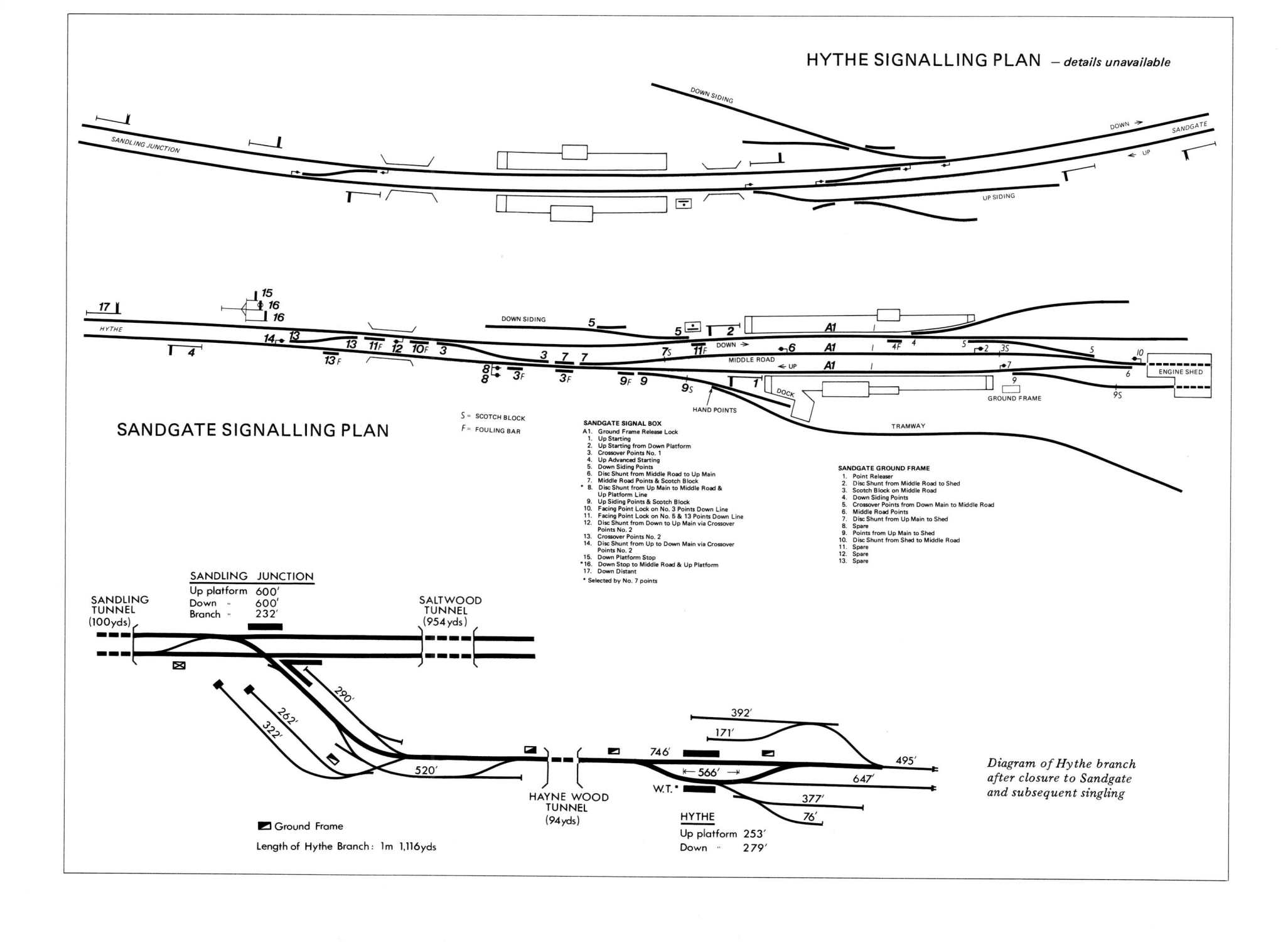

S = SCOTCH BLOCK
F = FOULING BAR

SANDLING JUNCTION
Up platform 600'
Down " 600'
Branch " 232'

HYTHE
Up platform 253'
Down " 279'

■ Ground Frame

Length of Hythe Branch: 1m 1,116yds

Diagram of Hythe branch after closure to Sandgate and subsequent singling

SANDLING TUNNEL (100yds)
SALTWOOD TUNNEL (954yds)
HAYNE WOOD TUNNEL (94yds)

James Pilcher and two conductresses wait hopefully for passengers at the Hythe terminus.

THE
HYTHE & SANDGATE TRAMWAY

A 1904 view of Sandgate High Street looking east.

Alan Taylor Collection

Introduction

The history of the Hythe & Sandgate Tramway is inextricably wound up with that of the South Eastern Railway's branch line to the district. Moreover, it had an effect on that other unique curiosity, the Sandgate Hill Lift. It is perhaps ironic that whereas Sandgate could once boast a railway, a tramway and a water-balance funicular, it ended up losing not one or two, but all three modes of transport.

The transport history of this area of Kent has been largely neglected and, generally speaking, falls into two main categories. Historical coverage has either been accurate, yet frustratingly scant, or that which has been detailed has often been grossly incorrect. When I began researching the tramway I naturally turned to magazine articles, books and newspaper features in an effort to gain an understanding of the task ahead. To my despair, however, almost everything written about it either carelessly repeated the mistakes of previous writers or precious little research had been carried out when asserting even basic facts. I therefore had no alternative but to abandon everything and begin afresh. Accordingly, I have relied on documented evidence, preferring to search out for myself the available official information dealing with its construction and operation, as well as contemporary newspaper files. The aim was to produce the most detailed and hopefully the most truthful account ever formulated. No effort was spared in the attempt for reliable and accurate facts. It is of course incomplete, but this is unavoidable since many vital records have been discarded over the years with, in most instances, only fragments remaining.

Apart from dealing with the necessary but cold figures and statistics, I have tried to inject a little life into the subject by including not only recollections of it from local people but also some of the more outstanding events which were reported in the newspapers. Unfortunately the short span of human life denies us much. For example, I would have cherished the opportunity to have met my great-grandfathers, one of whom lived a stone's throw from the Sandgate terminus of the tramway and who was employed as a brakesman on the Sandgate Hill Lift. Another, George Millgate, was foreman printer with J. English & Co. who produced many of the popular guides that found their way into the hands of tourists eager to explore the area. He loved Folkestone and spent many hours just walking or drawing and gathering specimens for his natural history collection.

When I was a small boy in the 1950s, before the mind-numbing television arrived, I would often sit with my gran, Lilian Millgate, pressing her to tell me about the 'olden days'. Sitting in the warm kitchen, while she darned some frayed garment, she'd pause from her sewing to recall her childhood in the 1890s. There were long walks with her sister Flo and their father through the wonderful Folkestone Warren, along the orchid and cowslip strewn ridges of the North Downs as well as sedate strolls along the Leas and down into Sandgate. Those hours made a great impression upon me and still endure vividly in my mind, especially the *essence* of that era when the bright prospects and hope had yet to be dashed by the awful consequences of August 1914.

The tragedy of the Hythe & Sandgate Tramway was its failure to establish itself as part of the regular public transport system. Nevertheless, had it been electrified and extended, its fate would surely have been sealed soon after the Second World War when Britain's once-prosperous tramways were foolishly ripped up and destroyed by myopic town planners. While our continental neighbours enjoy fast, frequent, smooth and quiet trams, we are now left waiting for buses that never turn up, are uncomfortable, slow, expensive, (even lacking opening windows) frequently end up in traffic jams and are little more than pawns in the chessgame of political overlords.

However, let us not dwell upon our miserable state today. Instead, I urge you to rummage for some friendly old pennies, yes, real money with Britannia on the reverse side, cast your mind back a hundred or so years and prepare yourself for a 'Four Mile Ride by the Sea'!

The lonely, windswept prospect along Princes Parade with a tram bound for Hythe. *Courtesy Marjory Rule*

The tramway along Sandgate Esplanade with the passing loop visible in the foreground. Across the road is the approximate site for the proposed 'Sandgate & Shorncliffe Camp Lift'.
Alan Taylor Collection

The new tramway laid down along Sandgate Esplanade, clearly showing the grooved rails and granite setts. *Alan Taylor Collection*

CHAPTER ONE

A Bright Augury

FOLLOWING the passing of the 1870 Tramways Act numerous towns throughout the British Isles laid down a tramway system during the ensuing decades. Whereas most Kent towns were at this time served by the railway, urban transport was relatively poor and although the well-to-do invariably owned a pony and trap, the rest of the populace had to contend with horse-drawn omnibuses which were expensive, infrequent, slow and in almost all cases, unable to match the demand.

In 1874, when the Sandgate branch had just opened, there were three separate concerns running omnibuses between Hythe, Sandgate and Folkestone. Henry Ovenden, the proprietor of the Swan Hotel at Hythe, operated daily buses to Folkestone at 9.45 a.m., 1.00 p.m. and 3.45 p.m., as well as arranging for an omnibus to meet every train. Up until the time when Hythe station opened, this bus operated to Westenhanger station. John Scott and Henry Laker also operated buses to and from Folkestone with each of them making three trips. By 1892, when the tramway had just opened, both Scott and Laker had increased their journeys to six a day.

Conveyance of goods in 1871 was handled by Henry Usher who drove the SER's horse-drawn van with a weekdays-only trip from Hythe High Street to Westenhanger station at 7.00 a.m. Messrs Mackett's and Messrs Capon's vans also passed through the district on alternating days between Romney Marsh and Dover.

It should be remembered that the siting of the railway was, for all intents and purposes, to enable the South Eastern Railway to open up a more expeditious route to the continent and, in spite of the many fine speeches delivered at its commencement and opening, it was not specifically built to serve Hythe or Sandgate. With the railway missing the centre of the towns it was hardly surprising that the discontent felt by both public and tradesmen should result in a clamour for better local communication. If the aspirations of the SER of getting the Sandgate to Folkestone extension had been fulfilled, these problems would have largely been solved, giving Hythe and Sandgate residents a quick and direct train service into Folkestone and would have dispensed with the absurdly circuitous route involving a change of trains at Westenhanger. Even with the opening of Sandling Junction station in 1888 the situation was no more convenient and passenger traffic between Hythe and Folkestone could hardly be relied upon as a mainstay of the Sandgate branch's income. It was therefore almost inevitable that at some point a tramway should have been proposed which would largely solve all these problems.

The first scheme to be suggested arrived just five years after the Sandgate branch had opened when, in 1879, a bill was presented for consultation. No less than 27 tramways were detailed in the bill, but this was merely for the approval and sanction of each section. Although it was not specifically mentioned, a gauge of 3ft. 6ins. was intimated, whilst the line was to commence at Albion Terrace in Folkestone, run along the entire length of the Upper Sandgate Road to the top of Sandgate Hill where it would descend into Sandgate, along the Broadway, through Seabrook to Hythe via the main road, terminating in the High Street at the Cinque Port Arms. Opposition to the scheme mainly came from tradesmen who feared a loss of business to Folkestone, as well as private residents along the route who were anxious that a drop in property values would ensue.

By 1880 the route had been altered and shortened so that it would overcome most of the objections. The *Folkestone Chronicle* announced that the tramway would now begin at the foot of Sandgate Hill, run through to Seabrook where, instead of venturing along the main road directly to Hythe, it would divert along the sea front to enter Hythe from the south. The *Chronicle* then pinned its colours firmly to the mast in summing up:

> 'The good news of the coming tramway is a distinct step forward in the march of progress, and we hope that it is a bright augury of that prosperous future for Hythe which must come if its people are wise in their own interest, and in their day and generation.'

On 21st July the SER's Seabrook Hotel was opened and in the autumn the board received a letter from the town clerk of Hythe who suggested that a tramway should be constructed between the town and the station for the conveyance of merchandise. The SER favoured a joint effort between themselves and the corporation for building this tramway, however the rather parsimonious attitude adopted by the council forestalled commencement at that time. In fact the only decision achieved at their meeting was that the roads be made wide enough to accommodate any future tramway.

The first tramway to be laid in the district was for the transportation of materials used in the construction of the sea wall. It ran, as far as can be ascertained, solely along the length of the works and did not at this time, as has frequently been erroneously related, cross the canal or venture up to Hythe station. Sir John Goode engineered the sea wall and parade project, whilst the building contractor was a Mr. James. Once the sea wall had been completed it is clear that James's tramway was left *in situ* for at a board meeting in April 1881 Watkin suggested his tramway should be purchased, extended and used for carrying passengers between the station, town and hotel. To have operated the tramway from the town to the station would have necessitated traction other than horsepower, for the gradients were far too steep. Perhaps it was because these difficulties could not be readily overcome at the time that the idea failed to take off.

The keenest proponents of a tramway were to be found in Sandgate where there existed a somewhat churlish attitude towards the railway. At a meeting of the local board in 1883 it was pointed out that whilst in 1879 provisional order to make a tramway was given, and granted, in the 1880 session, this had in consequence become extinct. Notice would therefore be given in November for the next session with an application of two years for construction. The opportunity was taken to discuss different routes as well as the thorny problem of entering Folkestone. Everyone knew that the easiest and most level route would have been to run the tramway along the Lower Sandgate Road at the foot of the Leas cliff but no one was in any doubt over the objections they would face if such proposals dared be put forward. Having been precluded from entering upon the Leas estate the only other direct alternative was up the long steep hill. Understandably, some anxiety was felt concerning

ROUTE OF HYTHE AND SANDGATE TRAMWAY

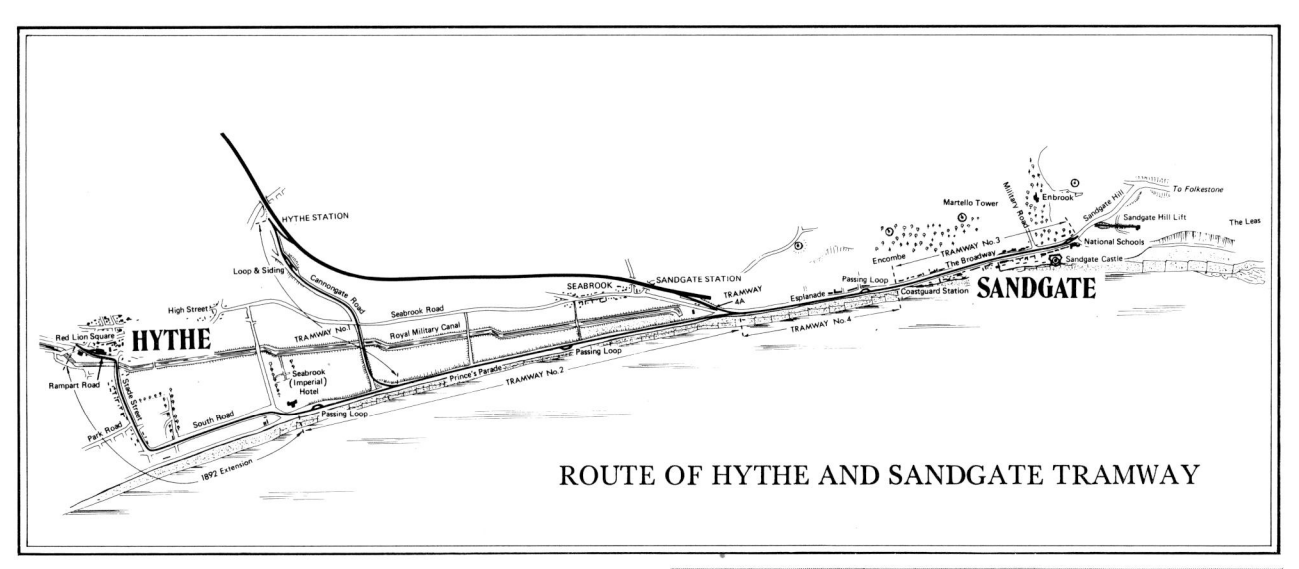

the safety of passengers in tram cars descending the hill, whilst the problems of ascending it, certainly with horse power, were insurmountable. Another facet which worried them was the width of the roads, the narrowest part of the Broadway being just under 20 ft., in front of the soldiers' convalescent home. However, as it was pointed out, a tramcar would only pass at intervals of about one an hour so it was agreed that this should be of no hindrance to other road users. One of the members, Mr. Franklin, wanted the tramway to be laid to Shorncliffe station which, having just been re-sited and rebuilt on a grand scale was, as he claimed, 'more used than Sandgate station'.

In the autumn of 1883 a nominally independent company, the 'Folkestone, Sandgate & Hythe Tramway Co. Ltd.' was formed and promoted by Benjamin Horton, John Vallier Bean, George Cobay and Henry Mackeson – all influential businessmen and figures on the local councils. Needless to say, behind the scenes loomed the South Eastern Railway, maintaining a watchful eye on the developments. The SER's chief engineer, Francis Brady, presented the company with an estimate of £30,000 for constructing a total of nine street tramways throughout Folkestone, Sandgate and Hythe. The rails would be standard grooved tramlines, flush with the road, whilst tolls not exceeding 2d a mile were stipulated. The scheme brought stiff opposition from not only the usual quarters but also another old enemy of the South Eastern Railway – the London, Chatham & Dover Railway. Quite why the LC & DR should be getting so hot under the collar over such a minor upstart as the little tramway is a thoroughly reasonable question and warrants an explanation. At this particular time the LC & DR were involved in one of the most vituperative of their spasmodic battles with the SER, perpetually haunting Watkin much like the ghost of Jacob Marley. The backdrop to this current squabble was none other than the establishment of a direct railway line between Canterbury and Folkestone, with the LC & DR and their Alkham Valley scheme in one corner, and the SER with their Elham Valley scheme in the other. The LC & DR's line was planned to run through part of the west end of Folkestone, terminating near Shorncliffe station, and the FS & HT Co.'s tramlines along Earls Avenue and Shorncliffe Road would interfere with the Alkham Valley Line currently being promoted in parliament. The score was eventually settled

Young James Alfred Pilcher in his Sunday best showing an early interest in horses, posing beside the bus at Hythe around 1885.
Courtesy Mr. & Mrs. Pilcher

in 1884 when the SER won a most dubious victory over the LC & DR only by agreeing to build a main line through the rural Elham Valley.

The FS & HT Act (1884) was passed on 28th July, permitting the SER to work, use, manage and maintain the tramway but as they were empowered to work it with only horses it is hardly surprising that nothing happened.

Exactly a year later to the day another estimate was ordered to be obtained for constructing a tramway between Seabrook and the western end of Sandgate which was referred to as tramway No. 4. A spur, known as 4a, was shown to lead from the seafront up to Sandgate station where a physical connection was made with a siding in the 'up' side goods yard.

Two months later Watkin told the board that he 'considered it in the interest of the company that a tram road should be constructed from Hythe station, over the Royal Military Canal, to connect with the new road which passes the Seabrook Hotel'. Subsequently Brady was instructed to carry out the work, as usual, 'without delay'. In November the *Folkestone Express* reported:

> 'A new bridge is being erected over the canal at some considerable distance to the east of the Bell bridge in order that a tramway might be made to run from the quarry with material for the repair of the sea wall.'

The tramway planned for the locality was divided into four sections although naturally once constructed it would operate as a whole. Tramway No. 1, costing £1,438 5s 0d, would commence in the approach road on the 'up' side of Hythe station. From here a left-hand fork was shown running directly into the goods yard where the tram lines should join the railway, whilst the right-hand fork ran down the left-hand side of Cannongate Road. A few hundred yards beyond, there was a loop and a short siding which may have been planned to act as a catch point in case of runaway vehicles. It has also been suggested that stone was quarried here. Continuing down Cannongate Road the line crossed over the main Hythe–Sandgate road before running across the canal and terminating in Princes Parade. Tramway No. 2 was a section which ran from the Seabrook Hotel, along the length of the parade as far as the junction with the Hythe–Sandgate road, near Sandgate station. The cost of this line was £1,851 3s 9d. From here began the section known as tramway No. 4, authorised under a previous act and confusingly appearing between Nos. 2 and 3! Tramway No. 3 commenced at the western end of Sandgate and ran eastwards along the Broadway, terminating at the foot of Sandgate Hill, adjacent to the National Schools. This section was costed at £1,494 12s 6d.

The Act for the 1886 session sought powers to build tramways 1, 2 and 3, including passing places as well as a provision for it to be worked by animal or mechanical traction, which included electricity.

Work soon began on laying tramways 1 and 2, from Hythe station down to and along the seafront. Francis Brady supervised its construction, spending much of his spare time on the project as he was ordinarily heavily committed with the building of the Elham Valley Line. To facilitate the laying of the tramway the SER made good use of the redundant plant from the Sudanese railway stored at Lydd which had been shipped back following General Gordon's disastrous campaign. Although it had originally been intended to use these materials on the proposed Hythe & New Romney railway, there was no reason why they shouldn't be put to good use on the tramway and repairing the sea wall as reported by the *Folkestone Express* of 9th January 1886

> 'The engine has commenced to run on the lines between the station (Hythe) and the sea wall. It is intended for the trucks to convey the stone from the quarries used to repair the breach in the sea wall. The engine is of small make. It was originally made for the Suakim–Berber Railway, and it bears those names on its plates.'

The locomotive, with its brightly polished dome, is said to have been stored in a shed at Hythe station where, at the beginning of the day, it manoeuvred the headshunt into the station approach before proceeding down Cannongate Road with a train loaded with stone. On the return journey the sight, from eye-witnesses of the day, was spectacular to behold as the gradient of the line up Cannongate Road varies from 1 in 28 to 1 in 16. With such gradients it isn't surprising the little engine puffed so violently that it alarmed residents and frightened many a horse, especially when it suddenly appeared across the Hythe–Sandgate road. To protect this crossing it is said that a signal post was erected 'close to the pillar box'.

Having completed sections 1 and 2, the SER now prepared itself to build the remainder through the Sandgate before applying to the Board of Trade for permission to open. Electric traction must have been their intention, in fact their only option, for horse power was completely out of the question as regards the line up to the station and they felt a steam locomotive could not haul a loaded train up such a severe gradient without a rack and pinion. Extensions 3 and 4 would involve running along public roads for which flushed, grooved rails would be necessary, as up until now ordinary raised railway lines had been used – this didn't matter as the tramway ran on private roads and land.

In the spring of 1888 tenders were received from suppliers across the country, notable examples coming from Messrs Dick Kerr & Co., The Ebbw Vale Steel & Iron Co., Darlington Steel & Iron Co. and Cammell & Co. It was considered the only reasonable one was Dick Kerr's, probably because it was the cheapest. Subsequently an order was placed comprising 130 tons of rails in 24 ft. lengths weighing 63 lbs per yard, a corresponding quantity of dog-eared spikes, fish plates – including nuts and bolts, and 4 sets of steel points and crossings. All was to be delivered within one month of order being placed. The estimate showed a breakdown of materials thus:

110 tons tram rails	£5 12s 6d per ton
Fish Plates	£5 12s 6d per ton
Bolts and nuts	12s 6d per cwt
Tiebars	9s 6d per cwt
Spikes	10s 6d per cwt
Points and Crossings	£10 10s 0d

All to be delivered to Angersteins Wharf

It was planned to pave between, and either side, of the tram lines with sets of local Kentish ragstone but sufficient quantities were hard to come by. It was therefore necessary to find a suitable alternative so tenders were sent out across the country. Messrs. J. S. Gabriel & Co. submitted a price of 32s 9d per ton for 3″ × 4″ Leicestershire granite sets including delivery by water to Folkestone harbour or 36/- per ton if sent by rail to Folkestone. This was turned down in favour of a cheaper price of 27s 6d per ton from Manuelle & Co. of Leadenhall St. which included delivery in Midland Railway trucks to London Bridge station.

In the meantime the *Folkestone Chronicle* reported on 10th March 1888:

> 'At a special meeting of the Sandgate Local Board, held on Saturday, present Major Fynmore, Messrs. Franklin, Kennett, Jenner, and Keeler, the plans of the construction of the lines, &c., in connection with the tramway, were approved of. Mr. Wilks attended on behalf of the company, and in reply to questions, said that tenders would be asked for immediately, and the work as soon as possible commenced.'

They were obliged to seek an outside contractor as Francis Brady, who had engineered sections 1 and 2, was unavailable, being hard-pressed by Watkin to oversee the long-overdue completion of the second stage of the Elham Valley Line, now being pushed with all due speed towards Canterbury. Therefore the services of Mr. Jeal were called upon yet again as he had carried out much of the SER's work in the area. His estimate for £1,660 was favourably received, which included building tramways 4 and 3 from Seabrook as far as the bottom of Sandgate Hill, as well as the short spur, 4a, up to Sandgate station. The late John Dunk recalled walking to Hythe during that summer and witnessing Jeal's workmen breaking up the road surface at Seabrook where they were engaged in connecting the new line to Brady's tramway along Princes Parade. In September the *Folkestone Chronicle* reported:

> 'The tramway in course of construction between Sandgate and Hythe, by Mr. Jeal, has made rapid progress during the past week, the section leading up to the Sandgate Railway Station having been completed.'

Whilst sections 4 and 4a progressed, the workmen were stopped from entering into Sandgate and continuing the laying of the tramlines to Sandgate Hill. This was because Lord Radnor exercised his powers of veto contained in the 1886 Act. If this wasn't enough trouble to contend with, more was soon to follow.

Locally the building of the tramway appears to have met with a mixed reception and there was both confusion as to where it would run as well as pressure from all quarters to extend it to all sorts of places. For instance, Colonel Tongue of the Hythe School of Musketry wrote to the SER begging that they might consider extending the tramway to the newly-opened Sandling Junction station. As this would undoubtedly have had detrimental effects on the Sandgate branch revenue, the SER were unimpressed and refused to even consider the idea.

Anxious to open the tramway for public use, in order that a revenue could be earned, the SER applied to the Board of Trade for an inspection. Major-General Hutchinson, the Board's Inspector of Railways, travelled down to his boyhood home but, following a perusal, refused to grant permission until his objections were remedied. His criticisms were:

1. That paving outside the rails on no. 4 section is only 13″ instead of the regulatory 18″. The outer edge of pavings are straight instead of being serated, also there is a difference in the sizes of the setts.
2. That tramway No. 1 and greater part of No. 2, constructed by Brady, are built as an ordinary railway instead of rails being level with the road as required by the General Tramways Act 1870.
3. That company had no parliamentary authority to use steam haulage upon tramway No. 2

Having just overseen the completion and opening of the Elham Valley Line on July 1st 1889, Brady was urgently summoned to go straight to Sandgate to see what he could do to rectify the situation. He soon remedied Hutchinson's first objection but as regards the other two points he felt they could only be provided for by parliamentary authority, the bill for which was awaiting the Royal Assent. It is almost certain that modifications to enable the tramway to conform to the accepted standards of the General Tramways Act 1870 were never sanctioned. This is because Tramway No. 1 from the station to the seafront never carried passengers, so it had no need to comply, and Tramway No. 2 – along the private Princes Parade, is said to have remained an ordinary railway on the unmetalled sections by those who remember riding upon it.

Complying to the order that only horses would be used to haul the trams, nothing, it seemed, could now prevent a public opening, but upon the horizon the storm clouds were rapidly gathering as intimated in a local newspaper report:

> 'The Hythe and Sandgate Tramway is now laid down within the limits of the original contract. The Sandgate end requires a few finishing touches, but on the whole Mr. Jeal may be fairly commended for having done his work so expeditiously and well. We hear that the cars have been taken in hand by a London firm, and this section may very likely be opened for traffic in the course of the month. The Sandgate people are not satisfied, however, with a terminus at the Coastguard Station, and will do all in their power to promote the extension of the line to the eastern boundary of their town. At Hythe, too, it is said to be quite decided that the tramway shall be carried along the rear of Beaconsfield Terrace (much enhancing the value of the property) and down Stade Street, so as to give access to the School of Musketry and the High Street. But all this will be of little practical good unless terms can be made with Lord Radnor for a nearer approach to Folkestone. Report declares that his lordship will not consent unless the gauge of the line is reduced. Such a proviso would amount to a practical veto, and rather than accept it the Company would have to devise another route. There is some talk of pushing on to Littlestone and New Romney, nor would such a development be at all impracticable.'

Those locals who had their coppers ready for the first celebratory trip were about to be disappointed, for the next two years proved every bit as frustrating as Watkin feared. The forces on either side closed ranks for the next battle.

CHAPTER TWO

Days of Adversity

SENSING that the South Eastern Railway were ready to commence operating the tramway, whereby they would bolster their case for extending through Sandgate, Radnor's agents fired the first salvo. On 26th September 1889 the FS & HT Co. received a letter from Messrs Norman, Brown & Norman, stating that the tramway company was forbidden to lay down a tramway through Sandgate of a greater gauge than 3′6″ as it would restrict other traffic through the narrow street. They continued: 'It is now understood the company will have power to operate tramway by steam instead of horse or other less objectionable power which adds important considerations concerning original agreement.' Three stipulations were then made:

1. Removal of rails through Sandgate if required by Lord Radnor.
2. Prohibition of steam on public roads through or within Sandgate district.
3. Provision stringently against any possibility of extension along Lower Sandgate Road.

The tramway company struck back with its three main intentions. Firstly, to complete the authorised extension to the foot of Sandgate Hill. Secondly, to complete an extension westwards to the shooting ranges at Pennypot and thirdly, apply for an extension through to Folkestone via Sandgate Hill. This provoked a speedy response from Radnor's solicitors:

> 'Announcing your intention of your company to go for parliamentary authority to extend this objectionable tramway into Folkestone – we sincerely hope you will abandon proposals – how will this influence proposed concession as to gauge of tramway through Sandgate?'

With Radnor adamant in his refusal to allow a wider gauge through Sandgate, Watkin decided he should visit Sandgate, which he did in the following January, where he walked over the route to the bottom of Sandgate Hill. Whilst he was there it is likely that he peered into yet another large hole in the sea wall, made by a storm in the previous week. The local paper reported:

> 'THE TRAMWAY – The Hythe & Sandgate tramway is again in use, not, however, for passenger traffic, but for the conveyance of truck loads of earth, which are brought down to the gap in the Sandgate sea wall in SER ballast trucks, the locomotive used being one of the little Suakim-Berber engines. By this means the dimensions of the hole are being rapidly reduced. A wooden fence is being erected by the side of the tramway, separating it and the sea wall road from the adjoining fields.'

By February it was reported that Folkestone Town Council had approved of the tramway extension through to the centre of their town as they were well aware of the benefits such communication would bring. However, the SER were still very mindful of the difficulties presented by the steep ascent into Folkestone as well as Radnor's intimations that he would oppose the scheme on the grounds of objections from tenants along the route. This caused the SER to hesitate and postpone the presentation of the next bill before parliament. It was then revealed that Radnor had agreed to the extension of the tramway as far as the bottom of Sandgate Hill and here was the nub of the confusion and furore that ensued. On one hand the SER believed they now had permission to proceed with the standard gauge tramway through the Broadway, whilst on the other, Radnor expected that the line would be extended on the smaller, 3′6″ gauge.

In March, Brady gave an estimate of £1,300 to complete tramway No. 3 through Sandgate and recommended the FS & HT Co. to now proceed with the work. Mr. J. Jeal was once again engaged and on 10th May 1890 it was reported:

> 'Mr. Jeal has had a large staff of workmen at work on the extension of the Hythe and Sandgate Tramway line to the East-end of Sandgate, with which he is making rapid progress. Whether the line will really be opened for traffic during the coming season is still, we suppose, an open question.'

This report, along with the fact that the gauge was 4′8½″, was conveyed to Lord Radnor who, it appears, immediately gave instructions through his solicitors that the work should cease. This enraged Watkin who, on 15th May, gave notice to the SER board that in the event of this matter not being amicably settled before the next board meeting, he should move that the tramway be taken up.

This odd state of affairs continued and the plot thickened as reported in a column entitled 'Local Talk', published in the *Folkestone Chronicle*.

> 'The tramway question has entered upon a new phase in respect to reaching Folkestone. The laying of the line through Sandgate was peremptorily stopped the other day and it was reported that this was in consequence of the apparent difficulties in getting the route completed to Folkestone. But the work has suddenly been resumed and now it is confidently asserted in Sandgate official circles that the line to Folkestone by the Lower Road shall be carried out without delay. That the traffic between the three towns is worth cultivating is clear from the fact that the proprietors of the expensive omnibus service find it expedient to commence running hourly from Hythe and Folkestone on the 1st June. The tramway service, however, is to be brought into requisition in connection with cheap SER trains from Sandgate to London, the proceeds of which will not come within the scope of the agreement between the rival Railway Companies. Apart from this the local patronage of visitors during the season between Folkestone and Hythe will be amply remunerative and prove a convenient mode of becoming acquainted with the various attractions of the united Borough. The fact that Lord Radnor recognises the proper route and consents to the Lower Road being used for the purpose, will give an impetus to the scheme which it could not otherwise command and in all probability, the tramway car will soon become a familiar sight running along the sea front between the Seabrook Hotel and the Pavilion*.'

* *The Royal Pavilion Hotel at Folkestone harbour*

This remarkable report contains much that was purely fanciful, for example no documented evidence has been found to prove that the SER intended to run the tramway along the Lower Sandgate Road, much as it may have liked to have done. It is true that popular belief at the time lampooned Watkin for secretly trying to reach the harbour by fair means or foul and that one dark night workmen would creep into Sandgate to clandestinely lay the rails. That the SER would do almost anything to avoid the agreement with the LC & DR over the pooling of the continental receipts admittedly sounds plausible enough but it could not have been a wholly serious proposition for the inconvenience of interchange from tram to train at Sandgate station which this would have entailed.

The item from the *Chronicle* was apparently cut out and forwarded to Lord Radnor at his home at Longford Castle in Wiltshire for on the 3rd June 1890 a telegram was sent to Mr. Wilks of the tramway company from Messrs. Bompas, Bischoff & Co., solicitors acting on Radnor's behalf. It read:

> 'HAVE JUST BEEN INFORMED TRAMWAY NO. 3 STILL BEING CONSTRUCTED. CONTRARY TO AGREEMENT 16-12-86. UNLESS YOU WRITE TONIGHT THAT WORK WILL BE STOPPED IMMEDIATELY WE SHALL APPLY FOR INJUNCTION.'

The following day a writ was served upon the SER by Radnor's solicitors and reluctantly a message was wired through to Sandgate asking Mr. Jeal to stop his workmen. Mr. Bischoff, Radnor's solicitor, then travelled down to Sandgate to meet representatives of the tramway company after which he wrote to the SER expressing his surprise when reading the tramway company minute book to find, in Watkin's handwriting, 'Negotiate – if object, pull up rails!' Perplexed and annoyed, the SER retaliated: 'I cannot understand why you should feel surprised at SE board recommending tramway company to pull up rails if Radnor persisted in refusal of extension to be same as other line – 4'8½". Could anything be more ridiculous than a break of gauge, necessitating a change of carriage, upon a tramway 2 miles in length?' Seeking to clarify their position and the situation the SER continued: 'By agreement of the 16th December 1886, the tramway covenanted that they would not at any time promote the extension tramway into or towards Folkestone and would not permit junction with other tramways without consent of Earl of Radnor. We understand you do not object to extension of tramway of same gauge as already constructed to National Schools, at the bottom of Sandgate Hill, provided SER enters similar agreement. If SER acquired tramway company they'd be bound by the same conditions.'

Bischoff then proposed the SER should indemnify Radnor against all costs in possible objections against extending the tramway to Folkestone. Understandably, the SER refused!

Having effectively put a stop to the progress of the tramway through Sandgate the inhabitants were left to wonder what might happen next with a broken-up road, stacked rails, and no trams. In the meantime the SER placed an order in September with G. F. Milnes & Co. of Cleveland St., Birkenhead for two tramway cars. Car No. 1 was built for £95 and comprised an overall roof with roll-down side curtains for wet weather. Car No. 2, costing £70 was built as an open car chiefly intended for use in the summer months. The accompanying section gives details.

> Specifications for SER Tramcars Nos. 1 & 2 for Hythe & Sandgate Tramway.
>
> <u>No.1 Tramcar.</u> The car has a roof supported with 2 end transverse partitions and 8 side pillars. 8 transverse seats to seat 40. Underframe of pitch pine, sole strengthened with 3/8ins steel edge plate. Length of underframe: 23ft. 1in. Width of underframe: 6ft. 3ins. Cast steel wheels, height 2ft. 6ins. Wheelbase 6ft. Centre of journal bearings 5ft. 11ins. coil spring between back of bearing and wheel. Steel coil side springs with rubber core. Axle boxes lubricated with oil. Spring cushions. One pair horse spring whippletrees, height of drawhead: 2ft. 5ins. Lever brake with cast iron brake blocks, 2 side stepboards, width overall 7ft. 3½ins. Body of pitch pine, 2 end partitions with 3 top lights in each. 2 oil lamps at opposite corners with ruby lenses. 8 side pillars bolted and clipped to underframe. Partitions and side pillars strengthened with iron brackets. Roof hoopsticks of ash, narrow pitch pine roof boards, 2 side destination boards fixed on top of roof. Sides of car fitted with waterproof drop curtains to fasten down with tabs. Width over side pillars 7ft. 0¾ins. There are 8 seats (transverse) to seat 5 each, viz, 2 each side of each partition, 4 centre seats with reversible backs. Weight of car complete 2T-6Cwts.-2lbs. Despatched to Sandgate 14th May 1891.
>
> <u>No. 2 Tramcar.</u> This is an open car without roof or sides. 8 transverse seats to seat 40. Underframe of pitch pine, sole strengthened with 3/8ins steel edge plate. Length of underframe: 22ft. 3ins, width: 6ft. 3ins. Cast steel wheels, height 2ft. 6ins. Wheelbase 6ft. Centre of journal bearings 5ft. 11ins. Coil spring between back of bearing and wheel. Steel coil side springs with rubber core. Axle boxes lubricated with oil. Spring cushions. 1 pair horse spring whippletrees. Height of drawhead 2ft. 5ins. Lever brake with cast iron brake blocks. 2 side stepboards, width overall 7ft. 3½ins. 2 candle lamps fixed on standards, one at each end of the car at opposite corners, with green and red glasses. 8 transverse seats with reversible backs to seat 5 passengers each. Timber pitch pine seats. Length of seat 6ft. 8ins. Car varnished and picked-out in brown. Weight of car complete 2T-2Cwts.-2lbs.

As the winter of 1890 approached, Bischoff wrote to the SER on 26th November reminding them that in their injunction, in the previous June, the tramway company was not permitted to allow No. 3 tramway through Sandgate to remain standard gauge after the 30th November. As no step had been taken to remove the rails it was now insisted that this order be carried out forthwith. The matter was brought before Watkin who instructed the secretary should write immediately to Lord Radnor himself. The letter read:

> 'My Lord,
> The Tramway Company and the South Eastern Railway were prohibited by injunction issued by your Lordship on the 13th June from using this piece of tramway or from allowing it after the 30th November to remain of a wider gauge than 3'6". Within the last few days your solicitors have written, warning they'd commit the directors for contempt of court if they don't remove section of tramway in question, or rather one line or part of it, so as to comply with order.
> Sir Edward does not see that it is necessary for your protection, and would subject company to expense and make them a laughing stock so he understands that all you desire is that tramway remains unused while at that gauge. Sir Edward cannot believe you would insist upon this if facts were brought to your notice and that even if his disobedience of court should subject him to imprisonment he will not be a party to removal of lines until he receives intimation from you that you insist it's done.'

The reply from Longford Castle read:

> 'Your letter, by hand, has just reached me. If you give me undertaking you'll not use it I'll not force injunction. I shall be in town tomorrow at the Carlton Club at 4.30 p.m. All this bother would have been avoided if the companies had agreed to the proposals I made originally for the gauge through Sandgate and if they had not laid it down in distinct contravention of the existing agreement with respect to its construction.'

One of the reasons why the SER wanted the tramway to be laid to the standard gauge was alluded to in a local newspaper:

Hustle and bustle in Sandgate High Street. The road on the left leads up Military Hill to Shorncliffe Camp. *Eamonn Rooney Collection*

'the company believe that a less gauge would be attended with an element of unsafety, as in the case of a gale, the car, if a large number was sitting on one side than on the other, might possibly turn over'.

Having averted the threat of legal action, the South Eastern were now in the ridiculous position of having a tramway laid to 4′ 8½″ upon which they could only run cars of 3′ 6″ gauge if they wanted to operate through Sandgate. Watkin was convinced that Radnor would never allow standard gauge trams through Sandgate and gave instruction to Mr. Jeal to begin tearing up one rail only on No. 3 section, adding that he very much regretted this but that it had been forced upon the SER by Lord Radnor.

There seemed little point in delaying the opening the rest of the tramway even though it would run from the Seabrook Hotel only as far as the outskirts of Sandgate. Accordingly the first public trams commenced on 18th May 1891 although it appears not many people realised it was running, as reported by 'Perambulator' in a local paper:

'One of the things not generally known is the fact that tramcars are running between Sandgate and Hythe. It hardly appears to matter how many conveyances are "put on" between the three towns of the parliamentary Borough – they are all crowded with passengers, and all well repay those who provide the accommodation. Whether it is that the lively scenes of witnessing the Boulogne boat's arrival at Folkestone palls upon the dissipation of the restless visitor and he requires a visit to the crypt of Hythe Church as a counterbalance, I know not. Perhaps, after all, it is the exhilaration of the ride along the seashore that is so enjoyable; and certainly this twopenny ride in an open-sided tramcar from Sandgate along the sea-wall between Seabrook and Hythe is an enjoyment of recuperative benefit to all who try it; while the view of Hythe and the surrounding landscape just now is well worth a visit to see.'

Whereas the sight of these two tramcars leisurely rumbling to and fro painted a picture of peace, behind the scenes the arguments raged on. The SER complained that the 1886 agreement between themselves and Radnor had restricted them only from approaching Folkestone and that hitherto hidden conditions and restrictions were now being forced upon them. Both the SER and the FS & HT Co. declined to enter into a revised agreement with Radnor and instructions were given for the extension tramway through Sandgate to be relaid at 3′ 6″. Besides this, the SER gave orders to prepare to lay down a third rail along the rest of the tramway to the Seabrook Hotel to accommodate 3′ 6″ tramcars, as well as arranging for the western extension to Hythe to be of the narrower gauge.

At the other end of the tramway there were no problems with obstinate landowners and tenders from Mr. Jeal for two new lines were approved by Francis Brady who recommended acceptance. They comprised:

A tramway from Princes Parade (Seabrook Hotel) along South Street, Stade Street and Rampart Road to terminate in Military Road or Red Lion Square. Materials were reckoned at 25/- per yard, labour at 13/6 a yard, making a total price of £3,865 8s 0d for the 2,008 yards extension. A further line to Pennypot of 1,540 yards, and costing £2,945 5s 0d, was deferred for further consideration.

As 1891 came to a close, the SER secretary met Radnor and his solicitors seeking consent for extending the tramway through Sandgate on the 3′ 6″ gauge as well as agreeing that

Car No. 1 proceeding along the esplanade on a sunny summer's day.

Alan Taylor Collection

his Lordship's veto as to any extension into Folkestone should be preserved. In the New Year a bill arrived from Bischoff for £54 3s 8d for costs against the FS & HT Co. At this time also, authority was given for 'a new tram carriage for the 3' 6" gauge section to be built at Ashford Works'.

In the spring General Hutchinson inspected the new extension to Red Lion Square, laid to standard, 4' 8½", gauge, and gave his approval for opening and to the agreement between the SER and the FS & HT Co. The *Hythe Reporter* commented:

> 'General Hutchinson from the Board of Trade made an official inspection of the newly-constructed line between the Seabrook hotel and the Red Lion on Tuesday last. There were present – the Mayor (Mr. B. Horton), Mr. G. Wilks, Mr. Jeal (the contractor), and the South Eastern Railway engineers. The tram was horsed by two animals belonging to Mr. J. P. Scott. The trial trip was accomplished successfully. Great interest was manifested in the proceedings both on the inspection day and on the previous day when the car ran along the line for the first time. It is not expected that the line will be opened for traffic before Whitsuntide. A shed for the cars and stabling for the horses ought to be provided at the terminus, and we should therefore suggest the old cattle market as the very spot, and this the Company ought to find no difficulty in procuring.'

Accordingly, the seal was affixed to the agreement on 25th May whereupon it was proposed to open the new section a week later, on 1st June 1892.

THE TRAMWAY.

To the Editor of the Hythe Reporter.

DEAR SIR,—Having taken, recently, several trips to Sandgate on the new tramway, I could not but notice the extreme danger to passengers from its close proximity to the lamp-posts on Sandgate Parade. If anyone happened to lean out of the car (more especially the open one) to look at any passing object a most serious accident might occur, should one's head come in contact with any one of the lamp-posts. I noticed the conductor had to be careful in dodging them when on the footboard collecting the fares. It is, of course, for the Company to consider whether it will be cheapest to run the risk of paying damages, or get leave to alter the position of the lamp-posts.

I enclose my card, but not for publication.

Yours faithfully,

A Visitor for last 22 years.

30th Sept, 1891.

Tramway terminus at Red Lion Square, Hythe, with covered tram standing outside shed. The bus and charabanc look equally well-loaded.
Tramway Museum Society

Car No. 1 at the Sandgate Hill terminus, outside the Royal Oak.
Tramway Museum Society

Time Tables.

SANDGATE AND HYTHE TRAMWAY.
WEEK-DAYS.
Leaves Hythe (Seabrook Hotel) 10 and 11 a.m., 12 noon, 2, 3, 4, 5, 6, 7, 8 p.m.

Leaves Sandgate (Bathing Establishment) 10.30, 11.30 and 12.30 am., 2.30, 3.30, 4.30, 5.30, 6.30, 7.30 and 8.30 p.m.

SUNDAYS.
Leaves Hythe 2, 3, 4, 5, 6 and 7 p.m.

Leaves Sandgaté 2.30, 3.30, 4.30, 5.30, 6.30 and 7.30 p.m.

Fare 2d. each way.

THE "VICTORIA" CHAR-A-BANC.
WEEK-DAYS.
·Leaves Wellington Terrace, Sandgate, for Folkestone, 10 a.m.

Leaves Town Hall, Folkestone, for Hythe.	Leaves Town Hall, Hythe, for Folkestone.
10.15 a.m. and 2.30 p.m.	12.20 and 4.20 p.m.

Leaves Town Hall, Folkestone, for Sandgate only, 5.45 p.m.

SUNDAYS.
Leaves Wellington Terrace, Sandgate, for Folkestone, 10 a.m.

Leaves Town Hall, Folkestone, for Hythe.	Leaves Town Hall, Hythe, for Folkestone.
10.45 a.m. and 2 45 p.m.	12.40 and 4.30 p.m.

Leaves Town Hall, Folkestone, for Sandgate only 5.50 p.m.

HYTHE, SANDGATE AND FOLKESTONE OMNIBUSES.
WEEK-DAYS.
Leave Swan and White Hart Hotels, Hythe, 9, 9.30, 10, and 11 a.m., 12 (noon), 1, 2, 3, 4, 4.30, 5, 6, 6.30, 7, 8 and 9.30 p.m., and on Wednesdays and Saturdays 10.15 p.m. to Sandgate only.

Leave Town Hall, Folkestone, 10, 10.30, and 11 a.m , 12 (noon), 1, 2, 3, 4, 5, 5.30, 6, 7, 7.30, 8, 9 and 10.30 p.m. On Wednesdays and Saturdays 10.40 p.m. from Sandgate only,

SUNDAYS.
Leave Hythe 10 a.m., 12 (noon), 2, 3, 5.30, 7, 8 and 9 p.m.

Leave Folkestone 11 a.m., 1, 3, 4, 6.30, 8, 9 and 10 p.m.

Passing through Sandgate and calling at the principal Hotels about Twenty Minutes after above times.

Booking and Parcel Office for Sandgate—Mr. A. Woollett.

The Sandgate Hill lift in operation. *G. L. Gundry Collection*

The events of the ensuing weeks remain something of a mystery and it can only be surmised that Radnor had a change of heart over his refusal to allow standard gauge trams through Sandgate. The precise reasons will likely never be known but it is worth recalling that at this time the Sandgate Hill Lift was under construction and, when completed, would be just a short walk from the intended terminus of the tramway. The Sandgate Hill Lift was a most curious and unique hybrid between a conventional water-balance lift and a normal tramway. The land over which it was to run was leased from Lord Radnor, who would also receive a royalty of $2\frac{1}{2}\%$ of the gross takings over and above £1,000 per annum. The Sandgate Hill Lift Company looked towards the tramway as a mainstay of income and may have been institutional in persuading Radnor that he'd only be spiting himself if he prevented the tramway from contributing to the lift's success.

When the letter from Radnor's solicitors arrived at SER headquarters, informing them that all objections towards the standard gauge trams through Sandgate had been withdrawn, there was probably a good deal of relief as well as surprise. It is apparent that No. 4 tramway, constructed by Brady and running between Sandgate station and the western extremity of Sandgate, was at the time being converted to 3′ 6″ for sanction was given for this portion to be restored to the full 4′ $8\frac{1}{2}″$ gauge. The end of this whole sorry affair came with the seal being affixed to a binding agreement dated 14th July 1892.

Over the next few weeks the work of completing the line was attended with all possible haste and on the morning of Friday, 30th July, a tram car ran to the bottom of the hill for the first time. Two days later, on Sunday 1st August, it was opened for public use with a half-hourly service and a tuppenny fare each way.

At last prospects looked bright for the FS & HT Co. and there was understandable relief when the yearly figures showed a profit on the first year's workings of £440 10s 10d, for which a dividend of 6% to shareholders was recommended.

The tramway came in useful for assisting the work on the Sandgate Hill Lift by transporting materials to the site. The wooden bodies of the lift cars, manufactured by Worthington Brothers of Hythe, are believed to have been carried over the

DAYS OF ADVERSITY

Tramcars Nos. 5 and 3 on Princes Parade.
Anne Bamford Collection

tramway but not on their wheels as has often been wrongly claimed, simply because the lift's gauge was 5′ 6″. Curiously enough, the FS & HT Co. had itself dallied with the idea of building a water-balance cliff lift between Sandgate and Shorncliffe Camp. It seems likely that the driving force behind the scheme, a parliamentary bill for which was presented in 1892, was Radnor's stubborn refusal to allow the tramway through Sandgate. Frustrated by this, there was only one direction left – northwards, straight up the hillside. The tramway company's Ernest Wilks surveyed the route and estimated it would cost £3,900, a fairly expensive venture. Partly due to the War Department's lack of interest and Radnor's eventual capitulation, the idea failed to pass the planning stage, yet remarkably the 'Shorncliffe Camp & Sandgate Lift' continued to make the news, even as late as 1908, with suggestions for its construction.

Now that the tramway was established, it was essential that suitable permanent accommodation be found for housing the two tramcars and stabling the horses. A property close to the Red Lion Inn was located and purchased for £1,400. Authority was given to secure further horses and an additional tramcar. By September the plans for the stable and car shed were drawn up and these were submitted and approved. Tenders for internal fittings were:

	Painted	Galvanised	Enamelled
Hope Foundry Company:	£207 10s 0d	£222 10s 0d	–
Musgraves:	£199 0s 0d	–	£227 0s 0d
Rownson, Drew & Company:	£185 0s 0d	£198 10s 0d	£215 0s 0d

Two more tramcars, Nos. 3 and 4, were built by the SER at their Ashford Works in 1892. Car No. 3, weighing 2 tons 10 cwt. 2 lbs was completed on 28th July 1892 and differed from all the other cars. It was designed specifically for winter use, being an enclosed car, glazed all round and with doors, to keep out the worst of the cold, wet and draughty winter weather. Car No. 4, weighing 2 tons 6 cwt. 0 lbs and completed at the same time, was built in the same fashion as No. 1, being a roofed car with side blinds. Some time after these cars were delivered to Hythe, open-car No. 2 was taken to Ashford where it was similarly roofed over to match cars 1 and 4.

The tramway had evidently been taken into the hearts of the locals and visitors for the local press reported that over 110,000 passengers were carried on the tramway throughout the season and this was in spite of the numerous buses and other conveyances all plying between the towns. In October a winter timetable was introduced comprising an hourly service, with the first tram leaving Hythe at 10.00 a.m. and the last departure from Sandgate at 10.00 p.m.

On 29th June 1893 the South Eastern Railway obtained an Act which, for £29,753, enabled them to officially take over the operation and maintenance of the tramway. Fortune, it seemed, was at last looking favourably upon this venture. The Sandgate Hill Lift had opened just four months earlier and the fact that at the end of its first financial year it was able to pay a staggering 20% premium to its investors, must have encouraged the SER that traffic on the tramway could only increase.

Mr. Jeal's estimate of £1,530 for the new tram shed at Hythe was accepted and this was erected in 1894, incorporating the large stone fascia reading 'Folkestone, Hythe & Sandgate Tramways 1894' although the reason why the names Sandgate and Hythe were transposed remains a mystery. Perhaps it was the stonemason's error!

Efforts to extend the tramway further westwards were frustrated despite the wishes of ordinary folk living on Romney Marsh. In 1895 a memorial from Dymchurch residents requesting that the company consider extending the line from Red Lion Square across the flat lands to their town had to be declined. The SER made it plain that whilst they were generally favourable to the idea, and had for this purpose gone so

The stone fascia above the tramway shed.
Tramway Museum Society

The rarely photographed car No. 3 for use in winter months.
R. C. Riley Collection

far as to introduce a bill of extension for the 1894 session, such 'onerous terms' had been sought to be imposed upon them by certain local bodies that they'd been obliged to withdraw it.

Three additional horses were purchased in April 1895 specifically for the busy summer season when hundreds of people took to riding on this most leisurely and delightful tram as it trundled sedately along the seashore. That it was an enjoyable experience is verified in a piece printed locally, yet somehow its theme rings true even today:

'There is a horse tram, open at the sides but covered at the top, which runs between Sandgate and Hythe, chiefly by the sea and it is really a delightful drive. Or may I amend that utterance by saying that it *would* be a most perfect drive if only the men who occupy seats would refrain from smoking strong tobacco and puffing it in the faces of those who sit opposite them!'

By May, the horse buses had increased until there were now a total of twenty-five daily departures from Hythe to Folkestone. A warm and sunny August Bank Holiday brought

Car. No. 4 terminating in Sandgate High Street, and not at the foot of Sandgate Hill, appears to be causing some congestion as the horses are led round to be coupled up again.
Tramway Museum Society

The sea wreaking its vengeance on Sandgate! *Alan Taylor Collection*

out the crowds, with it subsequently being reported that the trams had carried over 2,000 passengers compared to the omnibuses' 1,500.

While a journey by tram in summer, with the sun streaming down and the gentle splashing sound of a calm sea was enough to soothe even the most jangled nerves of those seeking recuperation, the journey in winter was quite often the opposite. Even within the comparative comfort of tramcar No. 3, the strong winds and high seas were at times alarming, frequently causing the suspension of the service. The prevailing south-westerly wind, whipping the sea up into a raging foam, brought havoc at high tides when huge breakers pounded the sea wall with the force of many tons. The most vulnerable stretch was, and still is, the length between Sandgate station and Sandgate itself, where large waves thumped into the wall, sending a curtain of water skywards which then crashed down upon the esplanade, raining pebbles, seaweed and debris to block the road. Drawing itself back with the familiar chatter of the beachstones, the sea would repeat the process until the tide had turned. Anyone finding themselves stranded at Sandgate station at high tide was well advised to heed the staff's advice to bide a while at the waiting room hearth until the sea receded. Pluckier souls might venture to risk a thorough soaking but the sea invariably ended up being the victor in these instances! Damage to the sea wall inevitably resulted after every winter and each spring the workmen would return to patch up yet another breach. Quite serious damage took place in 1896 and in the following year, when Sandgate Castle took a battering. Had the viaduct carrying the Sandgate–Folkestone railway been built, it would undoubtedly have suffered. The most ferocious storm, however, took place in 1899 when the sea wall was broken up for some distance, leaving the tramway track suspended in mid air. Clearing the huge quantites of shingle from the road after each storm is a problem still faced today. In the days of the tramway an old chap called 'Luchy' Hobbs was employed to walk the tracks to remove wedged-in pebbles. He was always to be seen after a storm, wearing his bowler hat, walking along with his old broom handle with its spike to knock out the stones.

For the summer season of 1897 the SER built a fifth car, designed for those all too short periods of warm settled weather.

The floods at the western boundary of Sandgate after the storm of February 1899.

Alan Taylor Collection

Two spectacular views of the wrecked tramway along Sandgate Esplanade after the 1899 storm. *Alan Taylor Collection*

A young girl and baby look on as car No. 5 prepares to leave for Sandgate. Mr. Powell's emporium can be seen on the left. The poster on his premises depicts a forthcoming attraction at the Alhambra Theatre in Sandgate, 'Nana – the rage of Paris'!

Peter Davies Collection

No. 5 pulls into Hythe. In the background stands the shed with one covered car visible in the doorway. *Alan Taylor Collection*

Colloquially known as the 'toast-rack', car No. 5 provided the best opportunity to enjoy the ride and the sunshine. During these times the traffic on the tramway was as heavy as ever with cars loaded to capacity. This is not surprising in view of the conduct of some of the motor bus and charabanc operators at that time, as recorded in a local paper:

> 'The ride from Hythe to Folkestone, and vice versa, is generally considered a pleasant little trip but the rivalry between the many charabancs and the bus service is not always a source of comfort and joy – particularly to the person with 'nerves'. The determined intention to 'lead the van' (or rather the 'bus) shown by one furious charabanc Jehu a few nights ago, resulted in much scraping of wheels to the detriment of the appearance of the 'bus and the consternation of the passengers. But Nemesis, in the shape of the police, overtook the offender as he was continuing his wild career through Sandgate with the result that he was 'hauled up' before the magistrates a few days later and fined to the amount of £2 with 9s costs.'

In the spring of 1898 an estimate of £25 from a Mr. B. A. Ainnes for a turret clock for the tramway shed was accepted and instructions given to proceed.

Expense of an entirely different nature was authorised at the same time when the SER began dallying with the idea of running its own horse-drawn omnibuses between Sandgate and Folkestone. In later years its successor, the Southern Railway, took the omnibus to its heart, much to the detriment of its rural branch lines. On 7th June 1898 a letter was despatched to Mr. H. S. Wainwright, the Carriage & Wagon Superintendent at Ashford Railway Works, informing him that within the next few days Mr. Ward, the manager of the FS & HT Co. would be calling in to discuss the proposed new bus. The purpose of the bus was that it should work in connection with the tramway for conveying passengers between the bottom of Sandgate hill and Folkestone town centre. London Bridge headquarters requested Wainwright to send on the designs and estimates. For Harry Wainwright this was a modest task, his blossoming genius in later years producing some of Britain's finest and most elegant engines, loved by crews and public alike. Although Wainwright met Mr. Ward, he didn't start work on the buses, simply because he had far too much work already and within a few months he was appointed Locomotive, Carriage & Wagon Superintendent. Instead, the buses were tendered out to Worthington Brothers of Hythe who had an enviable reputation for their workmanship, their customers ranging from the Folkestone Omnibus Co. to the Southport Tramway Co. Worthington's estimate of £148 3s 0d was accepted and the SER were informed that it would take three to four months to complete the job. One bus was ordered, which could carry ten passengers inside, or twelve in wet weather and eleven on the roof on 'garden' seats, as well as an extra four on the box with the driver. Further specifications included wheels with $2\frac{1}{4}''$ axles, driver's footbrake and conductor's screwbrake, trimmed interior with horsehair stuffing, coconut mats, wet-weather aprons, glass windows and a brass rod to the staircase. The exterior of the bus would be painted, written in gold leaf and varnished.

Although soundly constructed and handsome in their resplendent liveries, the early buses were not very comfortable, or particularly safe for that matter, as revealed in a local paper of September 1898:

> 'On Sunday last, at about a quarter past nine, a charabanc belonging to the Hythe, Sandgate & Folkestone Omnibus Co. arrived at the foot of Sandgate hill on its homeward journey when its nearside wheel caught the tram lines. This broke the nave of the wheel and resulted in the vehicle turning completely on its side, precipitating all its passengers onto the roadway. A large crowd assembled and a doctor and cabs were summoned. One passenger suffered a fractured collar bone and another had injuries to the head, otherwise injuries were slight. The conductor stated he'd felt the bus swaying shortly before it toppled. The horses were quite unharmed and remained motionless throughout the distressing commotion. Military personnel from Shorncliffe Camp assisted in clearing the vehicle from the road.'

In October 1898 more land was purchased in Rampart Road, Hythe where two old cottages, Nos. 6 and 7, already owned by the SER, were demolished to make way for the stables which were erected on the site. Up until the provision of stables at the tramway shed the horses were kept at the railway stables in Hythe station goods yard, where they were led each night. These horses officially belonged to the railway goods depot who were paid 35/- a week by the FS & HT Co. for their use, boarding and feeding.

At Sandgate a shelter, costing £60, was erected for the benefit of passengers changing from the tramway to the SER's new horse bus. Whether the bus failed its expectations, or the SER simply tired of venturing into this mode of transport is not known but a few months later, in January 1899, it was sold for £140 to the Hythe, Sandgate & Folkestone Omnibus Co. who were probably glad to have it to replace their wrecked charabanc.

By 1900 the tramway service consisted of sixteen journeys each way, with eleven on Sundays. Departure times were:

Weekdays
Leaving Hythe: 10, 11, 11.30, 12, 1, 2, 2.30, 3, 3.30, 4, 4.30, 5, 6, 7, 8, 9.40
Leaving Sandgate: 10.30, 11.30, 12, 12.30, 1.30, 2.30, 3, 3.30, 4, 4.30, 5, 5.30, 6.30, 7.30, 8.30, 10.15.

Sundays
Leaving Hythe: 10, 11, 12, 2, 3, 4, 5, 6, 7, 8, 9, Returning from Sandgate on the half hour.

The beginning of the twentieth century probably gave a psychological impetus to modernise and electrify the tramway and hopes that the sounds of hissing wires and whining electric motors would soon pervade Folkestone were frequently vaunted, putting all competitors out of business:

> 'From what I can gather, the Folkestone, Sandgate & Hythe Electric Tramway scheme stands a good chance of becoming an accomplished fact. If it does, I understand that the company are prepared to take over the Hythe, Sandgate & Folkestone Omnibus Co.'

A week later a headline declared:

'THE TRAMWAY – THE GREAT CRISIS – NOW OR NEVER'

GO TO

W. POWELL,

If you want to Buy or Hire

New or Second-hand Furniture,

Cheapest Place In Hythe.

Note Address—

RAMPART ROAD,

WHERE THE TRAM STARTS

Powell's emporium in Rampart Road. The man standing on the left is Leonard Maycock who later became the chief officer of Hythe Fire Brigade. Up until the First World War the tramway's horses were utilised by the Fire Brigade.
Courtesy Lister Maycock/Eamonn Rooney Collection

CHAPTER THREE

The Great Crisis

THE introduction of tramways onto the streets of Britain had proved a controversial matter although, in general, they were popular with the mass of the population who were hitherto unable to afford the high fares of the railways or omnibuses. Gradually the slow horse trams were replaced, in some cases, by steam traction but more usually by electric cars which offered the perfect solution.

The 1870 Tramways Act, in granting powers for private bodies to build and operate tramways, provided a clause to enable local municipal corporations, if need be, to compulsorily purchase the tramways within their district after 21 years had elapsed. This happened in the majority of the towns across Britain whereupon these lines benefited from being upgraded, extended and electrified. Cheap fares encouraged more and more ordinary folk to travel, thereby enabling them to journey to work or simply ride out of town on Sunday pleasure trips.

With this as a backdrop, the scene was set for the development of the Hythe and Sandgate tramway whose initial powers were set to pass into local authority hands in 1905. However, this was not the first time that electric traction had been proposed. Seven years earlier, in 1893, just months after the horse tram had commenced running, a plan was put forward and published in the paper:

'Electric tram communication is almost within reach of Sandgate, and Folkestone is about to be snuffed out. Mr. Sellon, C. E., has sent a letter to the local Sandgate Board in reference to the Folkestone, Sandgate & Hythe Tramway, and it is to be discussed at a special meeting of the Board. The writer says:- "I have been instructed to make arrangements for either the purchase or the lease of the above tramways, and in accordance with my instructions I have had certain business interviews with the Secretary of the South Eastern Railway Company, who has now informed me that he is willing to grant me a lease on terms which have so far not been arranged. I am, however, sufficiently forward with my negotiations with that Company to enable me to approach your Board on the question of electrical traction, which you are aware is now to be seen at work in nearly every town of consequence in the United States, and one example is now working at Leeds. As our proposals with the South Eastern Railway Company depend entirely upon the consent of your Board being obtained to the use of poles for the purpose of suspending our overhead wires, I am desirous, before proceeding any further, to obtain an idea as to how your Board would look upon an installation being placed in Sandgate, I would draw your attention to the fact that whereas it is usual to have cross lines from kerb to kerb for the purpose of suspending the longitudinal feeder, the tramways being laid along the side of the road will enable us to materially reduce any objection to cross wiring, as we propose to use, instead of such cross wiring, what is known as the side suspension. The poles we should put up would be of such a design as would be suitable to the views of your Board, and I have no doubt, should you view my preparations with favour, arrangements can be made for lighting with electric light the whole of the extent of the sea wall upon the poles or alternative poles, as the distance may require."'

Waiting for the tram from Hythe at the passing loop along Prince's Parade. *Courtesy H. C. Casserley*

Objections to the sight of wires appears to have caused this scheme to founder and this was also a contributory factor to the second plan which came along in 1897. A more ambitious layout was proposed by the 'Folkestone & District Electric Railway Co.' which was laid out in nine sections, stretching from East Cliff at Folkestone to Dymchurch Road in Hythe. Mr. S. G. Fraser, the engineer, estimated the total cost at £156,193 for a mainly double-track tramway at standard gauge, fed by overhead wires and used 'for the conveyance of passengers and parcels only'. From the outset the main stumbling block which, as events proved, would scupper all subsequent proposals, was the intrusion into Radnor's Folkestone Estate.

In 1900 a fresh attempt at electrifying the more useful lengths of the Hythe and Sandgate tramway, as well as extending it at both ends, was made when the 'Folkestone, Sandgate & Hythe Tramway Bill' was presented to parliament. Speaking for the bill were Mr. Balfour Brown, Q.C., Mr. Moon – representing the tramway company – and Mr. Brockman, the Mayor of Hythe. Directly opposed to the bill were the South Eastern Railway Company, the South Eastern & Chatham Railway Companies Managing Committee, the Folkestone, Cheriton & Shorncliffe Omnibus Co., the Corporations of Folkestone and Hythe, private occupiers in Seabrook Road and the Earl of Radnor.

It was proposed that a parallel line should be laid alongside the SE & CR's horse tramway through Sandgate but at Seabrook the electric tramway would carry on along the main road instead of Princes Parade. Powers to run over the SE & CR tramway were sought for, in their own words, 'Running over theirs could do no harm – they provided only one car an hour in winter and three or four in summer. There is plenty of room for extra cars and the SE & CR would profit from the extra traffic we'd bring in from New Romney and Hythe.'

At this point, residents in Seabrook Road voiced their objections, fearing not only a drop in property values but the alarming spectacle of omnibuses, charabancs and trams all racing one another to get there first with all the noise and dust that would create – there was even a rumour that these trams would be used to convey manure!

Lord Radnor then rose and intimated that if there were to be tramways in Folkestone then he would rather the Corporation construct them.

Mr. Moon, for the FS & HT Bill, then spoke of the grievances felt by Sandgate people at the poor communications they had to endure. In describing his proposed route it seems he couldn't resist ridiculing the SE & CR in referring to the tramway passing *Seabrook* station. He stressed that New Romney and Dymchurch people were just as anxious to see the tramway built as were Sandgate and Hythe folk, adding that the Sandgate Local Board had entered into an agreement with his company to purchase and hand over the section of the horse tramway 'from the bottom of Sandgate Hill to Seabrook station'.

In an effort to clarify the present transport arrangements it was suggested that the Sandgate Hill lift already catered for eastbound travellers, whereupon a number of witnesses protested that the drawback of the lift was that the lower station was situated a quarter of the way up the hill, it didn't open until 10.00 a.m. and, worst of all, its passengers were deposited at the top of the Leas with no option but to walk the mile into Folkestone. The Rev. Edward Bryan then complained that

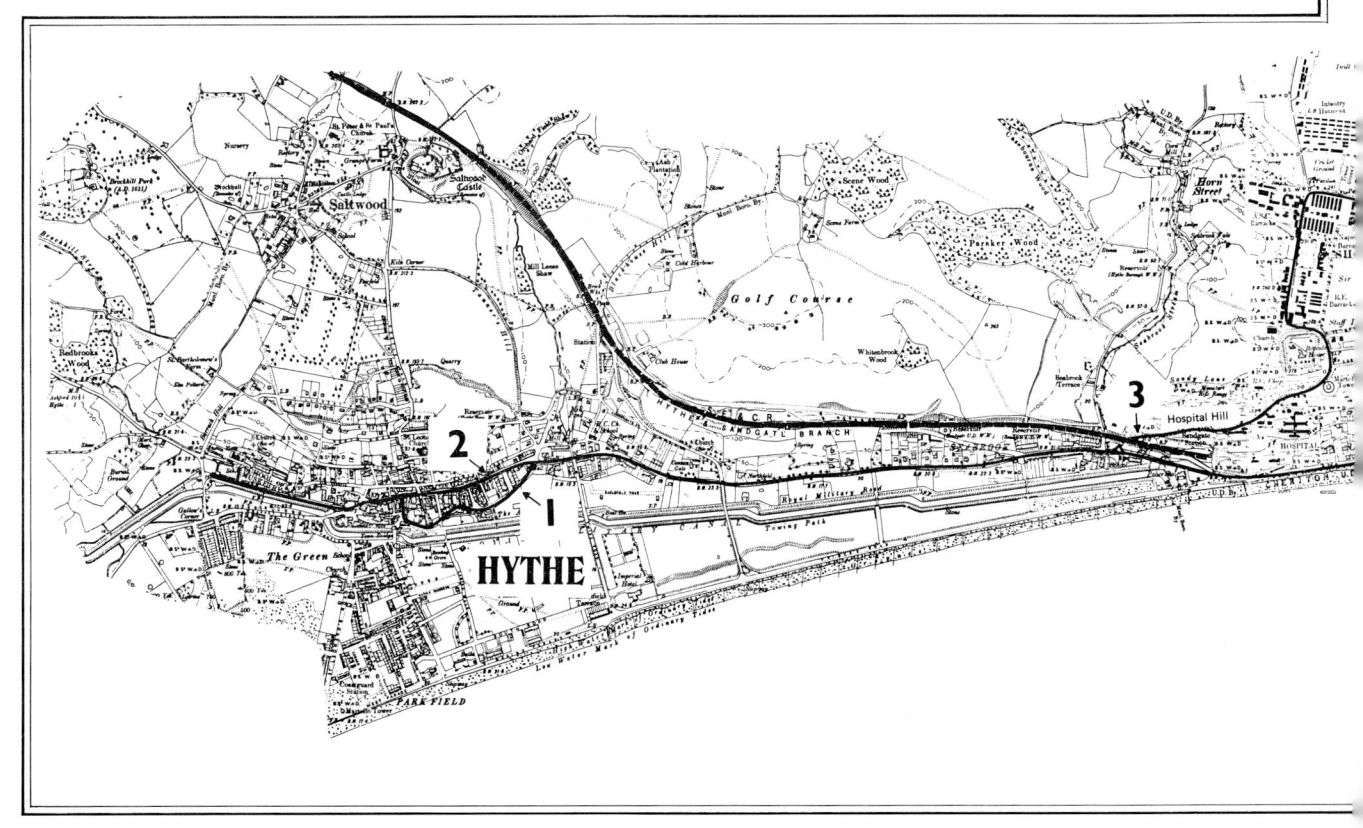

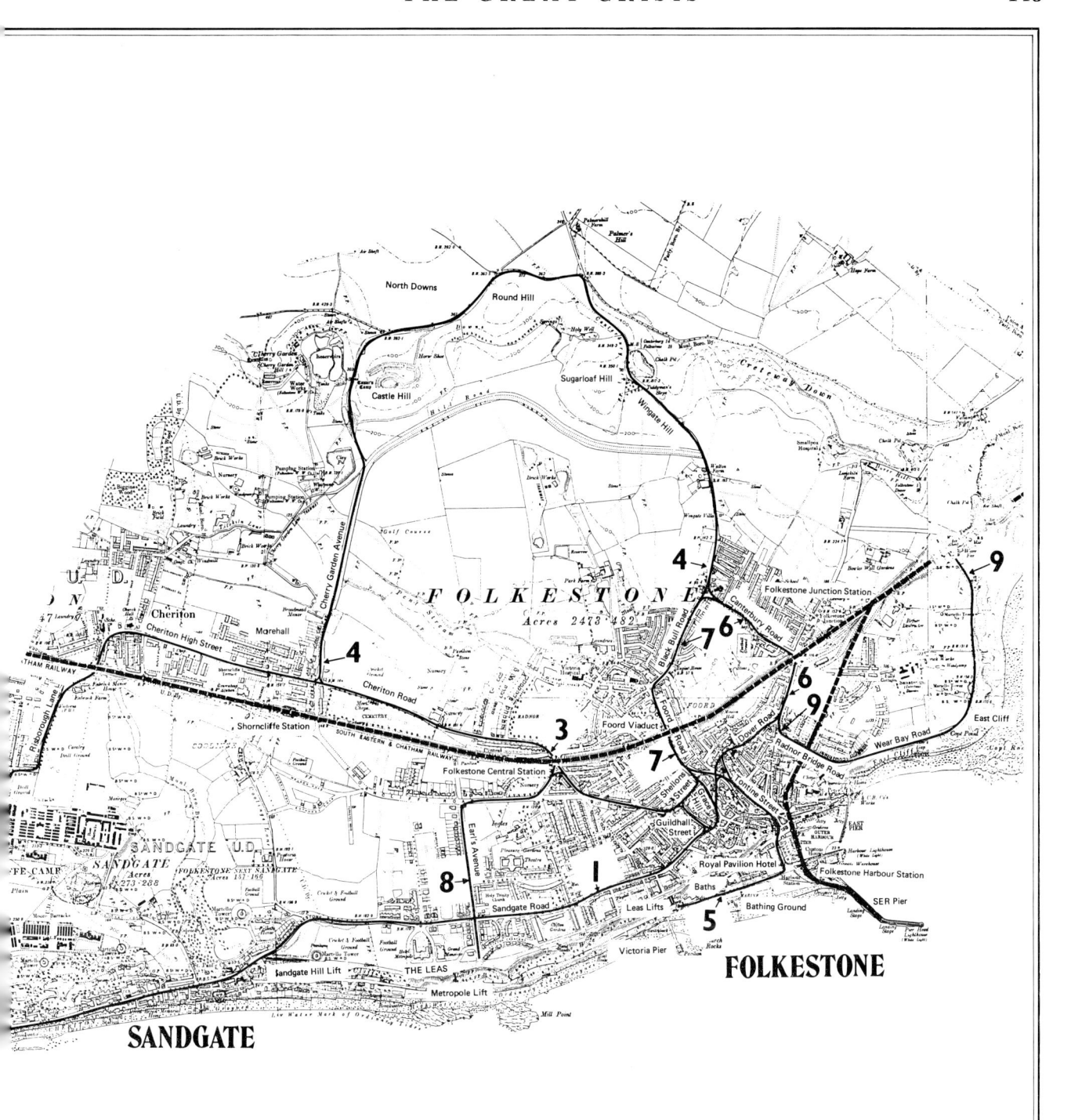

PROPOSED ELECTRIC TRAMWAY SYSTEM

The other face of fashionable Folkestone.

Author's Collection

A horse-bus begins the long climb up Sandgate Hill as a tramcar heads off for Hythe. *Author's Collection*

even though they had omnibuses and charabancs into Folkestone, they were most unreliable, never ran to a timetable and were quite expensive. He added that in the other direction the tramcars were subject to much overcrowding, as were the buses which were always being hauled up by a constable for carrying more passengers than their licence permitted. Mr. Worsley Taylor wished they could have something 'a good deal faster than horses' and criticised the SE & CR, saying that the tramway never ran at the times working people needed it and whenever a breach appeared in the sea wall the company took their time repairing it and restoring the service. As for communication between Cheriton and Sandgate, 'this is non-existent and a tram up Military Road to Cheriton would be of enormous benefit.'

The grievances of Cheriton were then sought. Being a growing suburb of Folkestone, its residents were 'mainly of the working or industrial classes' and had to walk into work, a distance of at least two miles. It was unanimously agreed that what buses plied to and fro were quite insufficient and a fast electric tramway along Cheriton Road would be just the thing.

Lord Radnor's views were then examined on the matter. Owning approximately seven-eighths of the west end of Folkestone, his involvement in its development showed a strong pecuniary interest as well as an acute awareness of the social implications that the tramway would have on the exclusive nature of the town. It was put to his lordship that although it was understood he had no objection to 'cheap trippers', he had no wish to attract them to Folkestone? Revealing his true objections, he bluntly replied: 'We do not want them at Folkestone.' Asserting his position, he explained that a tramway through the residential areas would be 'of serious detriment' and went on: 'If you want to have cheap trippers, have your tramways through your residential part, but the town has been built with high-class houses for high-class residents and high-class visitors and I believe if you have tramways going through the residential parts it will spoil the character of the place.'. Having large amounts of property on lease, Radnor opposed the introduction of tramways anywhere near the west end; however, he hinted he might consider the corporation introducing them in other parts of the town, provided an agreement on siting could be reached.

Referring to the western section of the tramway, Thomas Neal of Dymchurch spoke of the old South Eastern Railway's attempts at building a line between New Romney and Hythe, complaining that they'd done nothing except talk about it for years and years. Even though the route had been stumped-out at least four times and a station for Dymchurch planned, nothing of substance had materialised.

In summing up, the chairman expressed the view of his committee that in regard to the FS & HT bill, they were of the opinion that the preamble was not proved. Whereas this could be interpreted as a victory for Lord Radnor and those with egocentric interests, it was an undoubted setback for the ordinary inhabitants who would have benefited from the

The staff of Folkestone Motors Ltd. with one of their charabancs.
Tramway Museum Soc.

establishment of an efficient and co-ordinated public transport system. Their interests apparently came second to those who resided there purely in the 'fashionable seasons'.

There was little love lost between the two areas of Folkestone partitioned by barriers of social class and financial status. From Radnor's point of view, the town had grown and prospered under his guidance. Large houses and hotels in elegant avenues and squares now stood where once simple folk had grazed their sheep and tended allotments. The older inhabitants, who remembered the Folkestone of yore as just a fishing village, and those confined to the more squalid areas in the east end of the town, strongly resented the influx of the monied classes whom, they claimed, did nothing but force up prices in the shops. The town was almost divided into two areas and it was a division which, although to a far lesser extent, still surprisingly pervades to this day even though the barriers are almost indistinct and the once grand hotels and villas either lay derelict or are converted into flats. Perhaps Charles Harper, writing in 1906, in his book *The Ingoldsby Country* best summed up the atmosphere that persisted at that time:

'There is no love felt for modern Folkestone by the inhabitants of the old town, who resent the prices to which things have been forced up by the neighbourhood of the over-wealthy, and resent still more the occasional descent from the fashionable Leas of dainty parties bent on exploring the queer nooks, and amusing themselves with a sight of the quaint characters, that still abound by the fishing harbour. To those parties, every waterside lounger who sports a peaked cap and a blue jersey, and, resting his arms upon the railings by the quay and gazing inscrutably out to the horizon, presents a broad stern to the street, is a fisherman, and the feelings of a pilot, taken for a mere hauler upon nets and capturer of soles and mackerel, are often thus outraged.

'For the spiritual benefit of the fisherfolk and others of the old town, there is planted, by the Stade, a "St. Peter's Mission", established there by well-meaning but stupid folk who look down, actually and figuratively, from the modern town upon this spot, and appear to think of it as a sink of iniquity. But iniquities are not always, or solely resident in sinks; they have been found, shameless and flourishing in high places. There are those among the fisher population who take the creature comforts – the coals and the blankets – of the mission, and pocket the implied affront; but there are also those others who, with clearer vision or greater independence of character, do not scruple to think and say that a mission for the salvation of many in that new town that so proudly crowns the cliffs would be more appropriate. "What," asked an indignant fisherman – "what makes them 'ere hotels pay like they does?" and he answered his own query in language that shall not be printed here. "If them as goes there all had to show their marriage-lines first," he concluded, "it's little business they'd do"; and his remarks recalled and illuminated the story of a week-end frequenter of one of the great caravanserais whose Saturday to Monday spouses were so frequently changed that even the seared conscience of a German hotel manager was revolted.'

June 1900 brought the sudden and unexpected death of Lord Radnor. Aged just 59, he was the fifth earl and was succeeded by his son Viscount Folkestone, but attitudes towards the tramway did not change within the family and the new lord was as much an adversary as his father had been.

Other forms of transport now began to appear on the roads, or were proposed over the next few years. In 1901 the Folkestone Motor Company Limited commenced running a service of large open motorised charabancs between Folkestone and Hythe. Although fares were higher than on the tramway, for example, Folkestone to Sandgate 4d, to Seabrook 6d, and to Hythe 8d, the overwhelming advantage was not only its speedy, direct route but the benefit of a through ride.

An application for a steam-driven bus, weighing 2 tons and capable of carrying 25 passengers, came along in June 1902 from Messrs Salter Bros. but although it was approved it evidently never arrived. The horse tramway continued much as before, remaining especially popular in the summer months as witnessed by the fact that the SE & CR had to purchase three additional horses that season.

THE GREAT CRISIS

Mindful of the objections to overhead wires, in 1904 the Stirling Motor Construction Company put forward a plan for motor trams, utilising petrol-driven engines. Even though it was stated that running costs were cheaper than electricity, the idea failed to gain support and was never pursued.

In the summer a minor mishap took place on the tramway when one of the horses missed its footing and fell near the awkward curve from Rampart Road into Stade Street. Willing helpers assisted in getting the animal back on its feet and, thankfully, the horse was unharmed although dazed and after a few words of comfort, and perhaps a lump of sugar, all was well.

In the autumn one of the grandest schemes of all was put forward whereby a continuous electric tramway might extend from Hastings to Ramsgate, running through Winchelsea, Rye, Hythe, Shorncliffe Camp, Folkestone, Dover, Walmer, Deal and Sandwich. The promoters anticipated much tourist traffic as well as a considerable business in carrying agricultural produce. The idea was not new, in fact a similar plan, linking Hythe to the Isle of Thanet, had been mooted back in 1872. Not surprisingly, such an ambitious scheme failed to get any further than on paper or being discussed over a pint of beer at the public houses along the route.

In 1905 the 1884 Act, which allowed the construction of the length of tramway through Sandgate and known as No. 4, was 21 years old, so the clerk of Sandgate Urban District Council, J. Shera Atkinson, notified the SE & CR: 'My council claim power under the enactment (Tramways Act, October 1870, Sec. 43) to purchase compulsorily certain tramways within this district vested in the SE & CR Co.'

On 4th January 1906, the SE & CR wrote to the Board of Trade calling their attention to two competitive proposals then in hand for the construction of tramways within Folkestone, Sandgate and Hythe and, in one case, within the New Romney district. The SE & CR Board pointed out that it would perhaps be expedient to refer the purchase to parliament in order that it may be decided which would confer the greater benefit. Sandgate Council made no secret of the fact that it intended to hand over the tramway to either of the competing companies. It appears that no one had contemplated the likelihood of a local council purchasing a mere portion of a tramway and the SE & CR were concerned that the public, and ultimately themselves, would suffer with the loss of through communication. The railway company complained that no plans had been submitted revealing how the section would be worked. Without any depot, stables or other facilities, by reason of its position, numerous problems would have been presented for the council or lessee. The fact that Sandgate Council intended that the tramway be electrified seems to have escaped the SE & CR at this juncture.

The two contenders for the tramway were the British Electric Traction Company, represented by Mr. Sellon, and the National Electric Construction Company Limited, represented by Mr. Kennedy. Sandgate Council admitted they'd negotiated since 1899 with the BET Co. but felt they'd been let down, hence their intention to back the NEC Co., especially as the latter's plan didn't include 'that useless extension to Romney'. No record survives of what the inhabitants of the Marsh made of this remark! The SE & CR therefore consented to entering into a binding agreement for selling the tramway to the council who, in twelve months time, would hand it over to the NEC Co. to electrify and operate.

On hearing of this agreement, the new Lord of the Manor then instructed Bischoff to write to the Board of Trade:

'We believe you are aware of two bills before the House of Lords for acquiring the Hythe and Sandgate tramway and for extending it into Folkestone.

The Earl of Radnor has instructed us to present petitions against each of these bills and we shall probably call up the SE & CR to actively oppose them in pursuance with our agreement of 12th July 1892.

We should also be glad to hear that you will withhold your consent to the sale to the local authority or at any rate make the sale subject to the terms and conditions of the agreement of the 12th July 1892 so that the tramway may not be extended into Folkestone without his Lordship's consent.'

The SE & CR were now in the impossible situation of being obliged to oppose a sale they wanted to proceed with simply because of the 1892 agreement which required them to object to electrifying the tramway for that would mean overhead wires.

In an effort to break the stalemate, and wary of the opposition that would undoubtedly follow if overhead wires were proposed, the NEC Co. decided to opt for the 'Dolter' surface contact system and in 1906 obtained their own Light Railway Order for a 13 mile system. Bearing in mind that the late Lord Radnor had implied that he wished the corporation to make the tramways in Folkestone, if anyone had to, from 1900 to 1905 Folkestone Corporation in conjunction with Cheriton Urban District Council promoted their own electric tramway schemes, but this time on the 3'6" gauge. A provisional order, granting powers to construct the tramways, contained an undertaking, insisted upon by Radnor, that the overhead system of current collection would not be adopted.

Meanwhile, an agreement was drawn up for the sale to the NEC Co. of the Hythe and Sandgate tramway comprising all lines, plant, horses, rolling stock and premises for £20,000. A deposit of £2,000 was paid to the SE & CR who, quite likely, were glad of the prospect of being relieved of the tramway and all its troubles.

At last it seemed as though Folkestone would have an electric tramway for the Dolter system promised the solution. On 10th October 1906 a group of councillors from Folkestone visited Mexborough, in Yorkshire, to inspect and ride upon the town's newly-opened 1½ mile tramway which utilised the surface contact system. Perhaps mindful of Sandgate Hill, they were particularly impressed with the braking method which incorporated a magnetic clamp which acted upon the rail instead of the conventional type which gripped the wheel. Everything appeared to work most satisfactorily and the enthusiastic party returned 'most impressed and very satisfied'. Shortly before the NEC Co. were ready to begin work, however, serious problems began to manifest themselves at Mexborough. The studs in the road, which were intended only to be live when a tram passed over them, sometimes failed to operate correctly, causing a failure of power to the tram's electric motor. Worse still, the opposite happened with the studs remaining dangerously live, with possible dire consequences for those pedestrians and horses unfortunate enough to unwittingly tread on them. Thus the NEC Co were forced to think again and in 1909 attempted to introduce a bill to substitute overhead wires in place of the failed conduit system. At this point the secretary of the SE & CR met the manager of the NEC Co and warned them that they'd be obliged, by virtue of their binding agree-

No. 5 at Red Lion Square about to leave for its four-mile ride by the sea to Sandgate. Conductor Harry Jago is on the right.
Courtesy Mr. & Mrs. Pilcher

ment of 1892 with Radnor, to oppose the overhead wires. Notice was also served that the £2,000 deposit was forfeited by reason of failure to settle the balance in payment for the tramway. Thus the Hythe and Sandgate tramway remained in railway ownership.

The failure of the Dolter system was seen as the reason why tramways never entered Folkestone but it was the unrelenting opposition, not only to overhead wires, but the trams themselves, from certain quarters which finally killed the project stone dead. Whilst other towns enjoyed frequent, fast and cheap transport, Folkestone was left behind to be served only by the motor bus which, despite all its restrictions, was seen as the only answer to the area's public transport needs.

In May 1909 a poll card vote was carried out by the *Hythe Reporter* which showed that 403 of its readers were in favour of overhead wires, whilst 828 were against, but the newspaper's poll posed a biased question so it was hardly fair. A similar attitude was found, not surprisingly, amongst Folkestone's visitors and many wrote to the local papers. One letter castigated the town for its reluctance to press ahead with an electric tramway and listing the benefits – fast, frequent, clean, safe, plus the ½d workmen's fares as in other towns, he concluded: 'Wake-up Folkestone!'. A converse view begged the town not to follow Bournemouth's example: 'Business is bad because the visitors are more or less of the tripper element who go to Bournemouth to ride on a penny tram and eat their meals out of a paper bag.' Such absurd snobbery did nothing for the needs of the ordinary ratepayers of Folkestone who would undoubtedly have found the trams a boon. Opinions remained sharply divided. Whereas forty years previously the newspapers had enthused over the coming of the railway to Hythe and Sandgate and the development to follow, they now, it appears, had changed their minds:

'I do not intend to take sides in the controversy now raging at Hythe in regard to the question of trams or no trams. The orators, property owners, the unseen manipulators of the "chess board" and the general public may be left to fight the matter to the bitter end. However, taking another standpoint, and as one who for many years has written both locally and in several quarters of the London Press anent the remarkable beauties of Hythe, I could not help feeling something akin to regret that several parts of the ancient borough (especially in the neighbourhood of the Grove) are, if the promoters have their way, to "sing" or "hiss" to the music of the overhead wires of the trams. The sight, too, of the posts and wires will be out of all harmony with what Nature has so lavishly granted to Hythe. The tendency nowadays is for people to get away from the noise and clatter and hustle – to be at rest. And Hythe provides that rest. It is the moneyed people too, who are to be considered in this respect.

It was many years ago when the South Eastern Railway sought to extend their line from Sandgate station to Folkestone Harbour, via the Lower Sandgate Road. It was thought a few minutes would thus be saved on the journey to the Continent. It is probable that neither Hythe nor Sandgate Stations would have been in existence for many years after their erection but for the "grand idea" of that great railway king – the late Sir Edward Watkin. The Company purchased Sandgate Castle – they also acquired other rights. All, however, to no avail. Why? When the inhabitants of Folkestone realised that one of their greatest assets, the Lower Sandgate Road, would be ruined and disfigured by the railway they were up in arms. They joined issue with the then Lord of the Manor, and raised such a storm of opposition that the idea of the loop-line along the Undercliff was dropped. Even the great John Ruskin, who was then residing in the near vicinity, raised his noble voice against the proposal. And as I strolled through the quiet Grove and its vicinity on the glorious afternoon of Saturday last I could but think of those days when the preservation of natural beauty stood before the plans of great capitalists.'

The Hythe and Sandgate tramway was rapidly becoming something of an anachronism. The motor vehicle operators were no fools and were busily cashing in on the normal travelling needs of the locals who left the slow horse tramway for the summer visitors who had plenty of spare time to enjoy an amble along the seafront. Yet, in spite of its popularity with the summer tourists, its days were clearly numbered.

CHAPTER FOUR

A Fateful Sequel

THROUGHOUT the remaining few years of peace before the outbreak of the First World War, the arguments for and against tramways continued to rumble on, appearing in newspapers from time to time and likely providing a topic of conversation in the bus queues. It was, alas, nothing but vain rhetoric, the 'great crisis' was passed and there were very few people who believed that Folkestone might yet have its electric tramway.

Life on the Hythe and Sandgate tramway continued much as before, popular in summer, quiet in winter and frequently suspended due to bad weather. Although on most winter days the elements were braved, the service had to be cancelled on those occasions when the sea was whipped into a foaming fury. This happened yet again in October 1911 when a series of storms sent waves crashing over the promenade at Sandgate, causing the suspension of the tram service for a few days. The resulting damage meant that the SE & CR had to further strengthen the sea defences with a number of trainloads of redundant rails which were brought into Sandgate for this purpose. Another memorable period of inclement weather was the bitterly cold winter of 1909 when snow drifts, as late as March, brought chaos to East Kent. Consequently the trams were unable to venture out for over a week.

With the dreams of the Seabrook Estate Company turned to dust, economic reality began to dawn with a resulting contraction of expenditure as well as a surrendering of assets. It was decided that railway-owned Cannongate Road should be handed over to Hythe council to manage and maintain but the council would only agree to this once the tramlines had been removed. The headshunt into the approach road at Hythe station is thought to have been ripped up around 1900, but the rest of the old lines, right down to the Imperial Hotel, remained. During the summer of 1911 the rails were dug out of the roadway by a gang of labourers from the SE & CR's Permanent Way Department and the scrap material finally sold to Mr. W. G. Powell for £180 10s 0d. Cannongate Road was then repaired, with the SE & CR relinquishing its private right of way and handing it over to the borough in December 1912.

There were now just two summers left before the world would change irrevocably and we can only conjecture what it was like to be well-heeled and on a sojourn at this particular resort. A visit to Folkestone in the summer of 1913 or '14 was still a regular event in the society calendar. No other retreat anywhere in England had that certain *je ne sais quoi*. These were not only the dying days of the tramway, but the last vestiges of an unquestioned class system with all its trappings. Having arrived at Folkestone, the well-to-do generally kept to those areas of the town decreed for their amusement and relaxation. Excursions were, however, popular with all classes of visitors, when parties armed with a 'Ward Lock', 'Black's', or similar guidebook, took to the roads to explore the beautiful and ancient by-ways of Kent. Charabanc trips from Folkestone were always popular and apparently considered slightly daring by the younger generation, much to the consternation of their elders who, adhering to the stifling rules of convention, poured scorn on such whimsical foolery. Whereas riding in these hired charabancs was grudgingly allowed, a journey on a public omnibus was considered quite outrageous. In this context, riding on the tramway is believed to have been on a par with a charabanc and was therefore tolerable, although conduct not to be encouraged. The sensation of travelling in a charabanc is sadly almost an impossibility these days and only in the imagination can the delights be felt as the world swept by with the wind tugging at straw boaters, fancy hats and parasols.

For the monied classes Folkestone was indeed the 'gem of the south coast' as it liked to call itself in its publicity brochures. A typical day for its hotel residents began with an unhurried *petite déjeuner* amongst the huge palms of the sumptuous dining rooms. Suitably attired, a leisurely stroll westwards along the broad promenade of the Leas cliff bestowed unparalleled views of the English Channel with the French cliffs peeping above the horizon. Below, the sound of gentle surf lulled aged Victorians until they were soon dozing in their bathchairs, parked in grassy suntraps, while the more agile put their best foot forward and imbibed lungfuls of the freshest of air.

At the western end of the Leas stood the decorous and imposing red-brick upper station of the Sandgate Hill Lift. On

---

South Eastern and Chatham Railway TRAMS.

Revised List of Fares.

On and after June 1st the following fares will be charged on the Hythe and Sandgate Trams.

1d. Fares:
Sandgate Terminus and Lifeboat House (for Sandgate Station and Seabrook).
Brewer's Hill and Sea View Bridge.
Lifeboat House and Cannon Gate Bridge.
Sea View Bridge and Imperial Hotel.
Cannon Gate Bridge and Ladies' Walk, Hythe.
Imperial Hotel and Hythe Terminus

2d. Fares.
Sandgate Terminus and Cannon Gate Bridge.
Brewer's Hill and Imperial Hotel.
Lifeboat House and Ladies' Walk, Hythe.
Sea View Bridge & Hythe Terminus.

3d. Fares.
All the way.
Dogs 2d. each, any distance.

FRANCIS H. DENT,
General Manager.

THE HYTHE & SANDGATE TRAMWAY

The Sandgate Hill lift in operation in this view looking towards Shorncliffe Camp.

Eamonn Rooney Collection

The Sandgate Hill lift which ran from 1893 until 1918. The tramway terminated a few hundred yards further down the hill.

Folkestone Library

A FATEFUL SEQUEL

opening the glazed, heavy wooden doors, the faint smell of machinery assailed the nostrils while an indistinct rumbling impressed itself upon the ear as the huge iron wheel, concealed beneath the floor, allowed one car to climb the hill as the other descended. As the lift car slowly eased to a halt, the attendant would open the door to enable its load to disembark while those who had paid their penny toll, filed into the car. Sitting in a row along either side, their hearts would beat faster as water, gushing into the tank beneath, heralded its departure. Once the 'ready to go' bell had been rung from the lower station, the brakesman would pass along the side, step upon the canopied platform at the front end and grip the brake wheel, easing it until the car began to sink. The comparative gloom of the building was left behind, causing eyes to squint as the sun's rays burst through the windows. Running down the gentle gradient, most heads would be tempted to gaze seawards before looking ahead to watch the other car make its simultaneous journey uphill. Once the cars had passed each other, Radnor Cliff Crescent was immediately crossed via an ornate iron bridge, whereupon the steeper gradient resumed. A few moments later the brakesman turned his wheel, slowing the car to cause it to gently glide to a halt at the lower station. Here the sound of water gushing out of the car's tank accompanied the passengers exit as they followed one another, surrendering their tickets, before entering the impressive lower station. Here it was possible to make use of the commodious lavatories with their strikingly tiled patterns assimilating those so favoured by the Greeks. In the main hall a bookstall tempted a purchase of a newspaper, likely woefully portending the coming embroilment, or a journal to while away the loose hours, or maybe a picture postcard for that maiden aunt at Sydenham.

Out into the sunshine once more, it was impossible to resist one last look at this strange machine as the lift car ascended before turning to walk downhill to find the start of the tramway. If lucky, there would be no long wait for a tram and likely as not, No. 5, the 'toast-rack', would already be waiting whilst its equine power quenched a hearty thirst at the nearby horse trough. The conductor meanwhile busied himself with swinging over the backs of the reversible seats in preparation for the return trip to Hythe. While passengers jostled over their seats, the horses would be backed up towards the Hythe end of the car and coupled up ready for the command that would set them off. By now all seats would be full and disappointed latecomers would have to wait for the roofed car, which wasn't half as much fun as on days like these. Releasing the brake, the journey would commence, allowing the conductor to pass along the running board collecting fares and likely commenting on

With James Pilcher in charge, the journey to Hythe is about to commence. The fine array of remarkable hats is worthy of note as is the selection of whiskers sported by the gentlemen on board.
Eamonn Rooney Collection

THE HYTHE & SANDGATE TRAMWAY

Having just started its journey, the tram passes by an impressive line-up of cabs in Sandgate High Street. *Eamonn Rooney Collection*

Tramcar No. 1, 2 or 4 passing the bottom of Military Road in Sandgate on its way to Hythe. *Peter Bamford Collection*

A busy High Street as a covered tramcar makes its way to Hythe in 1904. *Author's Collection*

A loaded car rumbles through the High Street on a hot sunny day. On the hilltop, just to the right of the Martello tower, is the top station of the Sandgate Hill lift. *Eamonn Rooney Collection*

Parasols shade delicate complexions on the toast-rack as it trundles along through Sandgate in the peak of summer.
Peter Bamford Collection

Congestion in the narrowest part of Sandgate High Street and a moment of activity beautifully captured by the cameraman.
British Railways

Summer tranquillity along Sandgate Esplanade. *G. L. Gundry Collection*

the warm spell of weather currently being enjoyed. Through busy Sandgate High Street the tram would rumble, causing heads to turn and smile and where maybe class barriers would be transcended when a workman would wink at a pretty girl on board, causing her pale complexion to blush. Leaving the noise of the main street behind, the tram rolled onto the promenade alongside the sea which drowsily lapped the shore, hardly moving a pebble. Now and then a swell would cause a tiny wave to break, its soothing sound still one of life's great pleasures. A motor bus invariably whined past, its clanking gears and spluttering engine driving it faster to its destination, but who would want to hurry on such a perfect day? A pause at the entrance to Princes Parade enabled some passengers to disembark, perhaps to catch a train at Sandgate station, whilst

The foreshore and Esplanade at Sandgate. *Tramway Museum Society*

Tramway Museum Society

up in the yard the sound of an engine shunting wagons filled the air with the clattering ring of buffers meeting. From here the tram left the bustle of business and the main road to wander off with its happy band along the promenade. On the left the sea shimmered and sparkled whilst in the hazy distance Hythe could be seen standing out against the hillside. The empty promenade allowed the horses to quicken to a brisk pace towards the halfway passing place where the other tram was usually waiting. Ahead, the rails glinted in the sunshine whilst to the right the empty fields permitted an uninterrupted view across to the canal. How different it all might have been had Watkin's dreams come true and what fine houses might now have graced this pleasant aspect – Watkin Avenue, Watkin Square, Watkin Villas and so on! There was little else but the Imperial Hotel, even so, its proprietors attempted to make its isolation appear a positive asset:

'As a holiday resort Hythe possesses many advantages, amongst which may be mentioned its comparative quietude as against its

Waiting outside the Hotel Imperial on a sunny summer's evening. Conductor Richard Jago standing by the tram.

Tramway Museum Society

No. 5 entering South Road from Stade Street.
Tramway Museum Soc.

modern neighbour Folkestone, its close proximity to which, brings the more noisome pleasures of that town within easy reach, should a yearning for same be experienced.'

Once past the Seabrook Hotel frontage, the tram swung inland into Twiss Road, resuming its westwards course a few yards further when turning into South Road. At the end of the road the tram slowed once again while the driver operated the device for watering the wheels, thus enabling the curve to be negotiated as quietly and smoothly as possible. Heading inland once more, the tram passed along Stade Street, thereby taking it into the town. Crossing the canal via Town Bridge, punts and skiffs would be seen scattered upon the water where trailing fingers causing ripples upon the glassy surface idled away an hour or so. Once over the bridge the tram turned westwards along Rampart Road, passing the tramway shed and stables on the right, before entering Red Lion Square where this pleasant journey came to an end.

Here a variety of restaurants, luncheon and tearooms satisfied the pangs of hunger felt by the travellers, after which an afternoon spent lazily rowing along the canal might be enjoyed. Back at the square, a cream tea would beckon the palate before a return to Folkestone by tram and lift. In the evening, after a relaxed dinner, there was nothing quite the equal of a stroll eastwards along the Leas, the air scented with flowers and still warm as a rubescent sky heralded a glorious sunset. Descending the cliff face on the Leas water-balance lift, a few steps beyond the gaily-lit entrance to the Victoria Pier was reached. Here, the cooler air from the sea wafted welcomingly up through the wooden decking, whilst ahead the glittering lamps of the Pier Pavilion beckoned with the delights of the music hall. From the shore the pier took on the appearance of some titanic liner, with its lights reflecting in the water below. Within, came the sounds of music and laughter, from people who were likely just as unaware of an impending catastrophe as those poor souls

Stade Street Hythe looking towards the town with a horse-bus alongside the tramlines. The bus has 'S.E. & C. Railway' written across the back.
G. L. Gundry Collection

Town bridge, at the end of Stade Street, where the tramway crossed the canal before swinging westwards into Rampart Road.
G. L. Gundry Collection

Red Lion Square, at the end of the journey from Sandgate.

Eamonn Rooney Collection

A FATEFUL SEQUEL

Tramcar No. 3 makes a rare appearance in this view depicting military activity at Red Lion Square. *G. L. Gundry Collection*

Car No. 5 at Red Lion Square. In the background is Hythe Brewery. *Author's Collection*

who, two years earlier, had perished in the cruel, ice-bound waters of the North Atlantic.

On 7th August 1914, just three days after the First World War began, the tramway service was suspended, its horses requisitioned by the military authorities, whilst the depot at Red Lion Square is understood to have been taken over by the Canadian Military Police. The tramcars were put in store and those members of staff who had not enlisted were required to fill vacant posts in the railway's service elsewhere. For instance, James Pilcher, one of the drivers, went to work on the railway's horse buses, first of all at Hythe then later at Folkestone Junction.

The indescribable horrors of the years that followed will never be allowed to be forgotten, and rightly so, but a thought should be spared here for the tramway's horses whose happy lives pulling holidaymakers were abruptly ended, to perish, along with thousands of others, in the living hell of gore, mud and misery. They had no argument with their counterparts, for them there was no patriotic call to arms, no leave, and perhaps worst of all, no ability to reason. Their plight did not go unnoticed, however, and the sight of these good-natured creatures being shipped out to almost certain death broke many a heart. Edward Elgar, who had to endure the unbearable by hearing his glorious music commandeered by the tub-thumping war-mongers, was distraught at the prospect: 'The only thing that wrings my heart and soul is the thought of the horses. Oh, my beloved animals. The men and women can go to hell, but my horses. I walk round and round this room cursing God for allowing dumb brutes to be tortured. Let him kill his human beings but how *can* he. Oh, my horses!'.

The stark and dreadful consequences of war came to Folkestone on 25th May 1917 when a batch of bombs were shed over the town after a raid on London. They did little damage except for one which landed in Tontine Street just at the busiest shopping hour. The carnage was appalling and wrought the most terrible deaths and sickening injuries. At the time, James Pilcher was at the Junction station with the horse bus and the detonations caused the horse to panic and bolt. Only his prompt action in stopping the runaway averted an accident and for this he was awarded ten shillings by the SE & CR.

In March there were complaints to Hythe council over the state of the section of tramway in their borough. Apart from the accumulation of rubbish in the grooved rails, the cobbles needed repair. Shortly after the outbreak of war, wooden blocks had been tried in place of the unobtainable stones, but it appears they were quite unsuitable. For the duration of the war Sandgate Urban District Council was paid 10/- a week by

James Pilcher with one of the horse-buses outside the town office of the SE & CR which was part of the railway building. The sign reads: 'SE & C Rly Receiving Office for Parcels & Booking Office for Station Omnibus'.
Courtesy Mr. & Mrs. Pilcher

Conductress Ethel Harris with the mule-powered 'toast-rack' at Sandgate in 1919. The driver is Mr. W. H. Rowe.
Courtesy Ethel Harris

the SE & CR to keep the disused tramway throughout their borough in good order. Hythe had offered to do the same but the SE & CR had refused, replying that their own workmen would attend to it. As they never carried out their promise, Hythe council were obliged to eventually tidy it up.

In the spring, following the armistice, it was proposed to restart the tram service, but this was easier said than done for the tramway's own horses had met their death on foreign soil and no replacements could be found. This prompted yet another suggestion that a motorised locomotive be tried, but that met with little favour and the idea was eventually dropped. Soon after, it was suggested that some ex-army mules might provide the solution. The service was therefore able to be resumed, but earlier than Whit Monday, 9th June as is always quoted, for on 31st May 1919 the *Hythe Reporter* revealed:

> 'The SE & CR trams have commenced running between Hythe & Sandgate after an interval of nearly 5 years. When war broke out the Government commandeered all the horses. Everybody will be pleased to hear this service has been resumed. It would be even more welcomed if some arrangements could be made whereby the passengers could be taken into Folkestone by motor cars. As it is, the passengers will seldom manage to secure seats in Sandgate for Folkestone as the public cars are generally filled up by the time they reach Sandgate.'

No tram times were published, which was perhaps just as well for there may well have been difficulty in adhering to a punctual timetable. The mules, though quite capable and good-natured, displayed a singularly independent character, especially when it came to hauling trams. In spite of persistent coaxing from the drivers and conductors, the animals generally tended to commence the journey when it suited them. Once in motion it appears they were in no particular disposition to stop at the required places which meant that prospective passengers had to trot alongside in order to jump on the tram, whilst disembarkation was an equally hazardous affair. Worse still, and who knows what thoughts went through their minds, perhaps boredom at seeing the same old scenery, the mules often tried to go along roads without tramlines and had to be cajoled into following the authorised route. Altogether they were not a success and likely caused many a laugh or temper to fray, depending on how their antics were perceived.

Besides horses, there was also a shortage of manpower and whereas before the war it would have been unseemly to have employed women on such tasks, it was now an entirely different world. Having undertaken menial work for years, the women of Britain now stepped forward and saved the nation from grinding to a halt. It was indeed noticeable how quickly prejudice melted in the face of necessity as women were employed in all manner of manual jobs from driving buses and trams to operating signalboxes. On the Hythe & Sandgate tramway two conductresses were taken on when James Pilcher returned as foreman-in-charge. Occasionally, seemingly as an act of gratitude for their recent war efforts, the soldiers billeted at Shorncliffe Camp would be allowed to hitch a free ride to the Imperial Hotel on the empty trams returning from Sandgate.

Apparently only one accident took place during the period when the mules were in charge and this was through no fault of these stubborn beasts. It happened one afternoon in September 1919, when the tram was just passing the end of Park Road in Stade Street, Hythe, and involved a motor car which shot straight out and into the tram. The force of the impact was sufficient to loosen one of the mules from out of the traces. There was some commotion for a while as the tram occupants, the car's passengers, and the mules were calmed by passers-by and local shopkeepers but thankfully there was little damage and before long the tram was off again, leaving the car, which had fared worse, to be taken away for repair.

At last suitable horses were found to replace the mules which probably brought a sigh of relief all round. For the next few years only a summer service was operated as most local people now used the buses, and the tramway could only be viewed henceforth as a pleasure trip for the holidaymakers. How long it would survive was anybody's guess and it seems evident the SE & CR were about to pull out for in October 1919 they offered Princes Parade to the council, noting: 'It is probably of more importance to them than the railway.' Mr. Jeal, who died in the following year, estimated that £7,106 would have to be spent to remove the lines and make up the road.

The tramway was now a relic from the Victorian age and the new generation disparagingly shunned everything left over from the so-called 'age of elegance'. For three summers the tram continued to amuse those who unwittingly stumbled upon it, those who returned in vain in an effort to recapture those days before the Great War and those who saw the end was near and made the effort to see it in its twilight years. By now the track was in very poor condition, especially where the damage of winter storms was no longer properly repaired. The steel rails were badly corroded and noticeable holes were appearing in the trough of the grooves. Complaints were received from other road users as well as pedestrians who argued that workmen only appeared infrequently, tinkered about with the track and then left. The clerk of Hythe council reminded the borough that although legally the SE & CR were not obliged to run trams, they were required to maintain the track in good repair. The council surveyor remarked that he'd written to the railway on many occasions but they'd paid little notice to his complaints.

By this time the motor bus was firmly established as a number of small operators had combined together to form the East Kent Road Car Company. It was, however, still largely a free-for-all and some buses still dashed through Sandgate at top speed, in one case 'with its doors dangerously flapping and banging'. Over-crowding was another common complaint and the fact that a Captain Edwards troubled to write to the local paper concerning this on the Hythe–Ashford route perhaps implies that the train service was not even considered as an alternative.

The 1921 summer season of trams came to an end on Friday, 30th September. The horses were employed elsewhere during the winter whilst the cars were pushed to the back of the shed for storage.

After another winter the track had deteriorated so much that by January 1922 Sandgate UDC arranged to meet Mr. Shaw, the District Engineer of the SE & CR, in order to walk over the track with him and discuss its future. The chairman of Sandgate UDC suggested that they'd little use for the tramway any more and proposed that it should be abandoned and the track removed as soon as possible. Mr. Shaw readily agreed with him as the railway were anxious to be rid of it once and for all.

In the following April notices were served on the local authorities, announcing the intention to cease running the outdated horse trams. Before doing so, however, the railway company asked Sandgate Council if they were interested in exercising their option under the Tramways Act of 1870 to purchase that part within their borough. Whereas twenty years ago they had been so keen to do so, this time they were quite disinterested and replied that they required the lines to be taken out and the road resurfaced. A few weeks later the General Manager reported that he had, in fact, looked into the question of running trams between the station at Sandgate and Red Lion Square but it would probably run at a loss. It was estimated that running trams for the thirteen weeks, commencing 1st June, would cost £600 and receipts from fares would likely total only £200 unless good weather prevailed. After some discussion it was decided that the tramway should remain shut and to inform the councils of their decision.

Demolition of the tramway began in the first week of June when workmen arrived at the foot of Sandgate Hill to dig out the rails from the roadway. The work was, however, stopped soon after, following complaints from local tradesmen who feared a disruption of their summer takings. Just up the hill, the Sandgate Hill Lift lay derelict and disused since 1918 and, like the tramway, would soon be just a memory.

The portion of the tramway within the boundary of Hythe was offered for sale to the council at a moderate price but they were not interested in running trams themselves.

All five tramcars were taken into the stock of the Southern Railway at amalgamation in 1923 and were allocated numbers in the list of horse-drawn vehicles thus:

SER Tramcar No.1 became SR 3608
,, No.2 ,, SR 3609
,, No.3 ,, SR 3610
,, No.4 ,, SR 3611
,, No.5 ,, SR 3612

James Pilcher and his wife outside the tramway office soon after the service re-started for the timetable is dated Monday, June 16th 1919. *Courtesy Mr. & Mrs. Pilcher*

Rumbling along the weedy Princes Parade in 1919. *National Railway Museum*

Mule-powered car No. 1 leaves Marine Parade and joins the Seabrook Road in the post-Great War period. *Eamonn Rooney Collection*

The toast-rack in Sandgate High Street on a hot day but with noticeably fewer passengers on board than would have been the case before the war.
Eamonn Rooney Collection

The tramway in its last days.
Pamlin Prints

The shape of things to come!
Pamlin Prints

Whether the cars actually carried their SR numbers is not known and it is believed that they were all towed away via Sandgate station to Ashford works where they were stored prior to being broken up.

A proposal to lease the stables to a Mr. Chapman for £100 was cancelled after unacceptable stipulations were made. Meanwhile, the small yard and sheds adjoining Mr. Powell's photographic studio were sold to him for £210.

In February 1923 the Southern Railway agreed to take up the remaining tramlines and reinstate the road at no extra cost to the council but it was another year before tenders were invited. The Road Maintenance & Supply Company quoted £1,935 2s 10d for laying the course with Kentish ragstone and tarmac between Red Lion Square and the Imperial Hotel. At that same time, Hythe Council considered acquiring the tramway shed and stables, offered at £2,500, for conversion into public baths comprising a dozen cubicles. However, this would have cost £1,700 for the alterations and deemed too costly. Other suggestions included a fire station or a garage. All were voted down and eventually Mr. Powell took them over as a furniture and antique warehouse. Messrs Newmans used the building from 1947 as a repository for their removal business, whilst the front portion was converted into a restaurant.

Today, the restaurant still flourishes, whilst above the stone fascia still reads 'FOLKESTONE, HYTHE & SANDGATE TRAMWAYS 1894' and in the forecourt a section of tramlines can still be found. The sheds and stables have recently been splendidly renovated by their new occupants, architects Cheney & Thorpe, who have even proudly incorporated 'The Tramway Stables' into their address.

The epitaph of the Hythe & Sandgate Tramway might be that its long and difficult struggle to establish itself was eventually outweighed by the pleasure it gave to generations of all ages and classes. Perhaps if it had been situated elsewhere then it might have achieved its aim of electrification and would have ranked alongside other municipal tramways until those days when financial profit took precedence over public service. However, it remained firmly attached to the age which conceived it and it is perhaps somewhat surprising that it managed to last into the 1920s. The new era with its razzmatazz attitudes soon snuffed out this vestige of the Victorian age and so it passed into oblivion.

It is indeed most doubtful whether more than a mere handful of contemporary visitors to Hythe or Sandgate are even aware that both towns were once served by a railway and a tramway, nor are they likely to have an inkling of what might have been had the Seabrook Estate Company realised its ambition. Watkin may have been dead for nearly ninety years yet his dream of a Channel tunnel still lingers in the minds of the ambitious. That his more temperate aspirations should be recorded is only right and I believe the charm and appeal of this delightful tramway remains even today. Who, for example, could resist the prospect of a threepenny ride in a leisurely horsetram on a 'Four Mile Ride by the Sea'?

PAY A VISIT TO OUR NEW
SHOW-ROOM at the

Tramway Shed, Rampart Road.
NOW OPEN

Fresh consignment of Rugs and Stair-carpet.
China and Glass. Enamel Ware, Baths and Dust-Bins.
Clothes Baskets. Shopping Baskets.
Tea-pots from 1/-. Sets of Jugs from 3/3
Tumblers 3d. Bedroom Ware from 16/6 per set (6 pieces).
Mangles. Brass-rail Fenders at all prices.
Furniture & Bedding of every description at lowest prices
Lino 8/6 a yard (2 yards wide). Overmantels at all prices.
All-Wool Rugs from 8/6. Chests of Drawers of all kinds.
Dressing Glasses. China Tea-Sets from 17/6 (21 pieces).
Brushes and Brooms of every Description.
New Prams, Push-Carts and Cots. Camp-Bedsteads

Antique Furniture of all kinds.
INSPECTION INVITED

W. POWELL
RAMPART ROAD, HYTHE.

ACKNOWLEDGEMENTS

Compiling these acknowledgements allows me to reflect upon friendships old and new throughout the five years spent writing this book. First of all I should like to thank Peter Davies, to whom this book is dedicated, for his untiring efforts throughout his years as Reference Librarian at Folkestone. I am certain that without him much that has been secured for the historian would have been lost. I owe posthumous thanks to Cecil Barnard who first nurtured my serious interest in the Sandgate branch. I shall always remember his wit and charm as well as those unforgettable teas at his clifftop home overlooking Folkestone Harbour. I thank Alex Todd and his wife, not only for their warm welcome on my visits, but for having the presence of mind to save Cecil Barnard's little album of Sandgate photographs when his collection was auctioned after his death. Special thanks are due to Reg Randell, not only for his encouragement, but his considerable efforts on my behalf. Denis Cullum has my gratitude for finding the answer to many an irksome problem as well as for pointing me in the right direction on frequent occasions. Dick Roberts deserves praise for taking the train to Hythe in 1938, together with a loaded camera. To my great friends Eamonn Rooney, Alan Taylor and Peter Bamford I would like to record my sincere thanks for their tireless efforts in piecing together the history of the district and for allowing me access to their collections. My thanks go to George Gindry for sharing with me his tantalising memories of riding on the tramway, also to Charles Turner for his vivid account of his time on the line during the Second World War. Warm thanks go to Doug Lindsay, Bill Sparrowe, signalman Cowie, Sidney Burn, Dick Riley and Sid Nash. Sadly, posthumous thanks must go to Norman Wakeman with whom I briefly corresponded before his death. I thank Miss Eva Fright for her friendship and kind hospitality on my visits to her home and similarly thank former tramway conductress Ethel Harris. Such kindness has also been extended to me by Mr. & Mrs. Curtis of Cheriton, Mr. & Mrs. Pilcher of Hythe, driver George Halls of Ashford, and Mrs. Elaine Carter of West Malling.

Thanks are also due to The Rev. Colin Fleetney, John Kite, Tim L'Estrange, Alex Schwab, Douglas Thompson, Derek Stoyel, Mrs. Elaine Dawkins, George Barlow, David Banks, Geoffrey Balfour, Maurice Green, Richard Down, Donald Cheney, Marjory Rule, The Rev. Norman Woods, Michael Jack, Molly Griggs, H. C. Casserley, V. R. Webster, P. Batt, and John Smith (Lens of Sutton). I am also indebted to Richard Cross, son of the late Derek Cross, and would like to record my thanks to his father for his many interesting letters shortly before his untimely death.

To the following bodies and individuals I am thankful: The Southern Region of British Rail; Folkestone Reference Library (Brian Boreham); Kent County Library (Maureen Shaw, Area Archivist); Tonbridge Historical Society (Mrs. Gwenyth Hodge); The Tramway Museum Society (J. H. Price); The Saltwood Estate (The Rt. Hon. Alan Clark MP); The Public Record Office; The British Library; The Imperial War Museum; The National Railway Museum; The Ashford Railway Library; Aerofilms Ltd; The Francis Frith Collection; The Victoria and Albert Museum (Richard Cottingham).

It now remains for me to add my heartfelt thanks to my parents for the many cherished childhood memories of the railways of Kent which included Sunday walks upon long-lost lines. To Paul Karau and June Judge I give thanks for their warm hospitality and for their encouragement and assurance, but even more I thank them for transforming my humble manuscript into a truly beautiful work of art.

The impressive and decorative portal of Hayne tunnel. Photographed in 1950.

Denis Cullum